The Politics of Love in Myanmar

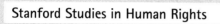

Stanford Studies in Human Rights

The Politics of Love in Myanmar

LGBT Mobilization and Human Rights as a Way of Life

Lynette J. Chua

Stanford University Press
Stanford, California

STANFORD UNIVERSITY PRESS
Stanford, California

Printed in the United States of America on acid-free, archival-quality paper

Library of Congress Cataloging-in-Publication Data

Names: Chua, Lynette J., 1977– author.

Title: The politics of love in Myanmar : LGBT mobilization and human rights as a way of life / Lynette J. Chua.

Description: Stanford, California : Stanford University Press, 2018.

Series: Stanford studies in human rights | Includes bibliographical references and index.

Identifiers: LCCN 2018013068 (print) | LCCN 2018014608 (ebook) | ISBN 9781503602236 (cloth) | ISBN 9781503607446 (paperback) | ISBN 9781503607453 (ebook)

Subjects: LCSH: Sexual minorities—Civil rights—Burma. | Sexual minorities—Political activity—Burma.

Classification: LCC HQ73.3.B93 (ebook) | LCC HQ73.3.B93 C48 2018 (print) | DDC 306.7609591—dc23

LC record available at https://lccn.loc.gov/2018013068

Cover design: Rob Ehle
Cover photograph: U Bein Bridge, Amarapura, Myanmar. 123rf.com | © Sasin Tipchai
Typeset by Bruce Lundquist in 10/14 Minion Pro

To Kristin Luker,
who taught me to trust my feelings

Contents

Foreword by Mark Goodale   ix

Acknowledgments   xi

Note on Language   xiii

List of Terms Related to Queer People, Queer Cultures,
    or the LGBT Movement in Myanmar   xv

Introduction   1

1   Human Rights Practice as a Way of Life   11

2   Forming the Movement: Founding Emotions and Social Ties   41

3   Transforming Grievances: Emotional Fealty to Human Rights   63

4   Building Community: Emotional Bonds Among Activists   89

5   Faults, Fault Lines, and the Complexities of Agency   109

Conclusion   133

Appendix: Fieldwork and Methods   145

Notes   157

References   177

Index   199

Foreword

When Lynette Chua introduces us to Tun Tun and Tin Hla, two central protagonists in her landmark book on the practice of LGBT activism in Myanmar, her description is riveting, revealing, and unforgettable. On the one side is Tun Tun, a university student who had fled the country after the suppression of the 1988 democracy movement by escaping into the jungles along the Myanmar-Thailand border, where he later joined the armed resistance against the military junta. And on the other side is Tin Hla, a ten-year-boy in 1988 who spent his early years living with his conservative military family while grappling with the implications of his emerging queer identity. Eventually, as Chua describes it, Tin Hla left his family home and "drifted across southern Myanmar trying to scrape together a livelihood, finding and losing lovers along the way." By the mid-2000s, Tun Tun, Tin Hla, and others had joined forces to create a pioneering human rights movement that would work to alter how Myanmar's LGBT community was perceived by the privileged within the country's gendered hierarchy. Even more important, as Chua's study reveals with nuanced ethnographic insight, the development of Myanmar's LGBT human rights movement transformed how the activists understood themselves, their rights as citizens, and their moral value as human beings.

By foregrounding the stories of Tun Tun and Tin Hla, among others, *The Politics of Love in Myanmar* signals a particularly compelling orientation to the book's broader themes, an approach in which the development of the book's innovative theoretical argument about the practice of human rights is always grounded in the complexities of lived experiences, life histories, and the trajectory of the inner self. In so doing, Chua's study makes several important contributions. First, it offers a robust justification for relocating the phenomenological subtleties of human rights subject formation to the very center of our empirical research. As she emphasizes, the ethnographic study of the practice of human rights has traditionally deemphasized the phenomenological, the affective, and the ethical dimensions of activism in favor of the social, the political economic, and the institutional. Chua's study does not deny the importance of these topics. Rather, it provides a blueprint for how a concern with both the social and the affective dimensions of human rights practice can and should be combined methodologically and conceptually.

Second, *The Politics of Love in Myanmar* serves as a particularly strong rejoinder to a line of critique that has too often oversimplified the broader ideological and geopolitical contexts in which the practice of human rights takes place. As Chua demonstrates, nothing is gained by framing research in terms of metanarratives of Western imperialism or with reference to the conventional dichotomies that have commonly been used to locate human rights: Global North–Global South, Global–Local, West–East, individual rights–collective rights, and so on. Instead, as she argues, the elasticity of human rights beyond legal and political categories, something I have described elsewhere as "connotative power," allowed the LGBT activists whose experiences suffuse her book to appropriate human rights against a background of other cultural values, other logics of actions, and other forms of motivation. After *The Politics of Love in Myanmar*, it seems to me, it is no longer possible to defend an approach to human rights activism—whether animated or not by a wider postcolonial critique—that reduces these overlapping phenomenologies to the implicit orientalism of savages, victims, and saviors.

And finally, Chua's study offers a sobering ethnographic reminder—one derived from research in extremely challenging and even improbable circumstances—of the ultimate limits of what she describes as "human rights practice as a way of life." Although the LGBT activists in *The Politics of Love in Myanmar* turned to human rights discourse with what Chua describes as "emotional fealty," the consequences for large-scale or structural change were much less certain. Instead, transformation was measured by much smaller emotional gestures, barely perceptible shifts in social relations, and the partial, yet still significant, relaxing of cultural pressures that had made the lives of queer Burmese historically ones of hardship, fear, and self-doubt.

Mark Goodale
Series Editor
Stanford Studies in Human Rights

Acknowledgments

The story in this book has a lot to do with the importance of affection and friendship. So do the research, writing, and publication of this book. Without the love, trust, and goodwill of friends, colleagues, and interviewees, it would have been far more difficult, if not impossible, to transform pages of scribbles, flickers of ideas, and surges of panic and excitement into the printed pages before you.

Andrew Harding gave me the encouragement and determination to pursue the fieldwork for this book. His intellectual leadership during the time he was director of the Centre for Asian Legal Studies at the National University of Singapore (NUS) inspired me to learn more about Myanmar. Otherwise I would not have come upon the news article about the 2012 International Day Against Homophobia (IDAHO) events in Myanmar and embarked on this life-changing journey.

Moora and Khine Khine not only provided language assistance but also laughter, kindness, and patience all these years. We gossiped, grumbled, and gobbled down hasty meals in between interviews, long car rides, and more interviews. Strangers to each other at first, we became friends and confidantes as we navigated the vicissitudes of fieldwork in solidarity.

Damian Chalmers, Nick Cheesman, John Dale, David Engel, Calvin Morrill, and Matthew Walton read drafts of the manuscript for this book and shared invaluable insights. They wrote copious comments and took time out of their busy schedules to chat. David was a Skype call away, willing to listen to my ramblings and offer advice that I will always hold dear to my heart.

Michelle Lipinski and Mark Goodale believed in the book when it was only a proposal. Their support for the project led to this opportunity to publish with Stanford University Press. Michelle readily answered my questions and ensured that I reached every milestone and crossed the finishing line successfully.

Friendship and guidance from colleagues and mentors, Catherine Albiston, Hillary Berk, Steve Boutcher, Ashley Currier, Jaruwan Engel, Marc Galanter, David Gilbert, Timothy Hildebrandt, Elaine Ho, Ho Hock Lai, Peter Jackson, Lynn C. Jones, Gwendolyn Leachman, Anna-Maria Marshall, Mark Massoud, Michael McCann, Frank Munger, Nyi Nyi Kyaw, Carroll Seron, Mary Nell Trautner, Keebet von Benda-Beckmann, and Barbara Yngvesson directly or indirectly helped me with the research and writing of this book; Minn Thu, Eugene Quah, Sai Nyi Nyi, and U Kyaw Maung provided assistance during the early stages of the project; Shaun Kang, Koh Wei Jie, Jannelle Lau, Nang Yin Kham, Phua Jun Han, Maria Acton Thomas, Intan Wirayadi, Daryl Yang, and Yeo Sam Jay carried out additional research and administrative work; Wendy Wee and Kris Zhao managed my research budget impeccably; the NUS library staff valiantly endured and handled my numerous questions and requests; and Cheah Wui Ling, Swati Jhaveri, Jaclyn Neo, and Tan Hsien Li supplied bountiful sisterhood, wicked humor, and countless emojis.

Trudging around doing fieldwork, deciphering stacks of field notes, and writing and rewriting a manuscript are time-consuming and often costly endeavors. The NUS Humanities and Social Sciences Research Grant (R-241-000-118-646) awarded generous funding for the fieldwork, the NUS Humanities and Social Sciences Fellowship enabled me to write the initial draft of the book on teaching leave, and the Centre for Asian Legal Studies supplemented a small grant for the final phase of writing and production. During earlier stages of the project, I presented drafts of articles or chapters at the Law and Society Association 2014 and 2015 meetings, the Center for the Study of Law and Society at the University of California, Berkeley, the Global Legal Studies Center and the Center for Southeast Asian Studies at the University of Wisconsin, Madison, and the Faculty of Law, NUS, where I received feedback and encouragement from the audience.

Last but not least, Burmese LGBT activists and everyone else who participated in the study allowed me to peer into their world, even if only momentarily. Each of them brought something specially theirs that has made who they are, what the movement is about, and what human rights mean: their emotions and their relationships. Thank you.

Lynette J. Chua
January 2018

Note on Language

Buddhism and Buddhist: When referring to "Buddhism" or "Buddhist," unless otherwise specified, I have in mind lived practices of Buddhism in Myanmar, an approach that resonates with the general trend of studying Buddhism as "deeply entangled with and constituted by other domains of life" (Schonthal and Ginsburg 2016, 9). Put another way, I treat Burmese Buddhism as a socially embedded religion and do not focus on doctrinal or textual constructs. Lived practices of Burmese Buddhism are diverse and ever changing, varying among social groups and individuals and across time and context.[1] They encompass interpretations and expressions of important elements of Theravada Buddhism, as well as beliefs and customs that purists consider to be non-Buddhist but are often observed by Buddhists (Brac de la Perrière 2009a).[2]

Burma and Myanmar: I use "Myanmar," the official name since 1989, to refer to the country and state, and "Burma" when specifically intending it to be a historical reference, such as "Union of Burma," or when quoting a text or interview.[3]

Burmese, Burman, and *Bamar*: I use "Burmese" as the adjectival form for the state of Myanmar, its society, and its citizens, and "Burman" or *Bamar* when referring to the dominant ethnic group.

Karma: Although "karma" is derived from the Sanskrit version of the word and not Pali (*kamma*) or Burmese (*kan*), I apply it as a word that has become part of the English language, spelling it without italics.

Nirvana: Although "nirvana" is derived from the Sanskrit version of the word and not Pali (*nibbana*) or Burmese (*neikban*), I use it as a word that has become part of the English language, spelling it without italics.

Pronoun use: My choice of pronouns for interviewees depends on their pre-ferred gender identity, which is not often easy to determine, so I can only claim to have done it to the best of my ability. I take my cue heavily from interviewees' chosen names, which are typically gendered as male or female, as well as their sexual or gender identity. I also consider their use of Burmese first-person pronouns in their interviews or conversations (but keeping in mind that they may switch to different pronouns when interacting with other people). For ex-ample, *kyun taw* and *kyun ma* are, respectively, male and female first-person pronouns. However, interviewees also refer to themselves in gender-neutral ways, such as using *ko doe* in the plural form, *doe* in the singular or plural form, or simply their own name. A few interviewees give themselves feminine names but refer to themselves in the male first-person pronoun of *kyun taw*; in these situations, I consider the person's sexual and gender identity, for example, whether the person self-identifies as a *gay* person or *trans woman* and how else they are known to other people—for example, if they are called, "Aunty," which is common for older *apwint*, or *trans women*.

Pseudonyms: I give pseudonyms to all interviewees and organizations of the Burmese LGBT movement. I chose interviewees' pseudonyms based on the various considerations for pronoun use, and whether their actual preferred names are Burmese (though Burmese names do not necessarily reflect ethnicity or religious affiliation). For a few non-Burman interviewees, I picked pseud-onyms based on their ethnicities or religious affiliations.

Queer and LGBT: When not referring to the Burmese LGBT movement or to specific persons or groups associated or self-identifying with a particular identity term, I use "queer" as a general reference for people who are nonhet-eronormative or gender nonconforming. Because "queer" is a less common term among my interviewees and Burmese LGBT activists generally, my use of the word helps to indicate clearly when I do not have in mind any particular identity—local or LGBT-related—that is widely adopted by individuals, groups, or the movement in Myanmar. I use the term "LGBT" where it specifically con-cerns the movement, its people, its work, or the identities its activists construct as part of their human rights practice. This approach is consistent with activists' own description of the movement as "LGBT." Where interviewees or the data refer to a particular identity term, local or otherwise, I use that specific word.[4]

Transliteration: I transliterate Burmese words based on how they are com-monly sounded and spelled out in English rather than follow a strict romaniza-tion standard.

List of Terms Related to Queer People, Queer Cultures, or the LGBT Movement in Myanmar

When using particular English words to refer to queer people, queer cultures, or the LGBT movement in Myanmar, queer Burmese often have meanings specific to their context that diverge from the English words' original meanings in places such as the United States. I use italics when the English loan words refer to distinctive meanings that Burmese queer people have in mind. For example, where the text refers to "gay" with and without italics, there are differences in the meanings.

achauk   Regarded by Burmese LGBT activists as a derogatory reference to *apwint*, the word literally refers to something dry and is commonly thought to connote the physical quality of having anal sex with somebody identified as such.

apone   "Hider," somebody who was assigned male at birth, identifies to some degree as feminine, and is attracted to men but appears and acts masculine.

apwint   "Open," somebody who was assigned male at birth, identifies to some degree as feminine, is attracted to men, and appears and acts feminine.[1]

baw pyar   Literally "flat balls," a derogatory reference to *tomboys*.

gandu   Regarded as a derogatory word for *apwint*.[2]

gay   Somebody who identifies as male and is attracted to men, most likely those who identify as *homo* or *gay*. Some *apwint* and *apone*, however, also refer to themselves alternatively as *gay*.

homo   Somebody who identifies as male and is attracted to men, most likely those who identify as *homo* or *gay*; the word, however, is often used to refer to *apone* as well.

IDAHO   International Day Against Homophobia, commemorated internationally on May 17 to draw attention to the violence and discrimination
experienced by people who do not conform to sexual or gender norms in
their society. In recent years, the name has been updated to IDAHOT and
IDAHOTB to include references to transphobia and biphobia.

ingahlan   *Apwint* who reverse their sexual role in relation to *tha nge* and become the penetrative partner or "top."[3]

lein tu chit thu   Literally "those who love the same sex [or gender]," the term
is often used interchangeably by LGBT activists to refer to "homosexual" or
"LGBT."

lesbian   Somebody who was assigned female at birth and is attracted to *lesbians*
or heterosexual, cisgender women. LGBT activists often use this term to include
tomboys and *trans men*.[4]

lesbian   Somebody who identifies as female and is attracted to or in a relationship with a lesbian.

meinmashar   "Man acting as woman," a term referring to *apwint*. Although
some *apwint* regard the term as derogatory, others use it for self-identification.

men who have sex with men (MSM)   An umbrella term in Burmese public
health parlance that includes *apwint, apone, homo, gay* men, *ingahlan, tha nge*,
and *offer*.

nat kadaw   Spirit medium, or literally, "spirit wife." This is a niche occupation
associated with *apwint*; however, not all *nat kadaw* are *apwint*. I use the term
to refer generally to those who engage in this occupation, although the term is
supposed to be reserved for the highest ranked in the occupation.[5]

offer   Sex worker who has sex with those who were assigned male at birth.
Offer includes *apwint, apone, tha nge, gay* men, and *homo*.

TDoR   Transgender Day of Remembrance, commemorated internationally
every year on November 20 to remember those who died as a result of transphobia violence.

T.G.   Short for *transgender*, an alternative self-reference for people who identify as *apwint*.

tha nge   "Guy," a person who identifies as heterosexual and cisgender and is the sexual or romantic interest of *apwint* and *apone*.[6] The LGBT movement does not regard *tha nge* as queer.

tomboy   Somebody who was assigned female at birth, identifies to some degree as masculine, is attracted to women, and appears and acts masculine.

transgender   Usually an alternative reference for those who identify as *apwint* or *tomboy*, though its stand-alone use (without being paired with "man" or "woman") is more often assumed to refer to *apwint*.

trans man   Usually an alternative reference for those who identify as a *tomboy*.

trans woman   Usually an alternative reference for those who identify as *apwint*.

UDHR   Universal Declaration of Human Rights, proclaimed by the United Nations General Assembly in 1948, setting out human rights that are to be universally protected. Burmese LGBT activists frequently refer to the UDHR in their human rights workshops and advocacy work.

yaukkashar   "Woman acting as man," a term referring to *tomboys*. Although some *tomboys* regard the term to be derogatory, others use it for self-identification.

Yogyakarta Principles   The Yogyakarta Principles on the Application of International Human Rights Law in Relation to Sexual Orientation and Gender Identity, developed and adopted in 2006 by human rights experts. Burmese LGBT activists sometimes refer to the Yogyakarta Principles in their human rights workshops and advocacy work.

The Politics of Love in Myanmar

Introduction

It's the first time I saw bloodshed and that made me really angry. . . . Some of my colleagues were shot. (Tun Tun, interview, February 21, 2013*)[1]

I could hear the demonstrators shouting. Sometimes I would go to the entrance of the barracks and look at the demonstrators. I could even hear the shootings. (Tin Hla, interview, June 26, 2015)

T HE YEAR WAS 1988, a tumultuous time in Myanmar when students and other Burmese rose up against the military's repressive rule and economic mismanagement and the regime responded with violence, killing thousands.[2] Back then, Tun Tun and Tin Hla, standing on opposite sides of the demonstrations, did not know each other. One was a Rangoon University student who escaped to the jungles along the Myanmar-Thailand border and took up arms against the junta. The other was a ten-year-old boy who lived in a Yangon barracks with his grandfather, an army major, and his family, shrouded by government propaganda.

It would be almost twenty years before the two met, and Tin Hla would come to describe many experiences in his life as human rights violations, including the military's actions in 1988 and the hardships he endured with his same-sex partners. After Tin Hla's grandfather retired from the army, his family moved out of the barracks. He drifted across southern Myanmar trying to scrape together a livelihood, finding and losing lovers along the way. Tin Hla's life and dozens of others' in this book converged and changed when they joined an obscure human rights movement that Tun Tun founded in the mid-2000s—an LGBT movement for queer people of Myanmar.

Today the LGBT movement is headquartered in Yangon with activists from around the country and all walks of life. They are city dwellers, small-town folk, villagers, political dissidents, children of military families, daily wage laborers, factory workers, shopkeepers, beauticians, *nat kadaw*, and students. Tun Tun, Tin Hla, and other movement leaders travel around the country to recruit and train new activists, educate lawyers, implement paralegal programs, file lawsuits, and speak to local media and politicians, all the while talking openly about human rights and their violations.

But when Tun Tun founded VIVID, the movement's national organization, he was still a political exile in Chiang Mai, Thailand. He did not know when he could go home. Leading a human rights movement in his homeland seemed a distant dream. From 2007 until early 2013, he and a few other Burmese, a mix of dissidents and economic migrants, operated VIVID out of Chiang Mai. They adopted human rights as their core strategy to achieve the goals of empowering queer Burmese to accept themselves, gaining social belonging, and reforming discriminatory legislation and law enforcement practices. They carried out human rights education workshops first among Burmese migrants in the Thai towns of Chiang Mai, Mae Sot, and Ranong, and then among such participants as Tin Hla, whom they surreptitiously brought over from Burmese cities, towns, and villages. After returning to Myanmar, some participants became grassroots organizers and spread word about the movement and their new knowledge. Tin Hla held gatherings in his little mattress shop.

The opportunity to bring home the LGBT movement arrived unexpectedly, when the military regime orchestrated elections in November 2010. The elections led to the formation of a semicivilian government in 2011 that showed signs of reforming the harsh regime.[3] In May 2012, grassroots organizers from five Burmese cities and towns organized the first International Day Against Homophobia (IDAHO) celebrations in Myanmar and distributed VIVID's magazines. Tun Tun went back to give speeches about the human rights of queer Burmese. The following year, his protégés at VIVID packed up and moved their office from Chiang Mai to Yangon.

Almost twenty-five years after Tun Tun marched in the front lines of pro-democracy protests, fellow Burmese trained and inspired by him boldly make human rights claims and put themselves forward as LGBT activists, representing a collective claimant of human rights, LGBT people of Myanmar. The

LGBT movement joins the post-2011 political landscape of Myanmar, where marginalized groups demand recognition and human rights advocacy attracts international support when it was once hostilely turned away by the state. It makes human rights claims in a society where the discourse was violently suppressed for decades, whose predominantly Buddhist population is unfamiliar with rights talk, and where queer people are hardly recognized as a discriminated group with legitimate grievances. It is not as prominent as movements with claims and claimants far more familiar in Burmese politics, such as those concerned with women and ethnic and religious minorities. Nevertheless, LGBT activists increasingly appear on TV, in newspapers, and at public events. They gain audience with leaders from political parties of all stripes, air to them the grievances of queer Burmese, and urge the government of the day to reform the law. Migrants who participated in VIVID's workshops gradually return from Thailand, bringing back human rights talk, advocacy skills, and connections to organize for the movement in their hometowns. They began their journey with the movement not knowing much about human rights. Eventually they formed their own ideas about what human rights mean to them and what they should and could do about their circumstances. Since the landslide victory of Aung San Suu Kyi's National League for Democracy (NLD) in the 2015 elections, the LGBT movement has expanded to twenty grassroots locations (Figure 1).[4]

How did Myanmar's LGBT movement emerge? This question inspired me to find out more when I came across a news report about a group of Burmese who were organizing IDAHO celebrations inside Myanmar. When I learned that they adopted a human rights strategy, I went on to ask: How do LGBT activists of the movement make sense of human rights and put them into action, that is, practice human rights? What are the implications of their human rights practice? These questions grew increasingly compelling as I carried out fieldwork from 2012 to 2017 to conduct a qualitative study of the LGBT movement's developments—from its inception in the mid-2000s among exiles and migrants in Thailand through the early years of Myanmar's political transition, when they shifted the movement headquarters to Yangon and spread the movement faster and faster across Myanmar.

The questions are compelling because of the promises and pitfalls of human rights. Debated tirelessly and proliferated across diverse societies (Santos 2002; McCann 2014; Osanloo 2009), human rights have, in recent times, been extended explicitly to sexuality and gender identity. The universal panacea that

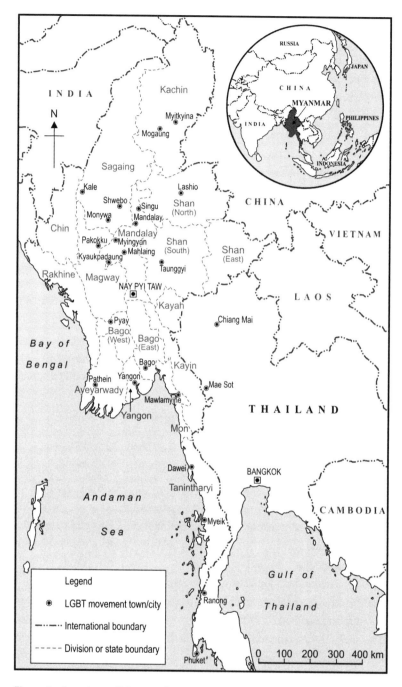

Figure 1. Locations of Myanmar's LGBT Movement (Map by Lee Li Kheng)

human rights purport to offer to human suffering, a prevalent phenomenon and strong motivation for the activists in this book, makes the discourse attractive yet objectionable. Some scholars find that human rights bring meaningful change, but others regard them as a Western imposition of power that is often ineffective as well—a long list of affirmations and criticisms that I elaborate on later in the book.

The questions make an even headier mix when we imagine a human rights movement in a country in political transition but mired in history of conflict and repression. What is geographically Myanmar today fell to British rule after the Anglo-Burmese wars between 1824 and 1885. To control widespread crime and disorder, which arose at least partly in response to their colonial invasion, British administrators introduced repressive laws that were retained by postcolonial regimes with long-lasting impact on civil-political liberties (Callahan 2003; Cheesman 2015). Immediately after independence in 1948, the Union of Burma succumbed to civil war and ethnic strife. The short period of liberal democracy ended when a caretaker military government took power in 1958 and cemented military rule with a coup in 1962. Subsequently, the military solidified its dictatorship under a centralized, totalitarian state structure, promulgating the 1974 Constitution that declared the Socialist Republic of the Union of Burma a one-party socialist state. Myanmar became synonymous with human rights violations, not the least the violent crackdowns of the 1988 demonstrations, the detention of Aung San Suu Kyi after the NLD's electorate victory in 1990, imprisonment of other political opponents, persecution of human rights activists, extrajudicial killings, displacement and systemic rape of ethnic minorities, and forced labor and relocation.[5]

Consistent with what we know about rights movements in times of political change (see, e.g., McAdam 1999b), Burmese activists enjoy greater freedom to make new claims, but their troubles remain despite the beginnings of democratization. The 2011 semicivilian government implemented partial reforms, such as releasing Aung San Suu Kyi and other political prisoners, and relaxing controls on civil-political liberties.[6] Foreign governments and international nongovernmental organizations (NGOs) more freely enter the country to assist a wide range of human rights–based projects. Yet the same government still arrested activists. Under its watch, Buddhist nationalists championed anti-Islamic causes to campaign successfully for Laws for the Protection of Race and Religion (Than 2015), which tightened the sexual regulation of women.[7] The 2015 elections resulted in the historic handover of government to Aung

San Suu Kyi's NLD, but armed conflict, marginalization of ethnic minorities, and abuse of power persist.[8] Legal reforms passed in Nay Pyi Taw, the capital, are slow to reach local authorities, towns, and villages. Efforts by international agencies and domestic activists struggle against ingrained social norms that perpetuate divisions and discrimination.

In light of Myanmar's past and present, human rights activists face stiff obstacles. Human rights were unfamiliar, even scary, to many Burmese. Being associated with human rights used to trigger state retaliation, and so they were something to avoid. Activists, whether working from within Myanmar's borders or without, had to find and persuade others to join their cause at great personal risks. They had to innovate strategies and tactics simply so that they and fellow activists could circumvent political constraints and evade punishment. Even after 2011, they still have to overcome the fear toward human rights and make them appealing instead.

The debates surrounding human rights and the challenges for human rights activism in Myanmar get amplified when we look at the LGBT movement. Internationally, the human rights of queer people—which Tun Tun and his fellow activists call "LGBT rights"—are still controversial. In Burmese society, queers are morally suspect. In contrast to popular Western portrayals that exoticize the celebrity of transgender *nat kadaw*, the "spectacularly gay" (Ho 2009), or idealize a tolerant Buddhist society, the reality for most queer Burmese is much grimmer.[9] They suffer from police persecution, aided by wide arrest powers and the criminalization of same-sex sexual conduct. They are commonly shunned by family and friends and experience bullying and harassment, sexual violence, other forms of attacks, and discrimination in education and employment.

These prejudices are rooted in norms and beliefs that shape the distribution of power and hierarchy. Myanmar is a society organized by a gendered hierarchy that privileges heterosexual, cisgender men. Queers generally occupy lower rungs of the hierarchy. According to Burmese Buddhist beliefs, people are reborn as queer due to the bad karma of having committed sexual transgressions in past lives. Coupled with sociopolitical conditions, they help legitimize queer discrimination and stigmatization and breed resignation. Suffering oppressive conditions, the result of deviating from accepted sexual and gender norms, is to be expected in this lifetime. Among Christian and Muslim minorities, homosexuality—often conflated with gender nonconformity—is generally regarded as sinful.[10] LGBT activists find that the perception of queers as deviants who deserve their plight runs so deep that it is widely internalized among queers themselves, festering self-hate, shame, and fear. Few people are able or willing to take up their cause because few comprehend or appreciate their issues.

Against this potent mix of concerns and issues as the backdrop, the story I tell in this book about the Burmese LGBT movement is an empirical account about human rights. It is not about human rights as moral or philosophical matters (Goodale 2006), as law defined in formal instruments, signed by governments, and interpreted by courts, or about their "cultural relativism" (Speed 2008). It is about how people who put human rights into practice interact with them and with the rest of society. Anchored in this scholarly tradition, in telling this story, I do not regard human rights as innately good, bad, powerful, or weak (Roberts 2015). They are empirically plural (Santos 2015). To know the good, the bad, and the ugly of human rights, I look to the ways in which people wield them to realize their hopes and dreams of a better life, the consequences they sow, and what those consequences mean to them.

Even more generally, then, this is a story about how human rights matter. Certainly, it concerns queer issues, LGBT rights, and Myanmar, a research site that until recently offered limited access and unusually difficult challenges (Aspinall and Farrelly 2014; Skidmore 2006).[11] But it is also more than that. It tells us how a human rights movement came to be and how a group of people relate to human rights in a country where they long meant state retaliation and were suppressed for decades. It is about why and how people can appeal to human rights and make them appealing to others, when their conception of the self has been informed not by human rights but by religious beliefs (in this case, Buddhism) and other cultural sources of feeling, knowing, and interacting with the world (Cowan 2006; Seligman 2000). And, at the end of it all, it is a story about the implications of human rights in action—both their prospects and their power.

. . .

In this story, we learn about human rights from the trials and fortunes of *human rights practice as a way of life*. This practice, a mode in which human rights are made sense of and put into action, is the pathway that Burmese LGBT activists take to win greater freedom for queers to live authentically as queer, that is, as people who love their queer self and are able to find social belonging and the dignity that comes with it. The journey begins with self-transformation, the rights bearer's change of personhood. It builds up to transformation of a collective, enacting an emotion culture made up of new means of feeling and bonding for queer Burmese. Then it connects them, individuals and the collective, to making changes to their country's politics. It is a way of life fueled by emotional fealty to human rights and the emotional bonds among those who share it. Born from a land bountiful with norms, beliefs, and distribution of power and hierarchy, and crafted by the people who live them, this way of life aspires to transcend and rise above its birth conditions, though as we will see, not entirely successfully.[12]

At the heart and soul of human rights practice as a way of life are emotions and interpersonal relationships, and at center stage are its protagonists: human agents like Tun Tun and Tin Hla. They give emotions and relationships body and motion, turning human rights from ideas and ideals into a living, breathing social thing. They steer the practice, sometimes in unison, sometimes in tension with one another, and always against those who oppose them. As they go on this journey, they also transform their very own social beings. They turn into somebody different, with a new sense of self, emotional bonds, and political demands. The result is recursive, overlapping social processes of formation, grievance transformation, and community building. The product of human agency, these processes emerge from human sufferings and triumphs, steeped in their pain and joy, fears and desires, loves and loathings.

The three sets of recursive, overlapping processes provide the theoretical link between the local adaptation of human rights and collective action. Without them, Tun Tun would not have founded the movement, and Tin Hla would not have met Tun Tun, learned about human rights, become an LGBT activist, joined the movement, and stuck with it all these years. Through *formation processes*, Tun Tun and other pioneers got together to establish the LGBT movement, circumvent obstacles before and during Myanmar's transition to recruit Tin Hla and other queer Burmese, develop the movement, and circulate their practice, laying the groundwork for the other two processes. Through *grievance transformation processes*, these activists redefine queer Burmese's sense of self by making human rights relevant to them, altering their understanding of queer suffering, and motivating them to take action and join the movement. Through *community-building processes*, they create a new community of LGBT activists, a politically united front of queer Burmese. They participate in these processes to keep up and develop the practice, creating and sustaining an ongoing cycle.

The three sets of processes are constituted by and constitute emotions and interpersonal relationships, extending the scope of how human rights matter beyond their substantive meanings. To find and draw people like Tin Hla into the movement and help them understand and relate to human rights, Tun Tun and other leaders make use of existing feelings and interpersonal ties, which stem from abuse of power, economic mismanagement, substandard health care, and queer suffering, the lived experiences of their country's sociopolitical conditions. They also reshape and cultivate emotions as part of their efforts to counter harmful norms and beliefs in Burmese society and find support from those beneficial to their cause. The norms and beliefs include karma in Buddhism, standards of socially acceptable conduct, and conceptions of social roles, responsibility, and dignity. Meanwhile, practicing human rights together as LGBT activists, they also foster relationships among themselves. Jointly, these emotions and social ties ignite inspiration, a "driving force" in Tin Hla's words (interview, June 26, 2015), to help queer Burmese, and persevere with the movement's practice.

Engaged in the three sets of processes, conditioned by and reciprocally conditioning emotions and interpersonal relationships, LGBT activists produce three interconnected outcomes that link the personal to the grassroots and to formal political institutions. The outcomes' interrelated nature highlights how social change can begin with *self-transformation* of the rights bearer. Tun Tun first altered the way he as a queer Burmese felt about himself and interacted with other people. Then he and fellow activists helped other queer Burmese do the same by shifting their understanding of queer suffering—that it should not be accepted or justified based on bad karma, but should be regarded as human rights violations for which somebody or something else is to blame—and by encouraging them to take up responsibility to the self and to queer Burmese collectively to fight for the remedy, human rights. Self-transformation culminates in the makeover of a social group, the creation of a *distinctive emotion culture* for queer Burmese. Those like Tin Hla, who undergo self-transformation and adopt the emotion culture, become LGBT activists—people who have emotional fealty to this human rights practice and are emotionally bound to one another as a result of practicing it together. With self-transformation and a new emotion culture, LGBT activists introduce to Burmese politics *new claims and claimant*, LGBT rights for LGBT people, to achieve the goals of self-empowerment for queers, their social belonging, and legal reform.

Pursuing their goals through human rights practice as a way of life, LGBT activists give human rights their own meanings that suggest the discourse does not necessarily impose so-called Western morality or individualism of which it is often accused. To these activists, human rights contain three essential meanings: *dignity*, *responsibility* (of the rights bearer), and *social belonging*. While they do draw from international human rights documents for the concept of dignity, they infuse it with local notions that stress the importance of social belonging and responsibility such that the rights bearer has to take action to earn it. They also reinterpret LGBT identities to connote dignity, mesh them with Burmese understandings of sexuality and gender, and construct a group of people who find belonging together and mobilize human rights collectively to gain greater membership in Burmese society at large. By linking dignity to social belonging through the rights bearer's exercise of responsibility, their interpretation of human rights and the accompanying LGBT identities render human rights a collective good that is to be collectively achieved.

This collective pursuit of human rights nevertheless is fraught with faults and fault lines. Being a diverse lot, national activists such as Tun Tun and grassroots organizers such as Tin Hla deal with unequal power dynamics between them, which have led to variations in the implementation of their practice. They each negotiate multiple selves, with LGBT identities existing alongside longstanding Burmese understandings. They move in and out of the movement and older queer communities, such as those concentrated around spirit mediumship, the female beauty industry, and lesbian social networks. They also remain divided along gender lines. What is more, their practice faces stubborn structural legacies, as well as entrenched norms regarding sexuality and gender among allies and among themselves. Their appeal to social conformity may end up affirming a hierarchy that disempowered queer Burmese in the first place. Furthermore, their practice embodies Burman and Buddhist privilege, marginalizing queer claimants who are non-Burman or non-Buddhist.

Thus, at the same time as human rights practice as a way of life brings meaningful impact, resonates with local folks, and galvanizes collective action, it is far from becoming the dominant mode of feeling, knowing, and interacting in LGBT activists' society, for one important reason: Human agency enables as well as constrains it. The individual and collective agencies of LGBT activists, and consequently their emotions, interpersonal relationships, and human rights practice, are socially embedded, structuring and structured by Myanmar's sociopolitical conditions, its norms, beliefs, and distribution of power and hierarchy. We must bear in mind such complexity and fluidity of agency, capable of lifting hopes and dashing dreams, as we follow the story of Burmese LGBT activists and come to understand the power and effectiveness of human rights.

Chapter 1

Human Rights Practice as a Way of Life

Tun Tun stood up and spoke in the front of the hotel conference room. Tin Hla and about fifteen other people gathered around tables arranged in a rectangular shape before him. They had come to Chiang Mai for this workshop from several Burmese regions and states and Thai towns bordering Myanmar. Along one wall, colorful letters spelled out in English, "Advanced Advocacy Training for LGBT Activists." Organized by [VIVID]." Throughout the day, Tun Tun, leaders of VIVID, the Burmese LGBT movement's national organization, and the workshop participants referred to the Universal Declaration of Human Rights (UDHR) and LGBT identities. They talked about what they could do to "get rights." They brought up the problem of social prejudices and discussed tactics for dealing with local authorities. There were raised voices, some agitated and others excited. Occasionally somebody interjected with a joke. At the end of the day, they lined up to collect VIVID's magazines and Burmese kyat, money for them to organize movement events in their hometowns. A few went up to Tun Tun's hotel room where VIVID leaders interviewed them for their future publications. About an hour later, groups of four or five headed out, dressed up for a night in town. (Field notes, Chiang Mai, Thailand, September 21, 2012)

THESE OBSERVATIONS from my first day of fieldwork embody the book's central concept: the practice of human rights as a way of life. The concept puts a theoretical framework around the story of the Burmese LGBT movement and its intertwined fate with human rights. It connects the 1988 events in Tun Tun's life to the movement's birth and growth and Tun Tun's journey to Tin Hla's. It explains how the two of them and everyone else at the workshop, a diverse lot from a society where human rights were suppressed for decades, ended up together in the conference room and became LGBT activists who embrace and collectively demand for human rights.

The concept has three salient features that advance human rights studies and research on the relationship between rights and social movements in sociolegal studies. First, human rights practice as a way of life comprises recursive, overlapping social processes of formation, grievance transformation, and community building, which I elaborate on to specify the theoretical links between human rights and collective action. Second, the processes are shaped by and shape emotions and interpersonal relationships, which I cast at the center of the analysis of human rights practice. Third, the processes produce three outcomes—self-transformation of queer Burmese, the rights bearer; the creation of a distinctive emotion culture; and the introduction of new claims by a new collective claimant, LGBT rights for LGBT people, to Burmese politics—which show how personal and grassroots dimensions of change are interrelated and have the potential to build up to formal institutional outcomes.

At the same time, because agency not only enables but also constrains ability and imagination, the conceptual framework explains how LGBT activists' practice contains faults and fault lines as well. Tracing processes and attending to emotions and relationships, it brings out the complexities of agency that lead to variations in practice across time, place, and people, an important consideration when assessing the power and prospects of human rights. The framework focuses attention on what human rights mean and how they matter, avoiding a binary, power-centric analysis that tends to juxtapose the global against the local. Thus, it allows me to appreciate LGBT activists as offering an alternative—one that is meaningful and hopeful but flawed and limited—to a place where it coexists with other modes of knowing, feeling, and interacting. And it compels me to do so by telling the empirically subjective with love, that is, with compassion for humanity in its emotional entanglements and relational messiness.

The Promises and Pitfalls of Human Rights

Ever since contemporary human rights emerged from post–World War II politics in the form of the 1948 UDHR (Baxi 2002; An-Na'im 2011), scholars have debated their pros and cons.[1] Their Janus-faced reality is perhaps unsurprising given their contentious birth and competing stories of origins (Roberts 2015; Somers and Roberts 2008). The debates intensified when human rights were extended to sexuality and gender identity in the early 1990s (Petchesky 2000; Mertus 2009), followed by the declaration of the Yogyakarta Principles on the Application of International Human Rights Law in Relation to Sexual Orientation and Gender Identity and United Nations resolutions in the past ten years (Farrior 2009; Swiebel 2009).[2]

Human rights are often meaningful to local populations and capable of doing good, say researchers from diverse disciplines, including law, political theory, history, sociology, and anthropology, some engaging in normative debates while others make observations informed by empirical studies. Human rights advocacy has promoted good governance and exposed serious wrongdoing (Kennedy 2012), and human rights treaties have resulted in changes to state practices (Cole 2012; Farris 2014; Tsutsui, Whitlinger, and Lim 2012). They possess connotative power (Goodale 2007b), the discursive, strategic, and symbolic capacity (Merry et al. 2010) to stir up ideas and passions for achieving social justice. They validate the claims of marginalized populations, empowering them to challenge dominant authorities (Ignatieff 2001; Holzer 2013, 2015). Activists who succeed at portraying their claims as human rights have won over allies (Richards 2005), international NGOs, and foreign governments (Bob 2005, 2009); secured funding and other resources to build organizational capacity (Holzmeyer 2009); catalyzed transnational activism (McCann 2014, citing Cichowski 2007); and pressured recalcitrant governments into taking action (Keck and Sikkink 1998; Heyer 2015). At the grassroots, human rights have struck a chord with local activists, even though they come from societies unfamiliar with them (Munger 2014, 2015; Holzmeyer 2009; Tripp 2004). They have managed to use human rights to persuade others to join their cause or recognize their claims (Mujica and Meza 2009; Rajaram and Zararia 2009) and build political communities (Smith 1998). Some are able to incorporate into human rights local notions of morality and personhood (Morreira 2016; Stychin 2004) or reconfigure them to challenge neoliberalism (Speed 2008). Human rights can also alter the manner in which people depict and talk about issues (McCann 2006), desire their society to be organized, perceive certain experiences in their lives, and understand who they are (Tsutsui 2017; Barclay, Bernstein, and Marshall 2009).

Nevertheless, human rights are ineffectual and represent another form of Western power, say scholars who also come from a broad range of disciplines, informed by different theoretical orientations or empirical findings. Despite achievements with human rights, vast segments of humankind still suffer from

violence and miserable conditions (Kurasawa 2007). Though filled with lofty
ideals, their narrow application has privileged individuals' civil-political rights
to the detriment of greater recognition of socioeconomic rights (Moyn 2010)
and collective rights (Engle 2010, 2011).[3] They impose Western ideas of moral
individualism (Kennedy 2002; Santos 2015) and lack cultural legitimacy (An-
Na'im 2011) or resonance (Engel 2012). They inhibit collective action (Brown
2004; Massoud 2013) and displace alternative modes of meaning making
(Subramaniam 2009; Morreira 2016) whose visions of social change could be
more transformative (Allen 2013) or community based (Kennedy 2002). Identities closely associated with human rights, such as LGBT, supplant indigenous
subjectivities (Waites 2009; Puri 2008), relegating them to the realm of the
backward (De la Dehesa 2010, citing Altman 2001 and Binnie 2004). Activists who adopt human rights strategies risk reinforcing unequal distribution
of power and resources (Merry 2006; Kennedy 2002), such as creating local
elites who alienate the rural majority's needs (Mutua 2004; Englund 2006).
Engrossed in fulfilling donor conditions, professional organizations eventually neglect local objectives (Massoud 2015; Igoe and Kelsall 2005), failing to
empower their target population (Swidler 2013; Englund 2006) or address de-
plorable material conditions (Mutua 2008). Human rights could even make
things worse. Their reliance on national laws for enforcement could end up
perpetuating the violence of law in postcolonies instead (Grewal 2016, citing
Comaroff and Comaroff 2006). Or they could attract backlash for allegedly
promoting undesirable Western culture (Currier 2012; Kollman and Waites
2009; Massad 2007; Boyd 2013).

The Empirical Inquiry of Human Rights

Looking at the debates about their promises and pitfalls, the paradoxically enabling and constraining nature of human rights (Cowan 2006) evokes contestations when people put them into action to fight for social change (Cowan
2003; Merry 2003a). When local activists use human rights to describe their
grievances, make demands, and build support, differences appear between the
human rights conceived in international documents and their home-grown
formulations (Cowan, Dembour, and Wilson 2001; Wilson 1997). They have
to mediate the tension between the purported universal claims of human rights
and domestic conditions (Levitt and Merry 2009). They have to deal with the
responses of politicians and officials and make the international discourse re-
latable to their movement constituents. Frequently they have to confront resis-

tance and opposition, especially where human rights lack familiarity or when the claims are relatively new to the human rights family, for instance, on issues of gender violence (Cheng 2011; Merry 2006) and sexuality (Mertus 2009; Petchesky 2000).

To understand the tensions and mediations, some scholars study the nature and impact of human rights as empirically open questions. They conduct empirical studies of human rights and bring nuanced, grounded insights from the field into the debates about their pros and cons, some of which I have already cited. They pay attention to the social nature of human rights, an approach that reflects the discourse's origins as the product of struggles over how society and social relations ought to be organized (Roberts 2015). Their starting point is that human rights are neither inherently liberating nor oppressive, but that their meanings, implementations, and consequences are social facts to be investigated. These scholars are motivated by questions such as: How do social actors, such as activists, make sense of human rights? How do they put human rights into action? How do their interpretations of human rights interact with local norms and beliefs? How do they struggle with other people and their governments to achieve their goals? What are the intended and unintended effects of these local interpretations and struggles?

Therefore, scholars in the empirical tradition focus on the interplay between the purported universalism and local variations of human rights in practice to draw out contextualized meanings and consequences (Cowan, Dembour, and Wilson 2001; Cowan 2006). They interrogate human rights as contested cultures (Cowan 2003; Merry 2003a), examine their implementation (Wilson and Mitchell 2003; Riles 2006; Rajagopal 2003), and trace their patterns of vernacularization (Levitt and Merry 2009) or circulation and adaptation (Merry 2006).[4] For example, Allen (2013) explores the struggles of Palestinian human rights organizations, Englund (2006) considers human rights education projects aimed at Malawi's poor, and Speed (2008) analyzes the appropriation of human rights by indigenous communities of Chiapas, Mexico, to mount resistance against their state. Merry (2006) is interested in the dissemination and "translation" of women's rights from international bodies to Hawaii, Fiji, India, and China. Selby (2011, 2012) observes how Thai people assert human rights through familiar tropes, symbols and beliefs, or everyday conventions in their society, whereas Osanloo (2009) explicates how Iranian women draw influence from liberal individualism, Islamic values, and pre-Islamic Iranian ideals to form their own understandings of human rights. In the area of sexuality and gender identity,

Thoreson examines the construction and institutionalization of LGBT rights by a transnational NGO (2014) and the local adaptation of LGBT politics in the Philippines (2012).

The Social Processes, Emotions, and Interpersonal Relationships of Human Rights Practice

Scholars who empirically study human rights bring out their social nature in a myriad of ways. The studies acknowledge that human rights come to life as ongoing series of social interactions, be they amicable, constructive, or contentious. Activists (or anyone else who puts human rights into action) interact with one another and with others such as allies, opponents, and politicians. They also interact with sociopolitical conditions, a place's norms, beliefs, and distribution of power and hierarchy, to help them interpret and implement human rights to achieve their goals.

Nonetheless, empirically informed research on human rights has overlooked two issues. The first two salient features of this book's central concept, human rights practice as a way of life, address these neglected issues and contribute to the study of human rights and sociolegal scholarship. Explaining the first two features leads to the third, the interrelated nature of the practice's outcomes, which follows later in this chapter.

First, the concept articulates the processes that are involved when a group of people adapt and use human rights to organize and advance a movement and specifies the theoretical link between human rights practice and collective action. Taking a process-oriented approach follows the general trend in sociolegal studies on rights and social movements (McCann 2006; Cummings 2017). However, studies on human rights practice rarely set out the types of processes involved, much less explicitly theorize their links to collective mobilization. In studies about the "translation" of human rights into the vernacular, authors do recognize the affinity of vernacularization patterns with collective action framing in social movements research (Levitt and Merry 2009; Merry 2006), but they do not expound on the relationship.[5]

Second, the concept takes into account not only the interpretation of human rights' substantive meanings but also emotions and interpersonal relationships inherent in the interpretation, as well as the circulation and implementation of human rights. Emotions and relationships constitute all of these processes and are constituted by them. Although research on human rights practice has in-depth analyses of the adaptation of their substantive meanings, these studies largely overlook the role of emotions and interpersonal relationships. Some do notice the feelings of solidarity and the creation of community (see, e.g., Mujica and Meza 2009; Rosen and Yoon 2009) or the uses and changes of emotions (see, e.g., Merry 2001)—as do sociolegal studies about movements based on domestic civil-political rights (see, e.g., McCann 1994; Silverstein 1996; Boutcher 2010)—but they rarely elucidate the significance of emotions and interpersonal relationships, especially their relevance to the social movement in question.

Hence, we find two of the book's scholarly contributions in this combination: theorizing the processes of human rights practice, thereby linking them to collective action, and integrating emotions and interpersonal relationships into the analysis. It is not new for social movements studies to pay attention to emotions and social ties. Neither is it new for sociolegal scholars to examine the contingent nature of rights and the impact of social relations on people's understanding and use of rights. Nor is it novel for legal scholars to emphasize the place of emotions in law. It is, however, less common to have such a combination, particularly when studying a human rights movement "from below" (Nash 2012; also see Grewal 2016). Fleshing out the social processes involving emotions and interpersonal relationships, the book's conceptual framework looks past formal legal regimes, domestic and international, and takes into account the ways in which human rights interact with local conditions and experiences and generate capacities as well as constraints in the struggles for justice (Kurasawa 2007).

These features make this book even more significant because of the research site and subject matter: a human rights–based LGBT movement in a Buddhist-majority country.[6] Save for a few notable exceptions, sociolegal scholars have yet to give Myanmar much attention. Among recent publications that draw on in-depth fieldwork to analyze legal repression and resistance (see, e.g., Dale 2011; Cheesman 2015), it stands apart with a framework that analyzes human rights practice as social processes and foregrounds emotions and interpersonal relationships in the analysis.[7]

The more I carried out my fieldwork and analyzed the data, the more I noticed the importance of the social nature of human rights practice. When LGBT activists try to make sense of human rights for fellow Burmese and use them to inspire action, they inevitably have to interact among themselves, with newcomers to the movement, and with others. And with social interactions come emotions and interpersonal relationships (Calhoun 2001; Turner and Stets 2005; Goodwin, Jasper, and Polletta 2001a).

From my fieldwork, I observed that emotions and interpersonal relationships are just as vital as cognition, for they are inseparable. Emotions permeate LGBT activists' thoughts and decisions about human rights and about themselves. Like other human beings, they feel their way through situations (Jasper 2014), including how they ought to make sense of and act on human rights. It is particularly important to consider emotions and interpersonal relationships in a society like Myanmar, once rampant with fear and ruled by fear and where fear led to distrust and the breakdown of social ties (Skidmore 2004; Fink 2009). But much more than fear, I found shame, self-hate, despair, hope, love, trust, and other emotions, to which I sometimes refer as "feelings."[8] Along with these emotions, I found a range of interpersonal relationships, such as friendships, professional connections, and alliances, which I interchangeably call social ties, emotional bonds, or affective ties.[9]

In fact, emotions and interpersonal relationships are the LGBT movement's genesis for political action, its heart and soul. "No action can occur in a society without emotional involvement. . . . Emotion is directly implicated in the actors' transformation of their circumstances, as well as the circumstances' transformation of the actors' disposition to act" (Barbalet 2002, 2–4). Emotions are also an inherent part of relationships. They emerge from and are experienced in the context of relationships, give meaning to the events and encounters for each person, and accordingly modulate their relationships within a social world (Bericat 2016; also see Emirbayer and Goldberg 2005).[10]

The attention given to emotions and interpersonal relationships in my conceptual framework resonates with the scholarly disciplines that I draw on: human rights studies, sociolegal research, social movements scholarship, sociology, anthropology, and legal scholarship on law and emotions.[11] In particular, by not treating cognition as distinct from or more important than emotions, the framework reflects recent developments across a diverse range of academic disciplines, including law, humanities, social sciences, and biological sciences. For a long time, a tendency in Western academia was to treat cognition and emotion as dichotomous (Emirbayer and Goldberg 2005; Nussbaum 2001). The former was associated with rationality and reason and the latter with irrationality, often in denigrating fashion (Goodwin, Jasper, and Polletta 2001a; Barbalet 1998), the unfortunate stuff that disrupts our lives and makes us do stupid things (Jasper 2014). Increasingly, however, scholars are reassessing this dualism in their respective areas of research.[12] For instance, sociologists and legal scholars look to neurological studies (see, e.g., Turner and Stets 2005;

Bandes and Blumenthal 2012) and point out that emotion is a key element of cognition and is not opposed to it; emotion influences thought and decision making, and cognition refers not only to conscious, deliberate, or rational thought.[13] "We need to recognize that feeling and thinking are parallel, interacting processes of evaluating and interacting with our worlds, composed of similar neurological building blocks" (Jasper 2011, 286).

To reiterate, emotions and interpersonal relationships embody all aspects of practicing human rights, such as meaning making, circulation, implementation, and the outcomes. Such emotions as fear and the desire to escape pain and suffering and such relationships as friendships and professional alliances shape decisions to join the LGBT movement and other movement-related actions. But a much deeper level is at work too. Emotions and relationships do not merely serve as the conduit or trigger of human rights practice, though they sometimes do so (and these aspects make up an important part of the LGBT movement's processes). Their roles go beyond strategic use and should not be simply analyzed instrumentally (Emirbayer and Goldberg 2005; Gould 2004). Emotions and interpersonal relationships and the very processes of human rights practice construct one another. The two arise from overlapping, recursive processes involving activists and other actors, all conditioned by the norms, beliefs, and distribution of power and hierarchy in their society. Reciprocally, more than being processual products, they reconstitute the actors involved in the processes, altering the processes as they continuously play out.

Human Agency and the Three Processes of Human Rights Practice as a Way of Life

With emotions and interpersonal relationships at the heart and soul of human rights practice as a way of life, human agents act as its protagonists. LGBT activists drive and produce the social processes of formation, grievance transformation, and community building that are mutually constitutive of emotions and relationships. They draw on and repurpose cultural schemas and resources so that they can effectively adapt human rights to redefine the status of queer Burmese, reimagine identities, and reconfigure relationships (Sewell 1992; also see Emirbayer 1997; Emirbayer and Goodwin 1994; Emirbayer and Mische 1998).

Cultural schemas are norms and beliefs, shared understandings of power and hierarchy, and common experiences, which comprise meanings, values, and subjectivities in a society (Dale 2011, citing Jordan and Weedon 1995), whereas resources include material and nonmaterial things like knowledge and money that help enhance or maintain power in that society (Sewell 1992). The same schemas and resources inhere in and compose all kinds of social structures, including gender, sexuality, law, and formal political institutions, intersecting with one another across the structures (Sewell 1992). Since emotions and relationships shape and are shaped by the norms, beliefs, shared understandings, and experiences, they are related to cultural schemas; for example, norms regulate the feelings one ought to possess and display (Hochschild 1983), such as at weddings and funerals, and common knowledge about an event may kindle such shared emotions as anger and bring people closer. Emotions and relationships can also serve as resources; for instance, affective loyalties, alliances, and professional connections can help increase power and influence.[14]

LGBT activists therefore enjoy bounded ability to create human rights practice. They borrow from cultural schemas and resources found in existing structures around them, reminiscent of American civil rights activists who developed "novel rights" by combining rights talk with the familiar discourse of Christianity (Polletta 2000). Yet their agency is presupposed, molded by the availability, nature, and rootedness of schemas and resources (Sewell 1992); it is why caregivers in American families often cannot envision more radical family care arrangements beyond existing welfare policies (Levitksy 2014). By practicing human rights, LGBT activists' agency emerges from and returns to the processes of human rights practice, continuously morphed by the experience. Individually, their agency also varies, for they each occupy different positions in their society due to the structures affecting gender, sexuality, education, class, and other conditions (Sewell 1992; also see Emirbayer 1997; Emirbayer and Mische 1998).

The complexities of LGBT activists' individual and collective agencies illuminate the effectiveness and power of human rights for collective action and social change, the big-picture conclusion for this book. For now, the enabling side of their agency shines through when I elaborate on the three sets of processes next. It continues when I discuss their infused meanings for human rights and LGBT identities, followed by their achievements of self-transformation, distinctive emotion culture, and new claims and claimant. However, the constraining side of their agency comes to the foreground when I turn to the practice's faults and fault lines toward the end of this chapter.

Formation

The LGBT movement's human rights practice first emerges from social processes known as formation. In Chapter 2, we see this more superficial, though critical, layer of dynamics involving emotions and interpersonal relationships. At this stage, a set of emotions and social ties shaped by Myanmar's sociopolitical forces converge to give rise to their movement and, as a result, its human rights practice and the subsequent two sets of processes.

Through interpersonal relationships predating the movement, Tun Tun and fellow pioneers meet one another, form the movement, and recruit others to join in their human rights practice. According to social movements scholarship, social ties are vital to recruitment (Diani 2004; Krinsky and Crossley 2014; McAdam 2003). Conversely, the lack of existing ties may hamper the ability to reach certain social groups. People coalesce to found or participate in a movement not only based on strategic motivations or instrumental calculations but also due to interpersonal relationships (Zurcher and Snow 1981; Snow, Zurcher, and Ekland-Olson 1980; Goodwin, Jasper, and Polletta 2001a). This consideration is especially relevant in high-risk situations (McAdam 1986, 1988; McAdam and Paulsen 1993), such as during the LGBT movement's founding years when grassroots organizers living under Myanmar's military regime traveled to its Thai-based headquarters for human rights workshops and meetings.

Significantly, preexisting social ties contain shared cultural meanings that are conducive for a movement's development (Taylor and Rupp 2002) and, in this case, its human rights practice. The social ties that led Tun Tun and fellow pioneers to found the movement and recruit new activists are rooted in their common experiences with pain and suffering in their homeland. They include ties of political disaffection among pro-democracy dissidents and activists, ties among economic migrants in search of "survival" or livelihood in Thailand, ties of altruism among workers and volunteers of HIV/AIDS organizations who seek to alleviate suffering caused by substandard social services and health care, and informal social networks formed by queer Burmese who seek refuge from abuse and discrimination. Even after 2011's political changes, LGBT activists continue to rely on such ties. That was how Tin Hla and many of the other grassroots organizers were recruited and later invited to the September 2012 workshop described at the opening of this chapter.

At the same time, emotions inherent in those social ties aid or motivate people to answer the movement's recruitment call. Having relied on preexisting ties, one type of emotion is obviously affective loyalties, such as trust, respect, or admiration newcomers have for Tun Tun and other movement pioneers. The second type is raw emotions of suffering that give rise to the interpersonal relationships in the first place. While grievances alone are insufficient for collective action (Jenkins and Perrow 1977; McCarthy and Zald 1977), they are nevertheless crucial motivators (Gamson 1992; Jasper 1997; Ferree and Merrill 2000). From the start of formation processes, grievous emotions generate feelings of desire to seek relief or escape and push people to take up the invitation to attend a human rights workshop.

In addition, a third type of emotions is triggered when preexisting social ties are put to use to found the movement or carry out recruitment. These emotions are most commonly fear and anxiety of getting caught for being associated with human rights activities, coupled with the courage and calmness needed to subdue them. They are triggered and experienced while physically taking the risk of answering the recruitment call—for example, during the movement's founding days, when a newly recruited person traveled across Burmese checkpoints to and back from Thailand to participate in movement activities.

Formation processes lay the foundation for LGBT activists to practice human rights as a way of life. By bringing a group of people together at workshops and other movement activities, they provide the means and opportunities for grievance transformation and community building to take place. Embodying shared experiences with sociopolitical conditions, the various emotions that constitute formation processes become relevant once more, to be remade by the two types of processes that follow.

Grievance Transformation

On their own, emotionally laden grievances and interpersonal relationships predating the movement are insufficient to motivate people to embrace the LGBT movement's human rights practice. Formation processes gather people who know one another, are connected through social ties arising from suffering, and thus share similar experiences. Nevertheless, as much as grievances fuel emotions that "put fire in the belly" (Gamson 1992, 32), they alone cannot get individuals to act together with a collective strategy and purpose (Jenkins and Perrow 1977; Goodwin, Jasper, and Polletta 2000).

Therefore, in Chapter 3, we see LGBT activists carry out grievance transformation. They remold and redirect queer Burmese's interpretation of their experiences, including their emotions, toward a collective understanding of injustice that they believe could and should be remedied by their taking up of collective action (McAdam 1999b) and, in this case, the specific solution of human rights. As Moore (1978) put it, the oppressed needs something else that pours iron into their souls, pushes them to overcome feelings of inevitability and resignation, and endows them with courage and optimism to challenge their oppressors.

Grievance transformation generates an important "something else"—changes to self-understanding that embrace human rights as the diagnosis and remedy to their grievances. To produce this change, LGBT activists mobilize emotions (Aminzade and McAdam 2001). They draw from cultural schemas and resources to elicit as well as reshape emotions. They recast into a human rights mode the way in which queer Burmese, their audience, "assign meaning to, and interpret relevant events and conditions" (Snow and Benford 1988, 198) and alter understandings of their problems (Tsutsui 2017). That is, they enable queer Burmese to blame external forces and reconceptualize the nature of their problems (Levitsky 2008, citing Ferree and Miller 1985). Hence, emotions more than play a part in instrumental purposes, such as overcoming fear (Goodwin and Pfaff 2001), mustering courage (Jasper 2011), and galvanizing collective action (Gamson 1992; Perry 2002), though LGBT activists certainly do those things as well. Grievance transformation also contains a deeper layer where we see more clearly the mutually constitutive dynamics between the social processes of human rights practice, and emotions and interpersonal relationships.

Grievance transformation therefore amounts to the cognitive work usually emphasized in social movements studies about collective action framing (Benford 1997) or consciousness raising involved in cognitive liberation (McAdam 1999b)—but in the sense that emotions are integral components of such activities.[15] This is the critical point: grievance transformation embodies and produces emotions that shape values and ideas (Ferree and Merrill 2000) in ways that are inseparable from cognition. "To frame an outcome as either injustice or as bad luck entails how we should feel about it . . . as much as how we understand it" (Jasper 1998, 411). Put differently, the work is inherently collective emotional labor (Whittier 2001). Its aim is emotional liberation (Flam 2005).

To make human rights resonate with queer Burmese so that they can change their self-understandings, LGBT activists call up the common emotions of suffering—the pain, fear, and despair experienced from being discriminated against and abused. It is a crucial step for turning grief into a mobilizing force (Flam 2015), because many ordinary Burmese, queers included, are unfamiliar with human rights. LGBT activists recharacterize grievous encounters of queer Burmese as the loss of human dignity, violations of human rights pronounced in the UDHR and the Yogyakarta Principles, and the emotions of suffering as stemming from such violations from which queer Burmese are entitled to be protected. They ask queer Burmese to imagine the opposite—what it is like to be free of such painful emotions—and try to get across the message that this is what having human rights feels like instead.

Then LGBT activists transform feeling rules (Hochschild 1979, 1983; Berk 2015) or emotion norms (Thoits 1989), that is, social norms regulating the emotions one ought to have in a given situation. LGBT activists offer queer Burmese positive feeling rules, so that they can cultivate for themselves stronger self-esteem, hope, and confidence. Having depicted queer suffering as human rights violations, these activists encourage queer Burmese to abandon feeling rules based on stigmatization, inferiority, and resignation, which breed self-hatred, shame, and fear of being queer. Aiming to erode acceptance and justification for their ill treatment as people with lower social station, a perspective sustained by beliefs about bad karma, they stress that sociopolitical conditions and other humans (Benford and Snow 2000), such as prejudicial norms, legal rules, the state, and the police, are the cause of queer suffering. They turn to the UDHR and Yogyakarta Principles for the authority that queers are entitled to human dignity just like anybody else. In other words, LGBT activists try to change the feelings that queer Burmese believe they ought to have about themselves so that they instead feel worthy of human rights. At the same time, they return to Buddhism, this time implicitly drawing support from the forward-looking, antideterministic aspects of karma, to instill in queer Burmese feelings of hopefulness and confidence that they can change their destinies (also see Gould 2002, 2004; Taylor 1996).[16]

Grievance transformation therefore involves the emotive power of law as well. Legal rules and rights (Abrams 2002; Bandes 1999; Nussbaum 2004; Berk 2015), their sustained patterns of enforcement (Pasquetti 2013), and their public expressions (Richman 2014) can cultivate, reshape, or validate emotions.[17] In Myanmar, police and courts perpetrate some of the queer suffering, abusing their power and inflicting penal provisions to shame and intimidate queer Burmese. In response, LGBT activists attempt to turn the situation around by emotionally appealing to rights. In order for queer Burmese to relate to human rights, LGBT activists summon their pain, fear, and despair and connect them to violations prohibited by human rights or the failure of rights commitment by the state. In addition, they harness the symbolic power of human rights (Merry et al. 2010) to empower their audience to feel deserving of dignity (Abrams 2011; Williams 1991).

Ultimately, LGBT activists make use of the new feeling rules and emotions to compel collective action (Abrams and Keren 2010), with the hope that one day their efforts will change the law and win them rights protection. Baxi (2002) describes human rights activism as a "labour of transformation" that works with the "raw material of human suffering arising from the denial of dignity, equal worth, and concern for all human beings" (58). For LGBT activists' practice, the transformation begins with changing one's emotions about one's sufferings followed by what one could do about them with human rights.

At this juncture, LGBT activists channel the feelings of optimism and confidence into a sense of responsibility, encouraging queer Burmese to join their struggle for human rights by helping to transform the sense of self of other queer Burmese and attain dignity in the form of social belonging and legal change. Drawing again from local norms, this time on behavior, roles, and obligations, LGBT activists conceive of responsibility as starting with making changes to oneself, the rights bearer—how queer Burmese should live, interact with other people, and conduct their interpersonal relationships in order to receive dignified treatment from others and gain their acceptance. Although they do not explicitly make the connection, their approach toward individual and collective responsibility implicitly finds grounding in their Buddhist understandings of the cause and effect of actions.[18] Then, harking back to the shared emotions of suffering, LGBT activists induce empathy to amplify the sense of responsibility so that queer Burmese see themselves as belonging to a collective of queers, feel motivated to join their human rights practice, and fight for a brighter future together.[19] In the example of the September 2012 workshop, Tun Tun and other movement leaders tapped that sense of responsibility among a select group of grassroots organizers and brought them back for leadership training.

Activities or actions count as grievance transformation if they are intended for that purpose. They can be human rights training or advocacy workshops, movement strategy meetings, rallies, and other movement events. They can take place less formally and on a smaller scale. For instance, during the early days of the LGBT movement, when founders and pioneers had informal conversations with potential recruits and discussed one another's backgrounds and motivations, they passed on their interpretation of human rights. Grievance transformation processes can also take place through the production and distribution of movement paraphernalia about human rights—for example, posters, audiovisual materials, and VIVID's magazines.

Community Building

Whereas grievance transformation establishes LGBT activists' emotional commitment to human rights, community building creates emotional bonds among the activists. In Chapter 4, we see community-building processes generate and modify emotions that foster new social ties, uniting them as a group of queer Burmese known as LGBT, activists who perpetuate the movement's human rights practice. LGBT activists are drawn to the movement not only by the aspirational qualities of human rights. They stay with the movement through thick and thin also because they feel they belong to a community of people who are doing this work together.

In one aspect of community building, LGBT activists construct a collective identity of LGBT. They cultivate the use of individual LGBT identities and invent *lein tu chit thu* ("those who love the same sex") as the Burmese equivalent. However, movement leaders do not enforce any definitions for these identities, letting fellow activists reinterpret them as they please for themselves, often meshed with prior understandings of Burmese sexuality and gender. More important to LGBT activists is the strategic value of deploying LGBT identities (Bernstein 2005). Similar to activists in Namibia and South Africa (Currier 2012), they intend LGBT identities to overcome what they believe to be stigma inherent in derogatory local words and thus to aid grievance transformation in engendering positive self-understandings. By doing so, they use "LGBT" to mark off their group (Taylor and Rupp 2002) and ultimately fashion feelings of affinity among a diverse lot of queer people based on what the collective marker represents: their shared practice of human rights.[20]

Apart from the deliberate construction of collective identity, the social interactions inevitably involved in human rights practice comprise community-building processes in and of themselves.[21] The interactions do not merely transmit information (Goodwin, Jasper, and Polletta 2001a; Mische 2003). They also produce emotions that cultivate affective ties, connecting people to one another through their shared practice, reshaping the interpersonal relationships they may already have with one another, and nurturing fresh bonds where they did not exist. Therefore, although the movement strengthens its community with a collective LGBT identity, explicit labels may be unnecessary if emotional bonds are strong enough to foster and hold together the community (Goodwin, Jasper, and Polletta 2000; Taylor and Rupp 2002). Such bonds can powerfully motivate individuals to act in accordance to what it entails to be a part of that community (Friedman and McAdam 1992), which in this book is the pursuit of human rights practice as a way of life to change the queer sense of self, society, and the law.

In fact, it is such emotional bonds that matter to whether some people stay on or even decide to join the movement after initially answering the recruitment call and participating in their first couple of workshops. The people who leave or turn away from LGBT activism appear to be attracted to the promise of human rights. They even openly adopt LGBT identity terms for themselves and keep using those terms afterward. However, they do not stay with or join the movement because their bonds to the activists are weak or because they feel more strongly attached to other queer communities to which they already belong, such as the social circles of spirit mediumship and the female beauty industry, or lesbian cliques in their hometowns.[22]

Some emotions that engender affective ties are feelings shared among activists about the sources of oppression (Jasper 1998). They are related to the emotions that constitute formation processes or are invoked as part of grievance transformation. During formation processes, getting involved with the movement and engaging with human rights come with fear and trepidation. When they arrive at the stage of community building, those emotions lead to camaraderie among new recruits and seasoned activists as they learn about one another's experiences, and sympathize with one another over similar worries and fears. During grievance transformation, participants relive their emotions of suffering, such as self-hatred, shame, and fear of being queer. As community building ensues, they realize from the sharing of these experiences and crying about them together that they are no longer alone. They develop feelings of solidarity that offer solace and mutual support (Coe and Schnabel 2011).

Other emotions are reciprocal feelings that activists have toward one another (Jasper 1998). Feelings of fellowship, such as trust, affection, and respect, arise from the social interactions at workshops, meetings, and other movement events. At the September 2012 workshop, for example, they manifest in the joking and banter during the workshop sessions and the social outings afterward. Unlike the other two types of emotions, feelings of fellowship may not seem to have any direct relevance to human rights practice. However, they are also critical to its perpetuation. Movement participation over time can create positive emotions and reinforce the sense of belonging (Goodwin, Jasper, and Polletta 2001a; Wood 2001; Bosco 2007), enticing activists to stay and increasing retention. In particular, intimacy is key to sustaining commitment (Taylor 1989) and persuading one another to act in dangerous circumstances (Robnett 1997).

Apart from the LGBT movement's meetings, rallies and workshops, where grievance transformation simultaneously occurs, community building can take place away from face-to-face interactions. Posters, flags, slogans, T-shirts, and other paraphernalia are the movement community's symbols or "totems" (Turner and Stets 2005, citing Durkheim 1965). Processes of community building follow when new participants or activists come into contact with these symbols, and activists use social ties to distribute them. The totems introduce people to the movement, jolt memories, and reaffirm affection for those who are physically away.

Infused Meanings of Human Rights and LGBT Identities

As LGBT activists take part in the social processes of human rights practice, they infuse human rights, *lu akwint ayay*, and accompanying LGBT identities with their own meanings. Influenced by queer suffering, as well as norms and beliefs in their society, they interpret three core meanings for human rights— dignity, responsibility (of the rights bearer), and social belonging—and mix LGBT definitions with local understandings of sexuality and gender. Together, these infused meanings and identities denote human rights as a collective good to be collectively achieved.

Through the rights bearer's responsibility, the attainment of dignity connects the individual self to the collective. To LGBT activists, dignity comes with social belonging, which improves their membership in Burmese society, something many queer Burmese have been denied and have long desired. Hence, human rights matter as a collective good in this regard. Furthermore, to achieve such dignity and thus social belonging, their practice calls on them to assume self-responsibility and collective responsibility on behalf of queer Burmese, based on notions of roles, duties, and obligations in their society. It constructs them, by practicing human rights together, as a community of activists called LGBT. Hence, human rights further matter as a collective good in the manner they are to be achieved—jointly by a group of people who belong to an LGBT community, who are expected to act according to norms of their society, and at the same time who exercise the responsibility of fighting for the collective lot of queer Burmese to gain fuller membership in society. The activist, despite maintaining unique queer identity and other self-understandings, is a social being bound to multiple groupings of people: queer Burmese, the LGBT community associated with the movement, and their society at large.

My findings seemingly deviate from those of scholars who doubt that rights (*akwint ayay*) discourse of any sort can make sense at all to Burmese people.

According to Keeler (2017), whereas rights embody the idea of equality for everyone, Burmese, in their highly hierarchical society, are positioned in relative standing to one another and advance their circumstances by gaining better placements within the hierarchy. He points out that *akwint ayay* tellingly refers to "people's opportunities" (17). Similarly, Prasse-Freeman (2015) argues that "Western concepts of rights and opportunities blur together, and tend to index an appeal to power" (96) in Myanmar, and rights therefore do not exist independent of power that flows from a given social status. To Houtman (1999), *lu akwint ayay* connotes the granting of permission by an authority; indeed, separately, *akwint* indicates "permission" and *ayay* refers to "matter."[23]

However, by treating human rights as socially contingent, I let my Burmese interviewees pour into the discourse their own understandings, aspirations, and claims. In other words, as the subject of empirical study, rights derive meaning not only from legal documents, jurisprudence, or political theories. They are not mere words to be translated from a foreign language. They can mean different things in different societies and to different people, or they can mean absolutely nothing. These possibilities are not exclusive to Burmese society or any other society where hierarchies prevail (though each society has its peculiarities). In his empirical study of rights in Japan, Feldman (2000) challenges the conventional view that the assertion of rights is fundamentally incompatible with Japanese legal, political, and social norms: rights do matter in Japan though they do "not have the same meaning as 'rights' in the United States, just as 'rights' in the United States does not have the same meaning as 'rights' in Germany" (13). It all depends on whether and how people make sense of and put rights into action, colored by who they are and where they come from—precisely what goes on in the processes of human rights practice as a way of life.

LGBT activists' interpretation of human rights, centered around dignity, responsibility, and social belonging, suggests that human rights need not foist Western ideas about morality, individualism, or identities on local populations, common criticisms mentioned already in this chapter. Consonant with other empirical studies of human rights practice (see, e.g., Speed 2008; Morreira 2016), LGBT activists do more than convey the meanings of human rights on international documents to a local audience. Although their funding mostly comes from Western donors, they set their own strategies for putting human rights into action (also see Tripp et al. 2009). Some may say the local version remains a derivative of the original and foreign, regardless of the amount of adaptation (Subramanian 2009); after all, LGBT activists undeniably refer to the

UDHR and Yogyakarta Principles. But the key is the approach I adopt to study the mediation between international and local meanings (Levitt and Merry 2009). I look to the emotions and social ties rooted in pain, suffering, and other experiences that emanate from Myanmar's sociopolitical conditions and how activists use those experiences and conditions to reconstitute emotions and ties. While LGBT activists do draw ideas from human rights instruments to counter certain local norms and beliefs, they also fill human rights with certain elements of the latter, which they find, conversely, to be helpful to their cause.

Arguably, Burmese LGBT activists render a more counterhegemonic version of human rights, whereby they produce core meanings for human rights based on dialogue with local conceptions and practices of dignity (Santos 2015). They believe that queers are equally worthy of dignity and entitled to rights, but they do not emphasize winning equality per se. They focus on increasing belonging to enhance the positions of queers in Burmese society. In their triad of meanings, human rights contain the supposed universal concept of dignity in such international documents as the UDHR, as well as their local understandings of dignity and their own method of achieving it—in ways that are relevant to ordinary Burmese. Seen in this light, their practice speaks to critics who urge a reexamination of core human rights concepts in diverse contexts (Santos 2015; Mutua 2002). Those scholars call out human rights activists for failing to account for contextualized meanings of dignity, shaped by poverty and other devastating conditions (Mutua 2008).

In the same vein, LGBT identities, integral to LGBT activists' human rights practice, need not be seen as overtaking more traditional or local subjectivities (Kollman and Waites 2009). To LGBT activists in my study, the imported terms are as much local as they are Western (also see Altman 2006, citing Jackson 1996, 118–119).[24] They do not consistently interpret and apply LGBT terms as they are usually defined in international parlance. Instead, they blend into LGBT vocabulary their prior understandings about gender and sexuality in Myanmar (also see Gilbert 2013, 2016). Hence, my findings on their engagement with LGBT identities resonate with queer studies about neighboring societies like Thailand (Jackson 2003, 2009; Sinnott 2004), Indonesia (Boellstorff 2005; Blackwood 2010), and Malaysia (Wong 2012). For example, writing about Indonesia, Tom Boellstorff describes the appropriation process of "gay" and "lesbian" into locally sensible concepts as one of "dubbing": the result is something different, unlike the older, local subjectivities but not quite the original version of the foreign either.

Intimately linked to the triad of human rights meanings, LGBT activists' employment of LGBT identities empowers a social and collective self rather than create individuated, automated persons as feared by human rights critics. Once more, the key is emotions and social ties that constitute and are constituted by the processes of their human rights practice. Consistent with studies defending LGBT identities against allegations of essentialism (Bernstein 2005) or Western imposition (Currier 2012), LGBT activists strategically use these identities to meet their needs and interests. When I explained community-building processes, I pointed out that the activists regard LGBT identities as the embodiment of dignity, a manner of enjoying human rights; they also intend LGBT as a collective marker for their community that coalesces around their human rights practice. Hence, movement leaders do not enforce any particular definition, letting queer Burmese reinterpret them in ways that even deviate from international parlance. More important to LGBT activists, they want the imported identities, untainted by derogation and insults in their society, to change queer Burmese's feelings about themselves. They also want LGBT identities to dispel some degree of isolation and unite queers with a new social form of belonging, the LGBT movement community, similar to their strategic use by movements in other countries to cohere diverse queer populations (Blackwood and Wieringa 2007). In return, the community of activists assumes the responsibility of winning for queer people greater belonging in Burmese society, therefore gaining greater dignity and collectively achieving the collective good of human rights.

The Interrelated Outcomes
of Human Rights Practice as a Way of Life

The processes of formation, grievance transformation, and community building, bearing infused meanings of human rights and LGBT identities, lead to three outcomes that bring out the third salient feature of human rights practice as a way of life. Emphasizing the interrelated nature of the effects of human rights practice, this feature demonstrates how personal changes are intimately connected to collective action from the grassroots and how personal and grassroots dimensions of change set in motion the push for formal institutional outcomes. The LGBT movement's practice cultivates the self-transformation of the rights bearer, queer Burmese. Starting with the rights bearer, changes to personhood or sense of self culminate in the creation of a distinctive emotion culture. The people who adopt the emotion culture make up a community of LGBT activists who maintain and spread the practice. They introduce to Burmese politics new claims and claimant, LGBT rights for LGBT people. The three outcomes bring the movement closer to the goals of self-acceptance of queer Burmese, their social belonging, and legal reform.

This third feature advances human rights scholarship and the sociolegal study of rights and social movements in the manner that it refines research on human rights outcomes, particularly their impact on collective action and social change. The contribution is not simply about reaffirming the significance of cultural outcomes in social movements literature, such as collective identity (Polletta and Jasper 2001), the expansion of social spaces (Armstrong 2002), and activists' postmovement biographies (McAdam 1988),[25] or confirming the indirect effects of rights known in sociolegal studies (McCann 1994; Albiston 2010; Engel and Munger 2003). Neither is it mainly concerned with the well-trodden debate about whether identity-based movements, as archetypes of "new social movements," are distinguishable from labor, peasant, and such "older" movements that demand the state provide better distribution of resources.[26] Of course, for the LGBT movement, the three outcomes do matter in and of themselves. Being inherently political, their practice seeks to redefine social positions and relations, and reimagine personhood and belonging in their society (Alvarez, Dagnino, and Escobar 1998; Jordan and Weedon 1995).

But even more pertinent, the conceptual framework of human rights practice as a way of life articulates how outcomes produced by human rights are interrelated and how this interrelatedness emerges through processes that make and are made by emotions and relationships. Social movements literature often points out the interrelatedness of different types of outcomes and their mutual effects on one another over time (Bosi, Guigni, and Uba 2016). For instance, Taylor (1989) finds that community and collective identity building during difficult political times prepared the American women's movements for future escalation of tactics. Gould (2009) examines the emotion work of AIDS activists to transform, generate, and mobilize emotions. Tsutsui (2017) observes that adopting human rights perspectives altered Ainu individuals' understandings of their problems and empowered them to organize a new movement. However, studies on human rights movements usually neglect to explain the social processes through which personal changes to activists or other consequences influence another outcome. Even more rarely do they consider the critical roles of emotions and social ties involved.

The LGBT movement's interrelated outcomes show that human rights practice from the bottom up can lay the foundation for formal institutional goals (also see Kurasawa 2007). Granted, the three outcomes alone may be insufficient to reach those goals. Activists need other breaks, such as democratization or greater access to the courts. Nonetheless, the outcomes so far come from and, in turn, sustain the recursive, overlapping processes. As Tilly (1984) noted, movements are sustained by those who keep on pressing their claims against the state—and, I would add, other targets.

Self-Transformation

By engaging with human rights practice as a way of life, movement newcomers eventually transform into a certain type of person with a certain sense of self or personhood—LGBT activists. Through grievance transformation processes, they learn and adopt fresh feeling rules on how to feel about themselves and alter their perception of queer suffering. Instead of pain, self-hate, and fear, they realize that they deserve dignity and perceive their suffering as human rights violations. They find hope and confidence, believing that their suffering, for which someone or something else is to blame, should and could be remedied. The adoption of LGBT identities, without the baggage of derogatory Burmese vocabulary, aids the transformation. To them, the new words affirm their sexuality or gender identity, relieving them of the reminders of prejudice and abuse that accompany the old and familiar.

Self-transformation goes on to alter interpersonal relationships in their lives. Adopting the new feeling rules further involves exercising self-responsibility, so that they as individuals should conduct themselves and social interactions differently and shoulder collective responsibility for queer Burmese to fight for their rights. We know from the earlier section that interpersonal relationships are experienced through and shaped by emotions. How queer Burmese interact with others and how they are treated by others inform who they are. Becoming LGBT activists who adopt more positive feeling rules alters—and, to them, improves—their interactions with family, friends, and others and perceptions of how they are regarded.

Improved interpersonal relationships entail greater social belonging and, accordingly, the enjoyment of dignity faraway from any formal recognition of human rights. The self is relationally constructed, contrary to its Western conception as a bounded and distinctive whole (Rosaldo 1980; Geertz 1984; Gergen 2009; Nedelsky 2011). Following this view, LGBT activists' personhoods are constituted by social ties. Embedded in a web of interdependent relationships (Fineman 2008),[27] who LGBT activists are (or were before they became activists) constantly changes according to their social positions, interactions, and experiences (Ewing 1990; Engel and Munger 2003, citing Bruner 1990) and, along with that, emotions. Their improved relationships connect their individual selves to other people, affirming them as social beings who belong to Burmese society, a crucial component of having dignity for LGBT activists—and many other Burmese, for that matter. The increased sense of belonging feeds back into ongoing intersubjective processes (Calhoun 1991; Emirbayer 1997; Liang and Liu 2018), further constructing their sense of self.[28]

Distinctive Emotion Culture

Human rights practice as a way of life also produces a distinctive emotion culture made up of two essential components: the feeling rules that facilitate self-transformation and inclusive bonding that aspires to bring together a diverse queer population. By taking part in the practice, queer Burmese are not merely socialized into a new emotion culture (Turner and Stets 2005; Gordon 1989). They actively and continuously construct it.[29] Uniquely the movement's creation, the feeling rules and bonds are a measure of its achievement (Goodwin, Jasper, and Polletta 2001a).[30]

The movement's emotion culture diverges from those of other queer communities in Myanmar. Its first essential component, feeling rules generated by grievance transformation processes, is grounded in the diagnosis of queer suffering as human rights violations and the pursuit of human rights as its remedy. They beseech queer Burmese to be hopeful and confident by taking action to change their conditions and gain greater belonging in society at large, not seek refuge from it—therefore turning them into activists. In contrast, more established queer communities, such as the ones coalesced around *nat* worship and female beauty, offer queer Burmese niche occupations and sanctuaries to escape from queer suffering.

The second essential component, an inclusive manner of queer bonding, ensues from community-building processes where shared affinities of being LGBT and affective ties are forged from their collective practice. By comparison, the older queer communities tend to be divided along gender lines, that is, how the queer person identifies in terms of gender, and tend to cater and keep to queers whom they perceive to be their own kind. For example, communities based in *nat* worship and the female beauty industry revolve around *apwint*, *apone*, and *trans women*, queers were assigned male at birth. Although LGBT activists recruit people who have social ties to these older queer communities and, as I will explain, have so far achieved limited success with inclusive queer bonding, they at least aim to unite a broad spectrum of queers regardless of their sexualities and gender identities. Tin Hla, for example, leads an organization for all LGBT persons and tries to reach out to lesbians.

This distinctive emotion culture composes a community of people who adopt its feeling rules and manner of queer bonding, connecting to one another through human rights practice as a way of life.[31] The practice emotionally ties them to human rights by way of the feeling rules and to one another by way of the inclusive queer bonding. Certainly, the movement's LGBT community is a place for queer people to find camaraderie, solidarity, and friendship, positive relationships that can alter personhood by providing a new sense of belonging (Jasper and Poulsen 1993; Krinsky and Crossley 2014). It is especially important for LGBT activists who did not previously belong to any queer community. But even for those who maintain social ties to other queer communities—and many of them do—the movement is not merely another option where they find commiseration and escape. It is a community of "people who act together in a particular way" and who understand "their problems as amenable to a particular type of action" (Clemens 1996, 205–206).[32]

New Claims and Claimant

The community of LGBT activists with their unique personhood and emotion culture represents a novel claimant and brings their novel claims to Burmese politics. Although human rights are gaining familiarity and political currency in Myanmar, the LGBT movement stands out for projecting queer Burmese as a collective claimant known as LGBT and asserting their entitlement to human rights—what they mean by "LGBT rights." At the same time, with human rights, they connect to a global movement, earn international legitimacy, and secure funding (Bob 2005, 2009).

In short, the LGBT movement advocates a discourse that once was taboo and brings attention to a population hitherto neglected to Nay Pyi Taw and town halls hundreds of miles away from Yangon. Its activists talk to the media and politicians about being LGBT in Myanmar, highlight their goals, and ask society and the government to play their parts in giving acceptance and reforming legal institutions. Bolstered by their international connection and money, they publish reports, hold public events such as IDAHO, organize petitions, and even file lawsuits to highlight the human rights violations of queer Burmese and lay claim to human rights and dignity.

A human rights–based LGBT movement can sometimes break new ground for activism and democratization (Thoreson 2014). Pressing for LGBT rights for LGBT people in their country, these activists push hard at the boundaries of change (De la Dehesa 2010) and the scope and meaning of rights (see, e.g., Polletta 2000; Silverstein 1996) that other Burmese activists and politicians have in mind. The LGBT movement's human rights practice has not won any formal institutional outcome in Myanmar; it faces limitations and contains flaws. However, it modifies Myanmar's sociopolitical landscape. In their study of the AIDS industry in Africa, Watkins and Swidler (2012) recognize that the organizations fail to meet their objectives but observe that they nevertheless bring to local people alternative understandings about their lives, new terminology embodied with its own meanings, different social relations and communities, and demands for how society could and should be. The same can be said of the LGBT movement's practice. The outcomes of self-transformation and emotion culture lead to the claim making of LGBT rights for LGBT people of Myanmar, a marginalized population who used to have little political voice. These groundbreaking claims and claimant, originating from human rights practice from below, have started to knock on the door of formal institutions.

Limitations of Human Rights Practice as a Way of Life

Up to this point, LGBT activists' practice comes across as an empowering way of life, an alternative mode of knowing, feeling, and interacting that shows human rights have the potential to bring social change through collective action. Contrary to some of the criticisms brought up about their pitfalls, human rights in this book resonate with locals from urban, rural, and provincial areas and all kinds of socioeconomic backgrounds. Human rights rally them to strive for social change together, form and join a movement, and sustain it from the times of repressive military rule through the contemporary period of democratization. Human rights seem effective, capable of local resonance and stimulating political action.

Nonetheless, the practice of human rights as a way of life embodies faults and fault lines. National and grassroots activists, roughly corresponding to the urban and the rural, differ in the extent to which they adopt the newly constructed feeling rules. National activists, who are full-time paid NGO staff, control the movement's funding and activities throughout the country. Grass-roots organizers, however, do not always go along. Though attracted to the movement, they are mostly volunteers. On top of fulfilling the requirements of national LGBT activists, they are interested in promoting their own local pa-tronage and hustling for daily wages, the realities of everyday life in Myanmar.

Depending on their social positions and interactions at hand, LGBT activists also diverge in how frequently they use LGBT identities on themselves and queer Burmese as a whole, which leads to variations in self-transformation. They navigate among the LGBT movement, other queer communities, and Burmese society at large, and they maintain various correlating identities and emotional bonds alongside one another. Tun Tun and Tin Hla, for example, describe themselves as *gay* (using the English word even when speaking in Burmese). But when they work at the grassroots, from time to time they return to local words, including the ones they accuse of being derogatory, to establish rapport and communicate more directly.

Trying to proliferate an inclusive form of queer bonding further runs into unequal gender dynamics, which are common in LGBT movements around the world (see, e.g., Mogrovejo 1999; Ross and Landstrom 1999; Stockdill 2003; Park-Kim, Lee-Kim, and Kwon-Lee 2007). As is evident at the September 2012 workshop, the movement is dominated by and inadvertently privileges queers who were designated male at birth, with the result of disadvantaging lesbians. Gender norms affect lesbians' chances of joining the movement, staying and becoming part of the movement community, and rising to leadership positions (also see McAdam 1992; Robnett 1996, 1997).[33]

Furthermore, external constraints and innate deficiencies dilute the transcendent nature of their claims of LGBT rights for Burmese LGBT. For one, in a country where abuse of power, corruption, and arbitrary rule reigned for decades over any semblance of rule of law by any definition, the LGBT movement encounters structural legacies that still pervade Myanmar's politics, courts, and law enforcement (Cheesman 2015) and obstruct its progress. For another, social norms are so entrenched that long-held biases are hard to overcome, even among potential allies. They infiltrate the practice, such that activists themselves risk affirming the hierarchy that sustains queer suffering and endorsing the uneven distribution of power immanent in social conventions (Selby 2012). The movement also privileges Burmans and Buddhists. Because they rely on interpersonal relationships for growth and expansion, LGBT activists, who are mostly Burmans and Buddhists, neglect people who fall outside their web of social ties, especially ethnic and religious minorities, and fail to address claims specific to non-Burman or non-Buddhist queers.

The Complications of Human Agency

Human rights practice as a way of life contains faults and fault lines because agency enables yet constrains it. Formation, grievance transformation, and community-building processes are embedded in the sociopolitical conditions of Myanmar, which give rise to emotions and interpersonal relationships. LGBT activists demonstrate innovation and the potential for change as they draw on and reconstitute cultural schemas and resources for their practice and produce encouraging outcomes. But as brave and creative as they are, overcoming deeply set distribution of power and hierarchy, norms, and beliefs is an arduous endeavor. These conditions made LGBT activists who they were and endowed them with a certain sort of agency (Sewell 1992) long before the movement, and they continue to exert their influence afterward.

To complicate matters, agency changes according to social positions (Sewell 1992), affecting individuals' interests and needs and their group's collective practice. As a stigmatized people, queer Burmese may tend to have similar emotions about their experiences, but their personal histories also distinguish them individually in the ways they feel and act (Gould 2009), especially if the power dynamics within their movement are asymmetrical (Flam 2015). For example, the fifteen to twenty participants and leaders at the September 2012 workshop show a wide spectrum of social positions that exists not only in terms of gender and sexuality but also class, education, geography, and other variables. The self-understandings, emotions, and interpersonal relationships that they bring into the LGBT movement are dissimilar. Thus, they engage and experience the processes of formation, grievance transformation, and community building differently, resulting in variations and deficiencies.

In light of the limitations, what should we make of the power and effectiveness of human rights to bring any good or mobilize people collectively? An obvious response is to point out, yet again, the inequalities and ineffectiveness of human rights practice. The differences in adoption of feeling rules between national and grassroots activists reflect power dynamics and local elitism that human rights critics have warned about. The movement's gender imbalance demonstrates patriarchal power at work, whereas its Buddhist and Burman centricity replicates Burman privilege (Walton 2013), an endemic problem of Myanmar's state and society. As for the existence of older queer identities and communities, the enduring structural legacies, and stubborn norms, they are yet more examples of why human rights are ineffective when put into local action.

All of that is valid, but it is only part of my answer. The concept of human rights practice as a way of life offers an understanding of the power and effectiveness of human rights by appreciating the multiplicity of humanity (Goodale 2009). It shows compassion for what makes all of us human (Jasper 2014) and less concern for binaries of global-local that mirror the power-powerless. Tracing social processes, especially their emotions and interpersonal relationships, I find a human rights practice that is ever changing and lacking in uniformity (Cowan 2006; Goodale 2007a), for the agency behind it is complex, fluid, and multiple within and across individuals. The people in this story enter the movement with prejudices, blind spots, and endearing loyalties, even as they embrace human rights with open arms and the best of intentions. Like the remarkable but flawed people they are, they render something that is hopeful and filled with possibilities and yet disappointing and full of letdowns.

In other words, LGBT activists create and offer an alternative way of life, but their human rights practice does not and cannot surpass other modes of knowing, feeling, and interacting in Burmese society. The meaningful outcomes of self-transformation, distinctive emotion culture, and new claims and claimant coexist with the practice's faults and fault lines. Sociopolitical forces more obstinate and powerful in Myanmar hamper the practice, posing obstacles and insinuating deficiencies into the practice. Ironically, it means that LGBT activists' practice cannot yet completely overcome structural constraints, local systems of patronage, struggles for livelihood, gender inequality, and prejudices toward queers and the non-Burman, non-Buddhist.

Rather than put at risk indigenous subjectivities, their practice also adds textures and layers to the diversity and fluidity of personhood. LGBT identities are remade and infused with local meanings and do not take over sexual and gender identities already there (also see De la Dehesa 2010). These include the derogatory terms that activists say they want to displace. Older forms of queer bonding, such as communities coalesced around *nat* worship and female beauty, remain well and alive.

Instead, in line with other writings on Myanmar (Keeler 2016; Gilbert 2016) and Southeast Asia (Chua and Engel 2015), LGBT activists strategically navigate multiple worlds and identities that exist alongside the community and identities shaped by the movement. They hold onto other identities, queer and otherwise, that attach them to other social groups with emotional bonds that are sometimes stronger than the movement's. Their multiple identities and belongings submerge or emerge to the surface as and when they are summoned, according to time, place, and people.[34] Unlike conceptions of the autonomous, bounded individual, personhood consists of unstable and multiple identities, constantly remade through social interactions (see Geertz 1984; Ewing 1990; Speed 2008; Gergen 2009). One identity is no less authentic than the other. For LGBT activists, personhood is plural, and they are capable of navigating each of their multiple selves.

. . .

What can we learn from human rights practice as a way of life? The book's central concept is informed by close analysis of the Burmese LGBT movement and the personal narratives of its leaders and participants, but the concept has broader relevance for the study of human rights and sociolegal research on the relationship between rights and social movements. Its emphasis on processes, emotions, and relationships, in particular, brings original insight into the capacity of human rights to advance collective action and social progress. In the Conclusion, I step back from the details of the LGBT movement to take up these discussions.

To close the book, I also reflect on what it entails to use the concept to study human rights empirically. Running throughout these pages, it is a commitment to subjectivities, especially emotions and relationships, and to telling them with love and compassion. Thus, in the following chapters, I tell the story of a group of people who give to human rights their emotional fealty and to one another fellowship and affection. Tun Tun, Tin Hla, and their compatriots, all of whom you will get to know, fight for human rights because they want to be happier about who they are, build better relationships with family and friends, and feel hopeful about their future. In the face of and in spite of faults and imperfections, they keep on fighting because they find a new creed for a better life in human rights.

Chapter 2

Forming the Movement

Founding Emotions and Social Ties

I didn't expect to end up with this life [laughs]. My family is a well-to-do family, kind of middle-class background with military and government servants. . . . But suddenly in 1988, the first student who was killed in March was my close friend. (Tun Tun, interview, February 21, 2013*)

T HE STORY of human rights practice as a way of life begins with the Burmese LGBT movement's origins, wrought of pain and suffering. Though founded in the mid-2000s in Chiang Mai, Thailand, the origins of the movement go back to 1988. The pain and suffering of those tumultuous days fomented political disaffection for Tun Tun. It provoked him to do things that forever changed his life and the lives of Tin Hla, the boy from the barracks, and other queer Burmese in the decades that followed.

As the LGBT movement emerges from formation processes, we begin to see how emotions and interpersonal relationships constitute the processes of human rights practice as a way of life. Through ties of political disaffection, ties of survival among economic migrants, and ties of altruism among workers and volunteers of HIV/AIDS organizations, Tun Tun and his mentees get in touch with and encourage Tin Hla and other Burmese to participate in human rights workshops and join the LGBT movement. All of these interpersonal relationships are rooted in suffering caused by the violence of the Burmese state—its brutal quelling of dissent, economic policies that devastated the livelihood of ordinary Burmese, and substandard social services and health care. Some of these relationships further connect to informal networks created by queer Burmese to help one another and hide from discrimination.

By tapping preexisting ties, LGBT movement leaders also awaken emotions that fuel the desire and grit that recruits need to answer the movement's calls. Pushed by raw emotions of suffering and pulled by affections of trust, respect, and admiration for movement leaders, the recruits want to find out about the new gathering of queer Burmese and the curious thing called "human rights." Once they decide to answer the movement's call, they come face-to-face with the fear of getting caught and punished by their government for dabbling in human rights, emotions that they often counter with courage and calm.

Seeds of Resistance: Political Disaffection and Fear of Being Queer

Fittingly, Tun Tun's tale offers the first illustration of how emotions and interpersonal relationships, shaped by Myanmar's sociopolitical conditions, constitute the LGBT movement's human rights practice. The 1988 demonstrations in which Tun Tun participated signified the disaffection toward the military regime, as well as the pain and suffering that ordinary Burmese felt about their lives and caused some of them to rise up. The violent repression Tun Tun encountered tells us why most Burmese dread their government. His life as a rebel who is also queer offers a taste of the shame, fear, and self-hatred that social prejudices wreak insidiously on queer Burmese. These deeply emotional experiences compelled Tun Tun to become a student protest leader, regime rebel, pro-democracy advocate, and then human rights activist—periods in his life when he built social ties that paved the long, circuitous road toward the birth of the LGBT movement.

At first, the pain of his friend's death "shocked" and awoke Tun Tun to the regime's brutality (interview, June 30, 2015*), kindling political disaffection that turned the young man with military family connections into a dissident and activist. In March 1988, police reportedly intervened in a conflict among college students in Yangon and killed some of them. The incident sparked off demonstrations that resulted in more killings (Steinberg 2010). One of the students who died was Tun Tun's friend. Tun Tun was studying English literature at Rangoon University, while his friend attended the Rangoon Institute of Technology. The two had volunteered together for the Red Cross. Angry that the government claimed his friend was killed by accident, Tun Tun joined the protests to demand the truth. "I was at the front, negotiating with the police to let us go and telling them that we are peaceful demonstrators. . . . And suddenly the riot police truck came to drive into us from the back . . . so we were totally stuck in between. They started beating the students" (interview, February 21, 2013*). Tun Tun escaped and hid in a stranger's house but returned to more protests.

His family was appalled when they found out. Tun Tun had more in common with Tin Hla than we would imagine from the opening paragraphs of the book. Tun Tun's father served in the army. His paternal grandfather was "high up" in the military ranks, a recognized "hero" who was given a "great position" to oversee governmental departments after retirement (interview, June 30, 2015*). When Tun Tun was arrested in June 1988, his mother bailed him out, and his father had him brought back to Mon State, his birthplace.

The protests in Yangon led to nationwide uprising, which erupted after decades of frustration and desperation. In the hands of the military government, Myanmar had descended into economic mismanagement, especially after the implementation of centrally planned economy and other "Burmese way to socialism" policies in the 1970s. On the eve of the 1988 uprising, the United Nations declared Myanmar a "least developed nation," and inflation was once again on the rise.[1]

In response to the nationwide uprising, the military staged a coup in September 1988 and installed the State Law and Order Restoration Council (later renamed the State Peace and Development Council), a development that eventually forced Tun Tun to flee into exile. After his parents brought him from Yangon back to Mon State, Tun Tun became a strike leader and a prominent target of the military. His family could not "control" him, he said (interview, June 30, 2015*). As the regime carried out widespread arrests and torture, he escaped to the Myanmar-Thailand border, took up arms with a student rebel army, and disappeared into the tropical forests where they joined ethnic minority armies in guerrilla warfare against the regime. Meanwhile, the military vowed to restore stability and claimed that it would hand over power after holding elections in 1990. However, when the NLD won 82 percent of the parliamentary seats, the military suppressed the NLD and held its leader, Aung San Suu Kyi, under house arrest (Steinberg 2001; Charney 2009). Eventually Tun Tun found out that his mother believed their family was being watched in case he secretly contacted them, and she disowned him publicly. Tun Tun would not reunite with his mother until 2012, after the semicivilian government permitted political exiles to return.[2]

In the rebel army, Tun Tun fell in love but met with another form of oppression. Although he did not disclose his sexuality, he had to be careful because he did not "appear macho." "In this kind of jungle life, men, particularly between twenty, twenty-five, hundreds without any pleasure, they think *gay* men are the free sex service doll" (interview, June 30, 2015*). Tun Tun's boyfriend felt pressured to prove that he was "macho"—so much so that Tun Tun believes it was why his boyfriend accepted a mission for the rebel army inside Myanmar (interview, June 30, 2015*). Tun Tun never saw him again; he later found out that the Burmese military had captured his boyfriend and tortured him to death. It was both homophobia and the junta, Tun Tun believes, that killed the young man who is leaning back in his arms in the faded photograph he still keeps (field notes, January 30, 2016).

Tun Tun's political disaffection and fear of being queer sowed seeds of his resistance, but the LGBT movement's bloom had to wait until his social ties connected him to other people who wanted to take up the cause together. By the mid-1990s, the junta had destroyed some of the rebel army camps. Tun Tun left guerrilla warfare to join a human rights group in Thailand and study overseas on a scholarship. He maintained ties with the rebel army and tried to convince the group to remove its punishment of homosexual acts in the early 2000s. He also set up an advocacy group to make contact with an international LGBT organization. However, none of these developments germinated right away into collective action for queer Burmese.

Ties of Disaffection and Escape from Self-Hatred

Instead, in the early 2000s, Tun Tun established a general human rights group, JUSTICE, which connected him to a sprawling network of political disaffection and gradually shored up momentum for the LGBT movement. Based out of Chiang Mai in northern Thailand, a popular center for Burmese exile activism, JUSTICE raised awareness about the rights of women, children, and ethnic minorities.[3] Compared to queer issues, those concerns resonated more easily with other Burmese activists. Queer issues were taboo and misunderstood even by Burmese pro-democracy and human rights advocates. Nonetheless, as Tun Tun traveled along the borders to speak about the military's oppressive rule and human rights violations, he expanded his interpersonal ties among dissidents and migrants that led him to other people who would play key roles in the LGBT movement's inception.

One critical figure was Seng Naw, whose ties of political disaffection put him in touch with Tun Tun and whose self-hatred and shame, and the desire to escape them, pushed him to follow Tun Tun to Chiang Mai. Born to a father in the Kachin Independence Army fighting a longstanding guerrilla war with the Myanmar state, Seng Naw was raised in a community of activists and a thorny web of ethnic-identity politics, which has implicated many of Myanmar's ethnic minority groups and troubled the state from one regime to the next.[4] When he was in his early twenties, Seng Naw joined an underground group in Myitkyina, his hometown and the capital of Kachin State. There, he organized discussions about human rights.

One issue, however, found no support in the human rights talk in Seng Naw's world: his sexuality, which he described to me as *gay* but for which he used to have no word. In those days, he had heard of *achauk*, which he associated with somebody who was assigned male at birth and identifies with being a woman, and not who he was.[5] He was one of the few LGBT activists who had heard of human rights before joining the movement but did not know about their relevance to queer people. "I'd see my image in the mirror and sometimes I even spit [at it]" (interview, April 25, 2013*).

Seng Naw was a young man filled with self-hatred and shame, praying to his Christian God to "take away these things" from him. A teacher from the theology college in Myitkyina told him that God rejected "*gay* people." When members of his church—the majority of Kachin people are Christians[6]—saw "*transgender* [women]" walking around, they would remark, "These people are really bad and they are going to hell for sure" (interview, April 25, 2013*). Seng Naw's grandparents, uncles, and aunts treated him harshly, even breaking his toys when he was boy because he did not seem masculine enough to them. His mother and sisters (his father had passed away) were not as harsh, but they were trying to persuade him to marry a woman (interview, April 25, 2013*).

In April 2002, news of Tun Tun's visit to nearby Liza, a Myanmar-China border post, spread through underground pro-democracy networks and reached Seng Naw: an *achauk* was coming to speak about human rights. Curious, Seng Naw headed to Liza. He introduced himself to Tun Tun and told him about his struggles, the first time he ever revealed them to anybody else. Tun Tun invited him to spend time with JUSTICE in Thailand (Seng Naw, interview, April 25, 2013*).

Seng Naw admired Tun Tun, the first person he had ever known to be "openly *gay*," and wanted to change the way he felt about himself. He decided to go to Chiang Mai: "I was not alone and I really wanted to come out from this pressure I have been living for over twenty years. . . . I really hate to lie to myself" (interview, April 25, 2013*). Before leaving, he slipped across the border to China to buy three handkerchiefs, one each for his mother and two sisters. "This is Kachin tradition. If you do something wrong, you must apologize to your elder. So I washed their feet. . . . I told them I just cannot marry a woman. . . . And, on that night, everyone was crying" (interview, April 25, 2013*). Seng Naw then set out for Chiang Mai.[7]

At JUSTICE, Seng Naw cultivated his desire to organize an LGBT movement. Arriving in March 2003 as an intern, he learned to type and use the Internet on the office computer, improved his English with lessons from a volunteer, and read books and articles he could not obtain in Kachin State. The organization could not afford to pay interns, so he lived at the office and helped cook and clean. He also learned about LGBT identities and LGBT rights (Seng Naw, interview, April 25, 2013*). Seeing that Seng Naw was "energetic" and had "potential," Tun Tun hired him as an assistant (Tun Tun, interview, January 19, 2013*). He sent Seng Naw to the Thai border town of Mae Sot to speak with Karen refugees, displaced by decades of ethnic violence by the Burmese state, and to Phuket to provide humanitarian aid to Burmese migrants after the December 2004 tsunami.[8] But when he learned about Tun Tun's earlier initiatives, what Seng Naw really wanted was to start an LGBT program under JUSTICE:

> Only a few people are doing [LGBT rights]. There are many smart ones . . . but they don't want to spend their lives on that issue so I will choose this road. . . . So I told colleagues in my organization, including [Tun Tun] and other administration department and committees, I really wanted to start an LGBT program. (Seng Naw, interview, April 25, 2013*)

Seng Naw first tried to convince Tun Tun to incorporate an "LGBT module" into JUSTICE's general human rights curriculum. Their JUSTICE colleagues did not support the idea, believing it to be premature for Burmese people. Tun Tun was also hesitant. He worried that the two could not sustain LGBT activism on their own. After all, his earlier group quickly became defunct.

Ties of Survival and Escape from Despair

This time it worked out differently, however, because Tun Tun and Seng Naw were able to nurture a set of relationships among Burmese economic migrants in southern Thailand. At this point, the LGBT movement's growth involved people who not only harbored political disaffection or experienced social prejudices against queer Burmese but also suffered from economic despair, another kind of violence under military rule. From the 1990s on, the reconstituted junta abandoned socialism and brought in foreign investment, but the lives of ordinary Burmese did not improve. Poor economic growth, forced labor for government projects, and unemployment drove hundreds of thousands of Burmese across the border into Thailand in search of livelihoods, frequently explained to me in English as needing to find "survival."[9]

From southern Thailand, among the hundreds of thousands of Burmese migrants, emerged three LGBT movement pioneers: Kyaw Kyaw, Pyae Soe, and Zwe Naung. A combination of social ties linked to pro-democracy activism and economic migration put the three into contact with Tun Tun and Seng Naw. Eventually Kyaw Kyaw and Pyae Soe turned to the fledging movement because they were ashamed and afraid of being queer and wanted to change how they felt about themselves. Zwe Naung was attracted to its human rights agenda because he detested the regime from which he had to flee. They were also encouraged by the affective nature of the relationships they eventually developed with Tun Tun and Seng Naw and among themselves.

As part of his travels along Myanmar's borders, Tun Tun used to frequent Ranong, Thailand, where he got to know queer Burmese, interpersonal relationships that became invaluable to the movement's recruitment of Kyaw Kyaw, Pyae Soe, and Zwe Naung a few years later. Through his pro-democracy ties, Tun Tun had tried to reach out to Burmese in the Thai fishing port, a popular destination for migrants from southern Myanmar. One of his contacts at an international NGO put him in touch with queer Burmese migrants who worked for or received services from its programs. "[Tun Tun] visited about once a month or bimonthly . . . and met [us] in karaoke bars and restaurants" (Moe Moe, interview, February 23, 2013). Once, Tun Tun donated 6,000 Thai baht to Moe Moe and her friends to organize a "fashion show for *transgender*," an event that she described with fond memories.

In 2007, not long after Seng Naw and Tun Tun decided to create an LGBT rights program at JUSTICE, Tun Tun's contact at the international NGO in Ranong asked him to conduct a human rights workshop for *apwint* migrants. Tun Tun delegated the task to Seng Naw. The workshop would be the first LGBT session that Seng Naw ever conducted on human rights and the first for Kyaw Kyaw and Pyae Soe, two village boys who would become leaders of the LGBT movement.

Economic despair drove Kyaw Kyaw from his village in Mon State toward Ranong, where his migrant ties led him to Seng Naw. After his father lost his factory job, Kyaw Kyaw's family sold their house and moved around. One day, the sixteen-year-old boy crammed himself on a boat with other villagers headed to Kawthaung and crossed the border into Ranong. He was determined to earn money to send home to his mother and siblings. In Ranong, he took up whatever job he could find—at a construction site, hotel, shop, and seafood plant. Gradually he met other Burmese and landed a full-time position at the international NGO where Tun Tun had contacts. As an outreach worker, he met more and more migrants, including the queer Burmese who knew Tun Tun from his visits.

Poor economic prospects at home also motivated Pyae Soe to leave for Ranong, where Burmese migrant ties too led him to Seng Naw's workshop. Pyae Soe grew up about ten miles from Dawei, the seat of Tanintharyi Region. His family farmed the paddy fields and traded on the black market to get by, as did many other Burmese (Taylor 1995). His uncles and cousins used to run away when the military came to demand a porter from each family for their fight against Karen rebels. Sometimes the authorities—he cannot remember which ones—would come with orders for each family to participate in "forced voluntary service." Whenever his family could not pay to get out of it, his mother would go to smash rocks for road projects and he to carry stones to construction sites (Pyae Soe, interview, July 3, 2015).[10] As the years went by, Pyae Soe's family increasingly struggled to make ends meet. It got harder to make money from toiling the land, and trading on the black market stopped being lucrative. When Pyae Soe turned twenty, he wanted to leave his village, as other young people had, in search of a brighter future. He contacted an uncle who was working at the international NGO in Ranong, where Seng Naw was going to conduct his first human rights workshop for queer Burmese.

Ties of survival thus converged with Tun Tun's pro-democracy network to put Seng Naw, Kyaw Kyaw, and Pyae Soe in the same room on that day in 2007. Kyaw Kyaw was working in the international NGO's office, and Pyae Soe was volunteering at its information counter, biding time to go to Phuket where he had found a job as a waiter. The two were not invited to the workshop, but they were curious and snuck inside. Seng Naw almost chuckled when he described seeing the two of them who were trying to avoid attention in the back of the room: "They said they were not *gay* and said they had just come to observe" (Seng Naw, interview, April 25, 2013*). Kyaw Kyaw and Pyae Soe recalled listening to Seng Naw in amazement. They had never before met anybody who talked about human rights, much less their relevance to queer people.

In addition to ties of survival, it was their desire to be free of self-loathing and shame, as well as their affection for movement leaders, that motivated Kyaw

Kyaw and Pyae Soe to take the next step: joining the movement. Growing up in his village, Kyaw Kyaw was teased for being "soft and feminine" and asked if he had "balls or a flap" (Kyaw Kyaw, interview, June 27, 2015). At the seafood plant in Ranong, Kyaw Kyaw met his then boyfriend, but he could not stop feeling that their relationship was somehow wrong. "Sometimes I even prayed [to Buddha], 'I'm tired of this life. In my next life, let me be a real man or real woman'" (Kyaw Kyaw, interview, June 27, 2015). After the Ranong workshop, Seng Naw told Tun Tun about Kyaw Kyaw. Tun Tun invited Kyaw Kyaw to a workshop in Mae Sot, where JUSTICE organized training for migrants and refugees from Myanmar.[11] Kyaw Kyaw admired Tun Tun's courage and was inspired by him: "I came to know one thing—in order for other people to accept who I am, I have to accept myself first . . . and I have to accept it bravely" (interview, June 27, 2015).

Life as a queer person was also "suffocating" for Pyae Soe (interview, July 3, 2015). When he was a schoolboy, he once felt so ashamed when a classmate chanted an insulting word for *apwint*, *gandu*, at him that he attacked the boy with a compass needle. Other schoolmates, noticing that he was "soft," forced him to touch their penises and tried to get on top of him to act as though they were having sexual intercourse with him (interview, July 3, 2015). Pyae Soe grew tired of hiding his attraction to men, but there was no escaping his own self-hatred and fear even after moving to Ranong. Immediately following Seng Naw's workshop, Pyae Soe departed for his job in Phuket, a five-hour drive away. He stayed in touch with Kyaw Kyaw but gave no thought to becoming an LGBT activist. In Phuket, he often felt lonely, confused, and anxious about his sexuality. One night he was crying when Kyaw Kyaw called. He confided in Kyaw Kyaw, blurting out that he "likes guys" (Pyae Soe, interview, January 18, 2013). The two have become close friends ever since. Pyae Soe affectionately refers to Kyaw Kyaw as his brother, somebody he trusts and looks up to. When Kyaw Kyaw encouraged him to take up an internship that opened up at JUSTICE in early 2008, Pyae Soe decided to go for it.

But before he left Phuket for Chiang Mai, the web of interpersonal relationships linking Pyae Soe and Kyaw Kyaw to Burmese migrants in Thailand and Tun Tun's human rights activism fortuitously led to the recruitment of Zwe Naung. Also from Tanintharyi Region, Zwe Naung had entered a Yangon monastery as a novice monk when he was fifteen years old. He had been a monk for about ten years when he participated in the 2007 demonstrations popularly dubbed the Saffron Revolution, which broke out in reaction to the military regime's sudden removal of fuel subsidies (Selth 2008; Steinberg 2008). At his monastery, Zwe Naung had joined an underground group affiliated with a dissident network stretching as far back as the '88 generation, activists involved in the 1988 demonstrations. He read and distributed censored materials on human rights, though he confessed he did not really understand them. He was unhappy with the government, but he could not remember exactly why. He simply enjoyed doing what the government forbade. On September 26, 2007, the first day of the crackdown, Zwe Naung marched in the frontline of the demonstrations up to the famous Shwedagon temple. Troops barricaded the front and rear of the demonstrations, where they beat the demonstrators and tear-gassed them.

Amid the chaos, Zwe Naung escaped through the bazaar on one side. Arrests swept across the city, and he dared not return to his monastery. Other monasteries turned him away for fear of courting trouble. Zwe Naung went home to Dawei, but his family was worried about his presence (interview, January 29, 2016). Having nowhere to stay, he kept moving south until he ran out of money at Kawthaung. In the end, a mutual friend contacted Pyae Soe telling him that Zwe Naung was in desperate need. Pyae Soe quickly asked Zwe Naung to join him in Phuket (interviews: Pyae Soe, July 3, 2015, and Zwe Naung, January 18, 2013). Crossing from Kawthaung to Ranong to make his way to Phuket, Zwe Naung shed his monkhood and became a Burmese laborer among the thousands employed in Thailand's tourism industry.

Zwe Naung's political disaffection did not dissipate with his new life; instead, it drew him into JUSTICE and the LGBT movement. "I was unhappy with what we were doing as waiters [in Phuket]. I wanted to be active in the political field, or work or learn from organizations. I was still very interested in politics, right after the 2007 Saffron Revolution" (interview, February 20, 2013). Through Pyae Soe, Zwe Naung got to know Kyaw Kyaw. When Kyaw Kyaw called about the internship at JUSTICE, the opportunity sounded much more appealing to the former dissident monk than waiting on tables. He decided to follow Pyae Soe to Chiang Mai and intern at JUSTICE as well.

Hence, Seng Naw's first meeting in Ranong with Kyaw Kyaw and Pyae Soe in 2007 came to define the course of the LGBT movement. Around 2008, Kyaw Kyaw became JUSTICE's part-time community organizer in Ranong. He formed a group, SUNSHINE, which served as the LGBT movement's base for recruiting, training, and organizing queer Burmese in southern Thailand. Seng Naw helped Kyaw Kyaw obtain international funding for SUNSHINE and administer the funds through JUSTICE with SUNSHINE as a subgrantee.[12] In 2011, SUNSHINE, with VIVID's assistance, secured sufficient funding for

Kyaw Kyaw to work as a full-time coordinator.[13] Other Burmese migrants volunteered or worked part time for the organization, including Moe Moe who met Tun Tun during his Ranong visits in the early 2000s.

Up north in Chiang Mai, Pyae Soe and Zwe Naung joined JUSTICE as full-time staff after their internships. Pyae Soe worked for VIVID, a program under JUSTICE at the time. Zwe Naung originally was put in charge of JUSTICE's videotape archives, library, and general human rights documentation. Months later, when Seng Naw fell ill and could no longer work regularly, Zwe Naung took over VIVID's website and its fledging magazine publication.[14] Although Zwe Naung regards himself as a heterosexual, cisgender man, it is "not difficult" for him to realize that fighting for the human rights of queer Burmese is part and parcel of their struggle for human rights in his country (interview, February 20, 2013).

Ties of Altruism and Escape from Pain

Under Tun Tun's tutelage, Seng Naw, Pyae Soe, and Zwe Naung scaled up the LGBT movement's recruitment and expansion efforts.[15] In addition to dissidents and migrants in Thailand, they looked across the border to their homeland. They started to invite queer Burmese living inside Myanmar to human rights workshops and other movement activities to train the movement's earliest grassroots organizers.

Again, they relied on interpersonal relationships and emotions to attract a geographically more diverse group of people to join in their practice. Using their own social ties rooted in political disaffection, they first contacted people who belonged to an existing web of relationships formed around the HIV/AIDS programs of international NGOs.[16] After the 1988 uprising, the junta tightened legal controls that effectively prevented the formation of most associations interested in civil society, political discourse, or activism.[17] However, among the limited scope of issues permitted for international NGOs was HIV/AIDS, which had reached epidemic levels of infection in Myanmar by the early 1990s, a situation exacerbated by the country's poor standard of social and health services.[18]

Under the junta's rule, HIV/AIDS programs thus offered a safe, albeit restricted, space for grassroots organizing among their targeted populations, including queer people who meet the definition of "men who have sex with men" (MSM) in the context of Burmese HIV/AIDS NGOs. Of course, international NGOs running HIV/AIDS programs were still subject to bureaucratic reviews, put under surveillance (Dar Dar, interview, September 23, 2012*), and prohibited from "engag[ement] in any political, economic, religious or social and cultural activities in conflict with the interests of the Government" (Memorandum of Understanding between the Myanmar Department of Health and an international HIV/AIDS NGO, 2012).[19] Before the 2011 transition, they did not explicitly relate HIV/AIDS work to human rights.[20] Nevertheless, their HIV/AIDS programs generated a network of community-based organizations and self-help groups that received their funding and assistance to implement the programs on outreach, testing, and treatment. These grassroots organizations usually lacked official status, but they were tolerated presumably because of the international NGOs' arrangements with the government. Among the grassroots organizations were those for and by *apwint* and *apone*.[21]

From HIV/AIDS-related ties, LGBT activists recruited queer Burmese whom they trusted and whose experiences with pain and suffering motivated them to take up the invitation and brave the risks of getting involved with human rights. Although the new recruits knew little about the movement or about human rights, they were all too familiar with suffering caused not only by HIV/AIDS but also by society's discrimination. Before HIV/AIDS programs reached their cities, towns, and villages, they had built informal networks of *apwint* and *apone* around occupations such as *nat kadaw*, beautician, and sex worker to help one another with survival and seek solace from the hostility of the outside world. So they answered the recruitment calls with a desire to alleviate the pain of queer Burmese, their physical torment, discrimination, and loneliness, curious about what the new movement had to offer.

The recruitment routes based on HIV/AIDS-related ties supplied the LGBT movement with most of their activists. I tracked the pathways into the movement of almost every person who attended the movement's workshops or meetings between 2013 and 2015. They came into initial contact with the movement through one of the two routes based on HIV/AIDS-related ties, or they were brought in by those who did; and they were affiliated with the HIV/AIDS program of an international NGO, one of their partner grassroots organizations, or an informal social network of *apwint* and *apone*.

First Route:
Linking Old Ties of Political Disaffection with Ties of Altruism

The first of two recruitment routes that tapped HIV/AIDS-related ties leaned on an even older set of emotions and interpersonal relationships: Tun Tun's '88 prodemocracy connections filled with political disaffection. Whereas Tun Tun had fled into exile, some of his compatriots had remained in Myanmar, going underground and concealing their political activism. Two of them ended up working for the HIV/AIDS program of an international NGO when the LGBT movement needed help. One was Maung Nyan, who had been secretly keeping in touch with Tun Tun. The other was Kaung Sat, then a second-year Rangoon University student and a younger schoolmate of Maung Nyan and Tun Tun. Years later, Kaung Sat reconnected with Maung Nyan on the international NGO circuit in Myanmar. Then, sometime in 2007–2008, Maung Nyan offered to help Tun Tun recruit participants for the LGBT movement's workshops and trainings.

To carry out this risky recruitment exercise, Kaung Sat traveled around the country to identify suitable candidates from community-based organizations and self-help groups affiliated with his NGO's HIV/AIDS programs. He and Maung Nyan selected people who were trustworthy, street smart, and courageous. They explained the risks of being associated with a human rights movement, as well as the expectations of sharing what they learned. Since most of those who were selected lived in small towns, local authorities would easily notice when they were planning a trip out of the country; relatives would want to probe and talk about it, because traveling abroad was considered a significant social occasion in most parts of Myanmar. Maung Nyan and Kaung Sat prepared them to devise personal strategies to satisfy the curiosity in their communities. In addition, explaining that the Thai embassy was "close" to the Burmese government, Kaung Sat said they had to come up with acceptable reasons for applying for Thai tourist visas. For instance, Tun Tun asked trusted friends in Chiang Mai to write letters inviting participants to the "Royal Floral Exhibition" (fieldwork, letter on LGBT HR training 2011–11) or to a "hotel and tourism conference" (fieldwork, letter on LGBT HR training 2010–05).

Gyo Kyar and Nay Win's journeys are typical of how grassroots organizers were recruited through this route and how they were emotionally drawn enough to take the chance. Maung Nyan and Kaung Sat contacted Gyo Kyar and Nay Win, whose grassroots organizations partnered with their NGO. Neither Gyo Kyar nor Nay Win knew about human rights from the HIV/AIDS programs, as "the political situation [before 2011] was very restricted. It was not okay to talk about human rights, any rights" (Nay Win, interview, May 13, 2013). But the two were curious about what the movement could do for queer Burmese. They understood the feeling of despair. They had founded their grassroots organizations after seeing *apwint* and *apone* in their towns dying of AIDS. They also felt the violence and discrimination against queer people. Nay Win was almost stabbed to death by a man who refused to keep on his condom when they were having sex. Although the two had an ongoing relationship, the man never disclosed to Nay Win his address or other personal details, behavior that Nay Win explained was quite common among *tha nge*, heterosexual, cisgender men who have relationships with *apwint* and *apone*. Gyo Kyar, who identifies as a *trans woman*, had a *tha nge* boyfriend who would date her only secretly and would not go out in public with her so that he could maintain the image of being "normal." Out of love for him, Gyo Kyar had to "stand it" all those years (interview, March 30, 2013).

Second Route:
New Ties of Political Disaffection Meet Ties of Altruism

The second route centered on HIV/AIDS-related ties connected to one individual, Cho Cho. Similar to the first route, LGBT activists relied on interpersonal relationships arising out of political disaffection. In this instance, the disaffection was directed at the military regime's actions in the late 2000s, including its mismanagement of the Cyclone Nargis crisis in May 2008. Those relationships of political disaffection then connected the LGBT movement to Cho Cho's HIV/AIDS-related ties.

Cho Cho was working for an international NGO's HIV/AIDs outreach program (not the same as Maung Nyan's) in Yangon in 2008 when JUSTICE asked her to assist with its no-vote campaign against the regime. Born in North Okkalapa, Yangon, Cho Cho had dropped out of school at sixteen to earn money for her family. She worked her way up from cleaning hotel rooms to the position with the international NGO (interview, August 18, 2015). Sometime in 2007–2008, she visited Chiang Mai to conduct research on HIV/AIDS programs on behalf of the international NGO. On that trip, she met the staff at JUSTICE. Soon after, the military regime announced a national referendum on the constitution it apparently had been drafting ever since it had disregarded the election results in 1990. Tun Tun wanted to hold a no-vote campaign to protest the constitution, which the NLD was also boycotting due to its limited participation (Williams 2009). One of his JUSTICE staff remembered Cho Cho and suggested to Tun Tun that they ask her to lead their campaign inside Myanmar (Cho Cho, interview, May 15, 2013).

On May 2, 2008, however, just before the national referendum, Cyclone Nargis made landfall in Yangon and the Ayeyarwady delta, causing a humanitarian crisis that ended up drawing Cho Cho and JUSTICE closer together. An estimated 150,000 people died or went missing, another 2.5 million lost their homes, and agricultural land, livestock, and rice stock were destroyed (Charney 2009; South 2008). The government insisted on holding the referendum as scheduled despite the cyclone's devastation to its population—part of the reason the referendum was widely perceived to be illegitimate (Williams 2009).[22] Meanwhile, it provided inadequate assistance to its citizens affected by Nargis and obstructed external aid (South 2008). Cho Cho was one among the many private citizens who took matters into their own hands.[23] With money from JUSTICE, she went around Yangon Region to find out the needs of the affected population and brought them supplies as basic as blankets, mosquito nets, candles, oil, rice, and noodles (Cho Cho, interview, May 15, 2013).

The collaboration between Cho Cho and JUSTICE in the wake of Nargis and the constitutional referendum forged a strong bond of mutual trust, turning her into the LGBT movement's one-woman base in Yangon until VIVID's relocation in 2013. Between 2008 and 2009, Tun Tun invited Cho Cho to Thailand for workshops on how to conduct human rights training and community organizing. Seng Naw asked her to participate in VIVID's workshops on LGBT rights.[24] Although Cho Cho identifies as a heterosexual, cisgender woman, she was familiar with the grievances of queer Burmese because of her work with the HIV/AIDS program. Using her contacts among *apwint* and *apone*, she recruited queer Burmese from communities in Yangon Region first to secretive one-day human rights discussions in the city between 2009 and 2010 and then to Thailand.

Tin Hla's pathway into the LGBT movement illustrates this recruitment route. After moving around the country for twelve years trying to make a living, he was back in Yangon by 2009, running a small mattress shop in North Dagon Township. During his free time, he volunteered for a grassroots organization affiliated with an international NGO's HIV/AIDS program. There, he met Cho Cho, who asked him to join the one-day discussions in Yangon. After they got to know one another, she put him in touch with Seng Naw, who invited him in 2011 to a VIVID workshop followed by the 2012 advocacy session into which I walked on my first day of fieldwork in Chiang Mai.

Tin Hla and other new activists who came through this route felt similarly drawn to the movement's call as those who took the first route. Like Gyo Kyar and Nay Win, wanting "to do something about" the plight of queer Burmese pushed Tin Hla to accept the invitation to learn about human rights (Tin Hla,

interview, August 2, 2016). He too was deeply affected by the pain and suffering he had encountered as a volunteer for the HIV/AIDS organization. He
also wrestled with the fear of being found out and felt the pangs of ostracism.
When he was living in the barracks, he had to conceal his same-sex attraction from his father, whom Tin Hla believed made warning hints with statements such as, "I know my children, who is who, who becomes who." Tin Hla
does not recall behaving in a "very feminine way" when he was a child, but
he remembers that other children sometimes punched him in the face and
called him *achauk*. Whenever that happened, he would stop playing "because
I was afraid that my father or siblings would hear" (interview, June 26, 2015).
After he grew up and left the barracks, Tin Hla struggled to maintain his same-
sex relationships in the face of prejudice, economic hardships, and objections
from his partners' families.

Recruiting Lesbians and Ties of Affection

The LGBT movement's efforts to organize lesbians further highlight the significance of emotions and interpersonal relationships to formation processes.
While lesbians have their own unique grievances, raw emotions, particularly
fear of being queer, sparked enough desire and curiosity in some lesbians to
accept the invitation to a workshop and learn about the movement.[25] The affective nature of the social ties also strongly mattered. Newly recruited lesbians
usually decided to venture out of their tightly knit social circles because they
trusted or respected the people who contacted them and because their friends
were going too.

LGBT activists, however, made progress with lesbian recruitment more
slowly compared to their recruitment of *trans women*, *apwint*, *apone*, and *gay*
men, who come under the MSM umbrella and are connected more directly to
the HIV/AIDS-related ties. Dominated by queers who were assigned male at
birth, the LGBT movement had difficulty gaining access to the social world of
lesbians in the beginning. Seng Naw attempted in the first couple of years to
recruit them but admitted he had failed to establish trust and rapport. Lesbians
generally distrust or feel uncomfortable socializing with strangers regarded as
male at birth, including *gay* men, *trans women*, *apwint*, and *apone*, explain Cho
Cho and other LGBT activists. Moreover, lesbians, being unfamiliar with these
other queer Burmese, harbor their own prejudices against them.

The movement made a breakthrough when they relied on offshoots of HIV/
AIDS-related ties, working through *apwint* and *apone* who are friends with

lesbians to gain access to the latter's social networks—for example, Dar Dar and Shwe Wah.[26] Dar Dar, who was assigned male at birth and identifies as *trans-gender*,[27] leads an HIV/AIDS grassroots organization, the same one where Tin Hla volunteered. Shwe Wah, who had known Dar Dar since she was young, sometimes distributes food to people living with HIV/AIDS served by Dar Dar's organization. Dar Dar was one of the first grassroots recruits who joined the movement through the first HIV/AIDS route of Maung Nyan and Kaung Sat. When VIVID asked Dar Dar for help, she brought in Shwe Wah. In 2009, Shwe Wah traveled to Chiang Mai to attend a VIVD workshop for the first time.

Shwe Wah was drawn to the possibility of alleviating lesbians' isolation and fears. She wanted to bring lesbians into "public life," by which she meant "feel less afraid of people," and interact more with other people outside their own social networks of lesbians (interview, May 10, 2013). That was the kind of life she was leading. Forty-eight years old at the time of our 2013 interview, Shwe Wah was unmarried and lived with her parents. They did not know she was a *lesbian*, but they noticed she hung out only with other lesbians. They were afraid Shwe Wah would become one because they would tell her, "'Instead of falling in love with another woman, why don't you get married with a man?'" (Shwe Wah, interview, May 10, 2013).

Aung Aung's journey into the movement is another important example of how LGBT activists recruited lesbians using HIV/AIDS-related ties connected to *apwint* and *apone*. A *trans man* from a southern Burmese town, Aung Aung attended his first human rights workshop by LGBT activists in 2012, after his T.G. uncle told him that they were looking for lesbian participants.[28] Aung Aung's uncle had heard the news from an employee at the international NGO that was partnering with his grassroots organization for *apwint* and *apone* to implement HIV/AIDS programs in their area (not the same NGO as Maung Nyan's or Cho Cho's).[29]

Once again, Aung Aung's journey contains the theme of wanting to escape isolation and fear. Aung Aung remembers a teacher in tenth grade who picked on him and other *tomboys* in class. The teacher pulled off the shirts that the *tomboys* wore over the mandatory uniform blouse, ordered them to stand in front of the class, and said to them, "Girls should behave like girls" (Aung Aung, interview, July 2, 2015). At school, Aung Aung socialized only with *tomboys*. He had no friends in his neighborhood because he did not know of any other *tomboys* living nearby. Still, he described himself as more fortunate than other lesbians in his town, some of whom suffered domestic violence. At least his mother tolerated his partner and let them live with her. Aung Aung is grateful to his *T.G.* uncle for persuading other family members to accept him. He also admires his uncle's group for *apwint* and *apone*, calling it "very strong" (interview, July 2, 2015). He wanted do the same for lesbians, and the movement's workshop seemed like an opportunity to find out how.

Making use of their existing social networks, emerging lesbian leaders like Shwe Wah and Aung Aung recruited more lesbians for the LGBT movement. After returning home from these workshops, Shwe Wah set up BRIGHT for lesbians in her Yangon township, and Aung Aung tried to consolidate existing social groups of lesbians into a new organization, GARUDA. Akin to the emotional appeal for Shwe Wah and Aung Aung, some of these lesbians were motivated by the desire to feel less afraid. With others, they had to harness the affective nature of existing relationships.

Activists such as Shwe Wah and Aung Aung understood that lesbians would be more likely to answer the movement's call if their friends agreed to go together. They visited places popular with lesbians—local bars known as beer stations, karaoke lounges, and soccer games—to persuade them to join their grassroots organizations or attend movement activities as a group of friends. Their approach has a practical side as well. Going out of town together gives lesbians safety in numbers and allows them to overcome the social restrictions on their physical freedom, because it is generally deemed inappropriate for unmarried women (those assigned female at birth) to be traveling alone. In some cases, these activists accompanied the new recruits to the movement events even though they had participated in a similar one before. As an older woman known in her neighborhood for doing charity work, Shwe Wah is an elder respected and trusted enough to "supervise" younger lesbians on overnight journeys (interview, May 10, 2013). Pa Dauk, a long-time friend recruited by Shwe Wah, also accompanied other lesbians because they "were uncomfortable going [alone] and wanted me to go along" (interview, May 9, 2013).

Overcoming Fear and Anxiety

Even a piece of paper can send you to many years of prison. (Maung Nyan, interview, May 18, 2013*)

After deciding to answer the LGBT movement's recruitment call, queer Burmese had to muster courage and composure to counter the fear and anxiety that permeated their society under military rule and lingered in the early years of political transition. During the movement's founding years, the junta still suppressed political activities and human rights discourse, sometimes taking extralegal measures and at other times applying draconian legislation. Being possibly associated with human rights was terrifying enough to discourage political resistance.[30] In the initial years of political transition, the situation remained unpredictable. Alongside its announcements about legal reform, the new government, led by a military-backed party, continued to arrest activists (Human Rights Watch 2014).

Until 2012, responding to the movement's recruitment call usually entailed traveling to and from Thailand. Regardless of whether they came through the first or second route based on HIV/AIDS-related ties or lesbians' social networks, they all had to pass through checkpoints between Myanmar and Thailand to get to the movement's base in Chiang Mai, or Ranong and Mae Sot, the two border towns where VIVID and JUSTICE reached out to heavy concentrations of Burmese migrants. They could cross over land, from Kawthaung to Ranong or Myawaddy to Mae Sot, or travel by bus to Yangon or Mandalay and then fly to Chiang Mai.

At the checkpoints, this mix of fear and composure would come into play. Kaung Sat describes going through checkpoints at airports as the most dangerous period of out-of-country travel for them. They would have to stay calm and display nonchalance, all the while keeping their fear and anxiety in check.[31] If questioned by immigration or special branch officers about their purpose for traveling, they would have to give credible explanations without inadvertently disclosing their real intention. "'You are going to Thailand?' 'Yes.' 'What is your purpose to go to Thailand?'" (Kaung Sat, interview, May 21, 2013*). Gyo Kyar, for instance, played up the stereotype of *apwint*, acted in a flamboyant manner, and replied that she was going "shopping" (interview, March 30, 2013). When Pa Dauk traveled with eleven other *tomboys* to Chiang Mai, immigration officers noticed they did not look gender conforming in appearance. They asked Pa Dauk why they were traveling abroad, and Pa Dauk kept her answer short and simple, "We are going there for a visit" (Pa Dauk, interview, May 9, 2013).

Arriving home, they had to compose themselves again if customs officers randomly selected their bags to check whether they had brought back prohibited items. Tin Hla's encounter vividly illustrates the mix of fright and composure of people who dared to bring home human rights–related materials, such as magazines and posters, from the LGBT movement's workshops. In 2011, on his return journey from Chiang Mai to Yangon, a customs officer at the

Yangon airport opened up his bag containing VIVID's publications and CDs about human rights:

> I was so afraid, so what I tried to do was say [to the officer], "Oh, I have seen you before. Where do you live? I'm from [name of place]. Where are you from?" Even the officer was quite confused about whether he knew me or not and said, "Yes, I think I've seen you before." [laughs] ... Because there were many CDs and many books, he felt something hard. He said, "What is it?" And I said, "Oh, it's just a hairdryer. Brought back from Chiang Mai." And then the officer said, "Okay, okay, you go." Otherwise, I could have gone to jail! (Tin Hla, interview, May 15, 2013)

Tin Hla is the only person in my study who reported coming close to getting caught. Some interviewees told me that they hid the materials underneath their *longyi* (sarong) or mixed them up with dirty underwear to discourage customs officers from rummaging deeper. Nay Win and others said they flirted with officers to distract them or bribed them with gifts.[32]

Laying the Foundation for Human Rights Practice as a Way of Life

As formation processes increasingly move outward, LGBT activists produce a "multiplier effect."[33] When VIVID was based in Chiang Mai from 2007 to March 2013, the movement started to establish grassroots locations, which it designated as "focal points." In addition to recruiting and training grassroots organizers, movement leaders held strategic meetings and celebrated IDAHO in Ranong in 2009 and in Chiang Mai the following two years. Cho Cho founded REGAL, a grassroots LGBT association based in Yangon Region that reached out to a diverse mix of queer Burmese. After she successfully obtained international funding for REGAL to provide modest staff salaries, Tin Hla quit the mattress shop business to work full time for it.

During this period, VIVID began to publish a magazine and produce a television show, important movement "totems" disseminated to queer Burmese.[34] The magazine, which remains a regular publication several times a year (the intervals vary), contains articles translated from sources around the world about LGBT personalities, legal reforms, and entertainment in other countries, and, whenever possible, stories about their own movement and the achievements and struggles of queer Burmese. The television show, no longer in production at the time of this book's writing due to VIVID's busy schedule, showcased interviews along similar themes.[35] Pyae Soe, who was responsible for the show, posted the episodes on the Internet and saved them on CDs. In Myanmar, where Internet access was—and still remains—difficult or nonexistent in many places, VIVID's magazines and CD recordings brought hope and support to queer Burmese in remote parts of the country.[36] In some instances, reading the magazines encompassed grievance transformation processes (see Chapter 3) that motivated people to join the movement.

Grassroots organizers across Myanmar serve as the movement's distribution system for the totems (beyond smuggling home a few publications in suitcases from Thailand). When VIVID was producing the materials out of Chiang Mai and Cho Cho visited there, she would bring as many copies of the magazines, CDs, and human rights posters as she could on her return journey. She would go down the road to Mae Sot, where she would pack the materials into bags mixed with household items and cover them up with blankets, load the bags on a bus, and explain to the driver that she was a factory worker moving home to Yangon. Later, VIVID found a trusted contact in Mae Sot to receive their deliveries from Chiang Mai and put them on Yangon-bound buses. When the materials arrived in Yangon, Cho Cho would contact grassroots organizers to collect their share or wait for them to come to Yangon for the next movement activity VIVID organized. Cho Cho improved the distribution system after VIVID moved to Yangon in 2013. For dissemination outside Yangon, she and her colleagues put the magazines, now published in the city, on passenger buses and address the packages to the respective grassroots organizers, who collect them when the buses arrive in their towns.[37]

After the political transition in 2011, Tun Tun gauged his communications with officials and other contacts and determined it was safe enough to carry out human rights activities under the semicivilian government (interview, September 22, 2012*). The time had come to take the LGBT movement home. He and VIVID leaders contacted Cho Cho to prepare the Yangon offices. Ahead of the relocation, Cho Cho also coordinated with grassroots organizers in Yangon, Mandalay, Monywar, Pathein, and Kyaukpadaung to hold the IDAHO 2012 celebrations for the first time inside Myanmar.[38] In March 2013, Pyae Soe, Zwe Naung, and their colleagues packed up and moved VIVID to Yangon. Under Kyaw Kyaw's leadership of SUNSHINE, the movement's Ranong base also produced leaders who returned to Myanmar in 2014 and set up a VIVID branch office in Dawei.

Working out of their headquarters in Yangon, VIVID leaders continue to expand the reach of their movement and practice. They board buses and visit new towns on advocacy trips. Ahead of their visits, they ask friends and acquaintances about informal social networks and popular hangouts for queer Burmese at their destinations. They try to arrive one day in advance and find queer Burmese at those places to invite them to the meeting. For remote small towns where residents have little or no access to the Internet, this is an effective method of outreach and recruitment. At the meetings, they introduce their movement and their human rights practice, with the aim of encouraging local queers to participate in future movement workshops and organize queer Burmese in their areas.

· · ·

In this chapter, we begin to see how human rights practice as a way of life comprises social processes and how they are inherently emotional and relational in nature. Through formation processes, Tun Tun and other movement pioneers came together, founded the movement, recruited new people, and expanded its reach. They made use of social ties predating the movement and stirred up raw emotions rooted in their country's suffering, affections toward movement leaders, and a mix of apprehension, courage, and composure. Gathering people at workshops, meetings, and other movement activities, formation processes provide the means and opportunity for grievance transformation and community building to take place.

Unlike formation processes, grievance transformation and community building are not simply constituted by emotions and interpersonal ties. In the next two chapters, we will learn that these two types of processes also make and remake emotions and relationships. In doing so, they produce the movement's three important outcomes: self-transformation, a distinctive emotion culture, and new claims and claimant.

Chapter 3

Transforming Grievances

Emotional Fealty to Human Rights

When I went for the first human rights training, we watched several video clips of what actually went on [in 1988]. Most of them were news reports by the foreign media. Those who personally lived through the entire event, like [Tun Tun] and several others, also shared with us their firsthand experiences.[1] That was when I realized just how much our rights had been violated all along. . . . By recounting these historical events, we came to know more about what human rights actually meant to us all. I still remember that there were about twenty to twenty-five of us in the course, and we were all shedding tears by the end of every video clip. (Tin Hla, interview, August 2, 2016)

WHEN THE 1988 DEMONSTRATIONS broke out and the military regime violently suppressed them, ten-year-old Tin Hla did not think of those events, happening outside his doorstep, executed by soldiers like his uncle, cousins, and neighbors under the direction of junta leaders, as having anything to do with human rights. Twenty years later, when he answered the LGBT movement's recruitment call, he was a typical newcomer who knew little about human rights. He was drawn to the movement by ties of altruism, wanting to alleviate pain and suffering of HIV/AIDS, and seeking relief from his own fear of being queer.

However, the pain, fear, and despair that push Tin Hla and other queer Burmese toward the LGBT movement are insufficient to motivate them to take the next step of putting human rights into action. Neither are the longings for escape from such emotions, nor the trust, respect, and admiration for movement leaders like Tun Tun. The relationships and emotions of formation processes only gather together willing and curious people.

Further processes known as grievance transformation are needed to cultivate emotional fealty to human rights. Whereas preexisting ties and emotions constitute formation processes, grievance transformation processes elicit, remake, and produce emotions to create resonance and make sense of human rights for queer Burmese. LGBT activists draw on familiar cultural schemas and resources, such as queer suffering, Buddhist karmic beliefs, and social norms that regulate behavior, roles, and obligations. They imbue human rights with these local understandings and experiences to produce three core meanings —dignity, social belonging, and responsibility—that portray human rights as a collective good to be collectively achieved. As a result, they transform the way they feel about themselves and what to do with queer suffering. They devise and adopt new feeling rules, which compose a distinctive emotion culture and motivate them to become LGBT activists. As they coalesce around their own emotion culture, they inject new claims of LGBT rights into Burmese politics.

Suffering and Karma: Queer Conditions and Queer Lives

If the surroundings say something bad or do something bad to me, I just think they can treat me like this as I am *gay*. (Yamin, interview, March 31, 2013)[2]

Burmese society is hierarchical, and Buddhist beliefs about karma reinforce its highly gendered order with grave consequences for queers. Yamin's statement contains the view that queers are born with lower social positions, and that is why they have to expect and endure their grievous conditions. It is a view rooted in the popular belief that people are born queer because they have committed certain misdeeds in their past lives, resulting in bad karma and suffering in this lifetime. Although some queers realize that their conditions are unfair, this belief helps legitimize their stigmatization, sense of inferiority, and resignation to fate that both queers and others in their society widely recognize. The conditions breed self-hatred, shame, and fear of being queer, emotions harbored among LGBT movement pioneers at the start of the movement.[3]

Most Burmese Buddhists are mainly concerned with karma and its impact on one's fortunes rather than the exalted goals of enlightenment and nirvana. Life is a cycle of birth, death, and rebirth. Social stations at birth are determined by karma, merit and demerit accumulated from good and bad deeds committed in previous lives. This belief is not deterministic or fatalistic, since Burmese Buddhists—as well as other Southeast Asian adherents of Buddhism (see, e.g.,

Tambiah 1970; Keyes and Daniel 1983; Engel and Engel 2010)—heavily focus their religious practices on improving karma and avoiding bad fortune. However, when they encounter circumstances that cannot be directly attributed to the consequences of their actions in this lifetime, Burmese Buddhists are known to identify bad karma as a causal explanation (Keyes 1983a, 1983b).[4]

According to such beliefs, people are born "male"—and thus regarded as men—because they accumulated more good karma than women in past lives. Therefore, men possess greater *hpone*, a spiritual form of power, and enjoy superior social status (Gilbert 2016; Keeler 2017). Women, having acquired less good karma in past lives, occupy lower social status and have to endure the "suffering" of menstruation, pregnancy, childbirth, separation from their parents, and "service" to their husbands (Harriden 2012).[5] Examples of women's lower status abound in Burmese society. For instance, the formal institution of Burmese Buddhism forbids women's ordainment,[6] Buddhist temples ban women from certain areas such as the top levels of pagodas, and women are not supposed to sit or stand physically higher than men to avoid placing their genitalia, considered "unclean," above men and causing them to lose *hpone*.

Sexual transgressions in past lives, such as adultery, rape, and sexual relations with monks, are believed to result in bad karma and rebirth as a queer person, especially as *apwint*. Based on a view that merit and demerit are transferable to other people (Keyes 1983b), some parents even attribute having *apwint* children to their own misdeeds in past lives. For example, Aung Aung said his mother in their "devout Buddhist family" believed "that because of the misdeeds of past life, they are like this—my uncle is *T.G.-ma*, and I am a *tomboy*" (interview, July 2, 2015).[7]

This belief about karma is so ingrained that queer Burmese are habitually conditioned to accept their ill treatment as expected, having to "pay back" for these misdeeds (Ma Aye, interview, October 16, 2014). It is a point repeatedly confirmed in my fieldwork and resonant with beliefs in such other societies as Thailand with a strong influence of Theravada Buddhism.[8] Put differently, according to this idea, although sociopolitical conditions or other people are the obvious offenders, queer lives are inherently defined by suffering that has to persist until the karmic consequences are worked out or expunged (Jackson 1998).

Buddhist beliefs in Myanmar therefore support a social hierarchy that casts queers as deviant and morally suspect people. *Apwint* are scorned for degrading themselves into "receptive" sexual partners, a role associated with women. That is why, in the previous chapter, Tun Tun, Kyaw Kyaw, and

Pyae Soe were not regarded as "real men" but treated as sexually available to other men. While *tomboys* are sometimes tolerated for trying to move up (rather than down) the hierarchy, they and their partners are also viewed as deviant, putting them at risk of being assaulted by those who do not accept their transgressions.

Apwint, lesbians, and other queers often feel immense pressure to conform to gender and sexual norms to avoid causing distress to their families.[9] *Apwint*, ridiculed and looked down on, reflect poorly on the entire family, especially male authority figures who are supposed to keep family members in line with social norms (Gilbert 2016). Some interviewees said there were parents who were glad that their daughters were lesbian, because they would unlikely have sex with men and become pregnant outside marriage—therefore disgracing the family—and would take care of them in their old age as is expected of unmarried female children. However, the unspoken bargain is that lesbians would not be chastised if they adhered to expected gender roles and did not assert themselves. As one scholar pointed out in another context, the privilege of those who live in quiet toleration is exchanged for keeping their sexuality and gender identity invisible, obscuring their subjugation (Boellstorff 2009).

While non-Buddhist populations, such as Christians and Muslims, have varying responses to queers, they generally subscribe to a similar social hierarchy that rejects sexual or gender nonconformity. I have documented incidents of bullying of lesbians in Karen refugee camps along the Myanmar-Thailand border and parental violence against *apwint* in Karen Christian families. In the previous chapter, Seng Naw's story illustrated the violence and pressure to conform among Kachin Christians.[10] My interviewees also report cases of queer Muslims who face strong family pressure to enter heterosexual marriages.[11]

The prejudices against queers affect their everyday lives, particularly their physical safety, education, and employment. *Apwint* and lesbians experience sexual violence, a common occurrence in Burmese society (Women's League of Burma 2014), as well as other forms of physical assaults by family members and strangers.[12] Lesbians worry about being pressured into marrying their rapists out of "honor," especially if they become pregnant.[13] Like most other people in Myanmar, queers distrust and do not seek assistance from the authorities. Notorious for corruption and abuse of power, Burmese police are known to disregard complaints, blame victims, and side with perpetrators.

Moreover, Burmese police take advantage of their wide powers to persecute queers. They frequently arrest *apwint* under Section 30(d) of the 1899 Rangoon

Police Act and Sections 35(c) and (d) of the 1945 Police Act, provisions col-loquially known as "in-the-shadow" laws.[14] According to my interviews, in-cidents documented by activists, and court cases, police persecution exhibits a pattern.[15] Usually police arrest *apwint* in public places popular with *apwint*, or when *apwint* are walking or standing on the streets at night (hence the laws' nickname). Following arrest, the officer often extorts monetary bribes or sexual favors in exchange for not pressing charges or escalating charges to Section 377 of the Penal Code, a law inherited from British colonial rule that criminalizes "carnal intercourse against the order of nature."[16] Sexual assaults and physical abuse of those in detention are also common.[17]

Wanting to avoid further entanglement with the legal system, even when factual evidence is lacking to make the threatened charges, arrestees typically submit to the extortions and demands of the police or, if they are arraigned, plead guilty rather than contest their charges. The litigation process is costly for the average Burmese. According to lawyers interviewed for my study, after pleading guilty, arrestees sometimes have to bribe the police, prosecutor, judge, or the judge's clerk to speed up their sentencing dates and secure shorter prison terms.[18] In court, it is usually the word of the arresting officer against the ar-restee, and judges are known to convict based on police testimony.[19]

At school, queers report peer bullying and ostracism by teachers for not appearing gender conforming, often to the extent that they drop out of school, which leads to problems with employment due to the lack of school creden-tials.[20] Even if they find employment, they face further discrimination in the workplace. While *apwint* manage to carve out self-employment in niche oc-cupations as beauticians and *nat kadaw*, only a handful ever achieve fame and succeed monetarily; most struggle with irregular work and income even in these niches. Discriminatory pay and hiring practices against women are pervasive (Ma Khin Mar Mar Kyi 2014; Than 2014) and are exacerbated for *tomboys* who lack formal qualifications but cannot or do not want to appear "feminine" in low-level office, service, or manufacturing jobs. Often they turn to traditionally male occupations, such as construction, but they receive lower wages than men do.

Yet despite their grievous conditions, the conventional response among queer Burmese is to do what Yamin said at the beginning of this section: Put up with it. Stigmatized as immoral or people with bad karma, queers and those around them expect and commonly accept their ill treatment and infe-rior social status. Many live with self-hatred, shame, and fear of being queer.

Among queer informants who do not believe they deserve to be discriminated against, they nevertheless emphasize not wanting to bring shame to their families because of who they are or are resigned to their fate. Some are fortunate to find relief and refuge among the informal social networks of queers. But having lived under repressive rule and abusive authority, they see little possibility for changing their conditions.

Suffering and Its Emotional Power: Making Human Rights Relevant

Grievance transformation therefore starts with changing the self-understanding of queer Burmese. Before LGBT activists can galvanize queer Burmese to fight for human rights together, they have to first empower them. And to do that, they have to change the way queer Burmese feel about themselves, so that they abandon feeling rules built on inferiority, stigmatization, and resignation.

Changing self-understanding entails, first and foremost, making human rights resonate with queer Burmese.[21] Although Aung San Suu Kyi, Myanmar's most famous pro-democracy activist and leader, advocated for human rights in her speeches and writings (1991), ordinary Burmese in Myanmar had little access to human rights discourse during military rule. The movement's founding and recruitment stories in the previous chapter show how human rights activism was suppressed. Before joining the LGBT movement, Pyae Soe had not heard of Aung San Suu Kyi. Nor did he realize what was wrong with the forced portering and labor that he and his family experienced in their village. Those incidents were simply part of their lives, the way things had always been. Tin Hla did not understand the 1988 protests or its aftermath. Most Burmese like him were unfamiliar with, even fearful of, human rights.

But LGBT activists have a rich cultural schema: the suffering of queers and other ordinary Burmese.[22] "Our people know human rights from their suffering. . . . The human rights concept comes from their lives. It comes from their real life, real suffering" (Tun Tun, interview, May 14, 2013*). All through their lives, whether it was suffering caused by family, other people around them, or state actors such as police, queer Burmese have felt pain, fear, and despair. Pyae Soe, Kyaw Kyaw, Aung Aung, and many other LGBT activists have experienced them in their own lives of which we caught glimpses in Chapter 2.

To make human rights relevant, LGBT activists evoke the emotional power of suffering. Emotions such as pain, fear, and despair are the antithesis of having human dignity, *lu gone theit khar*, a central tenet of human rights to LGBT activists. Hence, in Tun Tun's words above, Burmese people understand human rights by feeling what it is like to live in their absence. When queer Burmese experience the pangs of suffering, they lose human dignity, robbed by the violations of human rights. Although LGBT activists are informed by the UDHR, such as Article 1's reference to the equal entitlement of human beings to dignity, by "human rights violations," they do not mean claims according to the formal standards of international law. Rather, they mean human rights offer queers and other Burmese what they are deprived of, which has caused them to feel the emotions of suffering.

Tin Hla's story about discovering human rights, quoted at the beginning of this chapter, illustrates the emotional power of the shared cultural schema of suffering. He had traveled to Chiang Mai for a VIVID workshop where he first met Tun Tun, about twenty years after soldiers fired into demonstrators while he lived in the barracks and was still oblivious "in our own world, in our small world" (Tin Hla, interview, June 26, 2015). His story resembles the formative moment for Tun Tun when he realized the meaning of human rights. Although he was shouting for "human rights" during the 1988 protests, Tun Tun admitted he did not really understand what that meant at the time. After joining the rebel army, in "jungle university" along the Myanmar-Thailand border, he came across a UDHR booklet donated by an international organization to their camp library. "I started reading [the booklet] and compared it with the life in Burma. We don't have human rights, but we have violations of human rights [laughs]!" (Tun Tun, interview, February 21, 2013*).

While LGBT activists do not delve into major events of political oppression at every workshop, they usually encourage participants to share their encounters with oppression to summon the emotional power of suffering. At one workshop, Pyae Soe asked, "What are your experiences?" In response, the participants talked about feeling "pressed down"[23]—being beaten, disinherited, or kicked out of the house by family elders, bullying, verbal harassment, police abuse, expulsion from school, and dismissal from work (field notes, VIVID workshop, May 26–28, 2013)—personal stories reflecting the grievances of queer Burmese described earlier. Sometimes they watch a movie before sharing their stories. The movies, such as *The Wedding Banquet*, *Happy Together*, *Stonewall Inn*, and *Boys Don't Cry*, are not Burmese, but the participants see past their ostensible foreignness to find similarity in the prejudices that the characters encountered. In addition, since their first celebration in 2009 in Ranong, LGBT activists recount the discrimination and violence that queer Burmese face as part of their IDAHO celebrations. Usually they screen a video or give speeches that deliver a message to such effect. At IDAHO 2016, for instance, one activist told the audience about a *gay* student who "committed suicide because of discrimination from his family and school." A lesbian followed to tell her story: her parents sent her to a mental institution because they disapproved of her same-sex relationship (IDAHO 2016 report, VIVID).

Having evoked the emotional power of suffering, associating queer suffering with the absence of dignity, and construing it as the result of human rights violations, LGBT activists ask these fellow Burmese to imagine the opposite: what enjoying dignity and thus human rights would feel like when they are free from the pain of abuse, feel safe, and experience joy and happiness. Pyae Soe and other activists link the stories that workshop participants share to the UDHR (and sometimes the Yogyakarta Principles) to explain what it entails to have human rights. They take participants through the clauses in these international documents, which provide for rights to equality, life, personal security, fair trial, and education and illustrate them with relevant grievances mentioned in participants' stories. For example, they say, being detained under the Police Act just because they are *apwint* is a violation of "the right to life, liberty and security of person" under Article 3 of the UDHR.

From Shame to Blame: Shedding Negative Feeling Rules

By characterizing their suffering as human rights violations, LGBT activists try to help queer Burmese shed negative feeling rules, another necessary step to transform self-understanding. Steeped in stigmatization, feelings of inferiority, and resignation, negative feeling rules breed self-hatred, shame, and fear of being queer. Therefore, LGBT activists urge queer Burmese to jettison the internalized beliefs about karma to which Yamin referred earlier—that is, people are reborn queer due to bad karma from past lives and are expected to endure ill treatment and low social status. They remind them that prejudicial norms, state laws, authorities who abuse power, and other social actors are to blame for the pain, fear, and despair they feel. Their suffering should not be accepted or explained away on the basis of bad karma, for they are the fault of these other people and conditions, which violate their rights and human dignity.

LGBT activists explain that queers deserve human rights, just like everyone else. They again call upon human rights' promise of dignity. They point to human rights documents, such as the UDHR and Yogyakarta Principles, to persuade queer Burmese they are not inferior but are worthy of human dignity, regardless of their sexuality or gender and regardless of their past. In workshops and interviews, activists ranging from long-time VIVID leaders to new grass-roots organizers consistently stress that LGBT rights are the same as human rights and that they are asking for the same treatment.

The appreciation of human dignity—and thus human rights—by LGBT activists contains the meaning of a transformed sense of self as someone as deserving as other human beings. Chan Thar, like many others who recounted their experiences to me, described his amazement and wonder: "I felt like I was in a foreign country, seeing all the new things. . . . It was like when I went to Bangkok and saw the MBK shopping center. 'Whoa, it really exists!' That kind of feeling" (interview, May 15, 2013). He could not believe it when he first learned about human rights at VIVID's workshops. He remembered breaking down and crying as he rejoiced that he, a queer person, was entitled to human rights.

It would be easy to read LGBT activists' interpretation as a demand for the rights of LGBT persons to be recognized as human rights, akin to the ef-forts of international activists in the early 1990s (see, e.g., Mertus 2009; Farrior 2009). However, I find that it carries the much more significant meaning that queer people are equally deserving of rights. This meaning cannot be taken for granted in the Burmese context, for LGBT activists have to counter entrenched beliefs about karma and the related views on social hierarchy. I was particu-larly struck by the observations and interviews that contain statements along the following lines. At the movement meeting before IDAHO 2013, Tun Tun asked grassroots organizers how they would explain to local media the slogan for the event, "LGBT Rights Are Human Rights." Gyo Kyar, one of the earliest grassroots organizers, stood up and said, "We are all human beings, so there should not be discrimination of LGBT people" (field notes, movement meet-ing, May 11, 2013). When asked what he had learned about human rights, Min Min, a grassroots organizer who joined in 2013–2014, answered, "We are equal like other human beings. And we being like this doesn't mean that we are lower than other people" (Min Min, interview, July 7, 2015).

Hope and Karma: Constructing Positive Feeling Rules

In place of negative feeling rules, LGBT activists construct positive ones to instill in queer Burmese hope and confidence that they will be able to alter their conditions and alleviate their suffering. Having drawn from human rights documents to persuade queer Burmese that they are worthy of human dignity, LGBT activists return to karmic beliefs: Instead of focusing on the misdeeds of past lives, they appeal to the beliefs' antideterministic, forward-looking side.

While Burmese and other Buddhist adherents may accept that karma accumulated from the past has to work itself out (Jackson 1998; Keyes 1983b), at the same time, they do not readily accept its determination. Burmese Buddhists demonstrate their belief that anybody can improve their future karma and social status by accumulating good merit in this lifetime. Hence, they are often busy with charity work, donations to monasteries, and other merit-making activities. They also exhibit antideterminism in their customs concerning the supernatural and spiritual. Besides karma, Burmese Buddhists sometimes cite causing offense to *nat* as another explanation for misfortune. They may propitiate *nat* with the hope of placating the offended spirit and reversing their luck. Or they hope that *nat* worship can build up good merit, avoid being harmed by them, and lessen the harm if they already have bad karma (Spiro 1967).[24] Some protect themselves with amulets and other magical artifacts (Keeler 2017) or consult astrologers and specialty publications on supernatural and spiritual matters to deal with hardships or prepare for misfortunes (Maung Thawnghmung 2011).[25]

LGBT activists turn to this optimistic side of karmic beliefs to direct attention away from their backward-looking aspect, getting queer Burmese to focus on how they can improve their current situation and redirect their destinies. Although the movement's emphasis is primarily Buddhist, the forward-looking perspective covers both present and future lifetimes, and so it possibly appeals to non-Buddhists who may or may not believe in rebirth. During movement workshops and interviews for my study, both national leaders and grassroots organizers urged queer Burmese not to dwell on the past. The following are illustrative examples—the first two from national-level activists and the third from a grassroots organizer in a southern town:

> How many of us can see our past lives? So it is not important what happened and what is important is how we try to live our present lives. (Tun Tun, interview, December 12, 2015*)

> Can we look at our past lives? We don't know for sure. Maybe there was misdeed. But we should look at our present life. That is the important thing. Should we just live like this? Not care about anything because of our bad fate? (Pyae Soe, interview, January 29, 2016)

People come and say, "In this life, you become *achauk* because of your past." I would say that past life does not concern us. It is how we live this life. (Thura, interview, June 22, 2015)

The forward-looking perspective is also exemplified by LGBT activists' hopes for the dead. As part of the movement's Transgender Day of Remembrance (TDoR) commemoration in 2012, grassroots organizers from four towns—Monywar, Kyaukpadaung, Pyay, and Pathein—invited Buddhist monks and nuns to lead prayers for *transgender* persons who have died as a result of transphobia violence. They performed prayer chants, including the popular *Metta*, in hopes that the dead "will have better lives" (VIVID's TDoR 2012 report to funders). In his town, Nay Win asked those who joined in prayer to hold flowers because he wanted the dead to be "born again with a very beautiful life, like a flower" (interview, May 13, 2013).

The Individual to the Collective: Have Dignity, Earn Social Belonging, and Be Responsible

I want after their training, they can come up with their idea . . . and what they want to do in the future for their community, for their society. (Seng Naw, interview, April 25, 2013*)

Following the changes to self-understanding, LGBT activists channel freshly cultivated confidence and hope into collective action. As Seng Naw indicated in his interview, they want individual queer Burmese to expand their focus of grievance transformation. They want newcomers to join their efforts; become one of them, an LGBT activist; and work together to "get our rights"—that is, transform fellow queers' sense of self, gain social belonging, and reform the law.

The expansion from the individual to the collective builds from LGBT activists' interpretation of human rights as encompassing three core meanings: dignity, social belonging, and responsibility. Although they stress that queers are equally entitled to dignity and human rights, they do not focus "get rights" efforts on winning equality for queer Burmese in all aspects of life. Their approach centers on their three meanings of human rights, which connect to one another to characterize human rights as a collective good to be collectively achieved: LGBT activists define dignity—found in human rights documents—to include social belonging, which queer Burmese highly value for their personhood. To realize such dignity, they induce collective action by linking human rights to the exercise of responsibility by the rights bearer, whom they regard as a social being bound to social norms and related to multiple group-ings of people—queer Burmese and Burmese society at large.

Responsibility comes in two forms: exercising responsibility toward oneself and toward queer Burmese as a collective lot. Despite maintaining that queer people are entitled to human rights, LGBT activists insist they shoulder the re-sponsibility of earning them. Their workshops and meetings usually have seg-ments during which participants, new recruits and seasoned activists, break up into small groups to propose strategic actions. When they report back to the entire audience, they present several levels of action, which always progress from the personal level, taking responsibility for oneself, and move up to the state level, taking collective action aimed at formal legal institutions. VIVID's published recommendations also reflect this personal-to-state, multilevel na-ture of their strategy.

Responsibility to the Self: "Live Well" and "Change Behavior"

To LGBT activists, taking action to "get our rights" starts with having dignity, which starts with being responsible to themselves. LGBT activists regard the individual queer Burmese as a social being within Burmese society at large and require the individual to relate to its norms. Instead of formal rights recogni-tion, this form of responsibility focuses on changing social interactions, and thus interpersonal relationships, of queer Burmese to achieve the movement goal of social belonging. According to such responsibility, if queer Burmese want to enjoy human rights in the sense of being treated with dignity, they have to conduct themselves in a manner that meets behavioral norms expected of the rest of society so that they can be accepted into that society.

Being responsible to oneself, in the words of LGBT activists, entails living well and "changing" one's behavior. After urging queer Burmese to focus on their present lives, Tun Tun and Pyae Soe said, respectively, that they should "live well" and "live your life in a good way," and then they gave examples of habits and conduct that they should drop or alter. Urging queer Burmese to "change behavior" dates back to the movement's founding years. For instance, in a 2010 SUNSHINE report, Kyaw Kyaw summarized the group's discussion about human rights and wrote that they agreed on this statement: "We need to change some of our bad lifestyle for changing society's attitude toward us."[26]

The importance of "change behavior" is shared among national leaders and grassroots organizers of the movement. They bring up this point in interviews as well as movement activities such as the following. At a 2013 human rights workshop, "change behavior" was the first item that participants listed under the topic of what queer Burmese could do at the personal level to earn their rights (field notes, VIVID workshop, May 26–28, 2013). During a 2014 movement strategy meeting, when grassroots organizers from around the country gathered with VIVID activists, they highlighted "behavior of LGBT must change" in their discussion on the movement's "challenges and problems" (field notes, LGBT network meeting, June 14, 2014).

To "change behavior," LGBT activists ask queer Burmese to adopt dignified conduct, meaning conduct that comports with Burmese social norms.[27] When referring to queer people generally, LGBT activists mention such examples as making an honest living and not kissing or otherwise displaying physical intimacy in public (since heterosexual couples should not do so in Myanmar either). They usually admonish *tomboys* for the stereotypical conduct of getting drunk and provoking fights. Because *apwint* identify with the female gender, when LGBT activists talk about *apwint*, they often bring up *eain dre theit khar* to refer to the proper conduct that Burmese society expects of women, such as the manner in which they dress, talk, walk, and sit.[28] The activists clarify they do not object to *apwint* expressing themselves and dressing as women, but they do not condone wearing provocative outfits, exaggerated mannerisms, flirtatious speech, and other conduct stereotypically associated with *apwint* (such conduct is also considered improper for heterosexual, cisgender women).

My fieldwork contains many examples on this point. For instance, after a workshop presentation about gay pride parades in Australia and Europe, Gyo Kyar, a *trans woman*, said the costumes worn in those parades exposed a lot of skin and "would get negative remarks from society . . . and do not fit with our own Burmese culture and society's values" (field notes, movement workshop, September 22, 2012). Thein Gi, an *apwint*, told me that she wanted "to live like a 'real lady' and not fool around" (interview, November 14, 2014). She explained this meant dressing modestly such as in the traditional *longyi* (sarong) and demure blouses, which she was wearing when I saw her in November 2014 and December 2015. It also means going about with one's life "without shouting at other people, or talking to or teasing *tha nge*" (Naing Lin, interview, June 23, 2015).

LGBT activists' calls for "live well" and "change behavior" are also grounded in Burmese norms about roles and obligations, which contain an implicit reciprocity found in Khin Kyine's words: "You will only be respected, if you know how to behave appropriately and live in a dignified way" (interview, August 5, 2016). Everyone in Myanmar, from the country's leaders to ordinary folks, has roles defined by certain obligations (Keeler 2017).[29] They are entitled to treatment befitting their social roles and in return are expected to conduct themselves properly by fulfilling the obligations flowing from those roles. The obligations and conduct are measured against a set of corresponding social norms. Therefore, as part of their human rights practice, LGBT activists ask queer Burmese to "respect societal values and norms" (VIVID 2014 publication on the impact of laws and practices) if they want fellow Burmese to treat them with dignity.

In addition to dignified conduct, LGBT activists stress the importance of fulfilling other social roles. According to their approach, living up to the other roles is even more important, since the sexual and gender roles with which queers identify are transgressive. When I asked about their childhoods, interviewees like Tun Tun, Nay Win, Kyaw Kyaw, and Zin Yaw said their school teachers did not mistreat them even though they did not quite meet the normative standard of masculinity, because they were hard working and studious. LGBT activists also extol the virtues of being "good" sons and daughters, who take care of their parents and provide them with material support, and being "good" partners who are faithful and financially secure so that their families would be more likely to tolerate, even accept, their nonheteronormative or gender-nonconforming relationships. During the workshops, LGBT activists discuss how they can build on behavioral change to become role models for other queer people in their hometowns and improve their relationships with their parents, siblings, and other relatives.

"Change behavior" finds support in LGBT activists' dealings with social actors whom their movement is trying to influence to gain social belonging. One particular public dialogue between an activist and business leaders helps us appreciate why LGBT activists emphasize "changing behavior." During the dialogue, the activist brought up the problem of employment discrimination against queer Burmese. The representative of a regional commercial organization replied that "society's views" were changing in their favor but went on to qualify, "But they still need to behave in a socially acceptable way." A leader of a major business association agreed and listed three points queer people ought to fulfill to avoid discrimination: "Be well-disciplined, behave like a good citizen, and have good character" (media report, October 11, 2016).[30]

Moreover, "live well" and "change behavior" have implicit basis in Buddhist notions of personal responsibility—people are responsible for their own actions and their consequences—an understanding related to their interpretation of social norms, roles, and obligations. Queer Burmese have to be mindful of their positions in relation to the norms of their society if they do not wish to suffer undesirable consequences. Only by appreciating this aspect of their moral universe can we truly grasp Cho Cho's meaning: "So we want society to accept LGBT people, but one important thing is, we have to look at why, why society is treating them like that" (interview, May 15, 2013). In my conversations with many other interviewees, both LGBT activists and those involved in Burmese civil society more generally talk about responsibility in the same manner as Cho Cho. Being responsible to oneself and for one's actions does not absolve the offending party; that party may suffer consequences for the offense, including social opprobrium and legal sanction. It also does not negate any correlative duty the state or other parties owe to the rights bearer, queer Burmese. If state and society do not act against the offending party or fulfill their correlative duties, others may try to change the rules or those parties' behavior (something LGBT activists also pursue). However, the consequences for the offending party are separate concerns. Self-responsibility coexists and is consistent with LGBT activists' forward-looking perspective on karma. Queer people can change their destinies, but they have to behave responsibly too. Being irresponsible about one's conduct can lead to suffering negative consequences. It can also result in demerit or the accumulation of bad karma that brings about future misfortune.

To LGBT activists, "living well" and "changing behavior" affirm the agency of queer Burmese, even though outsiders may object to its potential reinforcement of status quo norms and promotion of "homonormativity" (Duggan 2003), an issue examined in Chapter 5. LGBT activists do understand that norms and beliefs lead to harsh conditions and the suffering of queer people. Their internal discussions and published recommendations clearly identify the problem. In my interviews, the more astute activists point out that *apwint* and *tomboys* often display socially inappropriate conduct to shield their self-hatred, shame, or fear, emotions bred by having an inferior and stigmatized status. But it is because LGBT activists are acutely aware of the low social position of queer Burmese that they urge "live well" and "change behavior."

Here, LGBT activists return to queer suffering and its emotional power with which they begin the processes of grievance transformation. To them, queer Burmese grew up and still live in a society that put them down as lesser beings. VIVID leader Khant Nyar has traveled around the world to conferences on human rights and LGBT activism. He knows "change behavior" may be criticized for being conservative. However, his foremost concern lies with not "giv[ing] any more reason" (Khant Nyar, interview, July 28, 2016) for others in their society to discriminate against queers. From the viewpoint of Khant Nyar and other LGBT activists, "change behavior" is empowering, despite what outsider critics may say. It aspires to raise queers up from the lower rungs of Burmese social hierarchy so that they are treated like everybody else in accordance with their other social roles (not the status of being a queer person) and the rest of society's norms. In other words, to enjoy human rights, queer Burmese must obtain fuller membership (Roberts 2015) in their society. LGBT activists' approach may not openly challenge existing social norms regulating behavior, but it still requires courageous and deliberate decisions not to accept a mandated form of the present and future (Skidmore 2003, 2004).[31]

Responsibility to the Collective: Have Empathy and "Get Our Rights"

Fighting for change is our obligation. That is my feeling. . . . When doing the training and learning about others' experiences, I could feel for them—the rigid family and community. I felt saddened by such severe discrimination. (Pyae Soe, interview, February 21, 2013)

On top of being responsible to oneself, "getting our rights" as an LGBT activist involves the exercise of a second form of responsibility, which connects the individual to a different social group: a sense of duty to fight for the human rights of queer Burmese, linking the individual to the latter, a collective. Such collective responsibility coexists with the first on self-responsibility. The first focuses on the pursuit of dignity for the individual queer Burmese—a realization of human rights in LGBT activists' books—that does not directly concern formal rights recognition. The second, exercising collective responsibility toward queer Burmese, pursues human rights for the betterment of other lives. It aims not only to transform other queer selves, but also to change social norms and formal legal rules to realize their human rights.

Since their movement's founding days, national leaders and grassroots organizers have followed up with initiatives on bolder tactics for newcomers. VIVID invites those who stand out or indicate interest in assuming more prominent roles to workshops on leadership or practical skills such as bookkeeping and grant writing. Since 2007, LGBT activists have expanded their state and societal levels of action to film festivals and photo exhibitions to educate the public about queer lives in Myanmar, human rights documentation programs, workshops for lawyers and other allies, and engagement with politicians and the media to advocate for legal reform.

As Pyae Soe puts it, this collective form of responsibility emerges as LGBT activists develop feelings of empathy amplifying self-responsibility into a sense of greater obligation. At this stage, LGBT activists' human rights practice once more turns to suffering and its emotional power. In addition to creating resonance for human rights, sharing their experiences with discrimination and oppression makes activists and newcomers realize that other people suffer similar, or even worse, grievances. Pyae Soe, who remembers the self-hatred, shame, and fear when he was teased and bullied, described empathy as his "driving force" to prevent "the younger generation" from going through what he had to endure. Chan Thar, who was recruited through the HIV/AIDS-related ties examined in Chapter 2, felt the same way. At his first human rights workshop, besides crying for himself, happy that he is entitled to human rights, Chan Thar wept for other queer Burmese. He "felt sorry" for them, for they did not know about human rights and deserved to be treated with dignity:

> Even for a person like me, who lives in Yangon, this was the first exposure to these kinds of things [human rights]. I was thinking about the people from the remote areas, *gay* people from the remote areas, very faraway places. So how about them? They also should know about these rights. The information must be spread out. (Chan Thar, interview, May 15, 2013)

Chan Thar's empathy amplified his sense of responsibility and directed it from himself to others. He packed VIVID's human rights publications into his suitcase and carried them across the border into Myanmar, braving the risk of detection at the checkpoints. Since his first workshop in Chiang Mai, Chan Thar has joined REGAL and served as a media spokesperson for the movement.[32]

Empathy is also why activists who are heterosexual and cisgender, such as Zwe Naung, Cho Cho, and Cindy, develop collective responsibility and feel compelled to take up the cause of the LGBT movement. In 2007, when Zwe Naung was a dissident monk fleeing the military regime, he could not have imagined becoming an LGBT activist. However, he does have memories of being bullied as a child because others thought he was *achauk*. After participating in JUSTICE and VIVID human rights workshops, Zwe Naung saw those childhood experiences in a new light: "I am not *gay*, and I didn't like it. So what about *gay* people themselves? They would not like it" (interview, February 20, 2013). Cho Cho was already exposed to the hardships of queer Burmese when she was working for an international NGO's HIV/AIDS program. Subsequently, from VIVID's workshops she learned that everyone, including queers, deserves human rights: "All these years, all I had heard was how they were discriminated, how they were treated badly, how people called them bad things. . . . I wanted to do something for them" (Cho Cho, interview, May 15, 2013). Similarly, for Cindy, learning about human rights from LGBT activists motivated her to join their movement. The Yangon lawyer had been representing *apwint* arrested under the notorious in-the-shadow laws, but she was unaware of human rights, which were left out of her Burmese legal education.[33] She discovered human rights only after LGBT activists invited her to participate in VIVID's activities. Then she began to construe her cases as human rights violations: "These people feel lower than straight people, and I don't want them to feel that way, so that's why I am in this field" (interview, May 11, 2013).

The sense of collective responsibility, a duty to do something about the suffering of queer Burmese, perhaps resonates with another type of Buddhist understanding in their society: the moral obligation to resist oppression and injustice (Hayward 2015; Schober 2011) and therefore take action to change the future (Walton 2017a). Although LGBT activists do not explicitly underscore their collective responsibility with such a moral undertaking, they situate their movement in Myanmar's political transformation and their collective responsibility as enabling queer Burmese to contribute to their country's future. During public dialogues, it is common for LGBT activists to explain in the following manner why they want human rights for queer Burmese:

> We may be in the minority in terms of numbers but we are ready to take part in any sector, including peace and politics, whatever or however so for the society, and for the country. But . . . we are currently being prevented from undertaking a role as a citizen in the country's political transformation. Once the laws that are targeted toward suppressing us have been considerably abolished, along with the discrimination toward us by the mainstream media, . . . we can then take part in any peace and development missions that the country shall need us for. (Media report, January 1, 2017)

Grievance Transformation and the Interrelated Outcomes of Human Rights Practice as a Way of Life

With grievance transformation, LGBT activists show that human rights, when put into action, can resonate with local residents in cities as well as provincial towns and villages, and even rally them to organize and join a movement, potentially leading to wide-reaching impact on formal political and legal institutions. As newcomers to the movement participate in grievance transformation, they develop emotional bonds to human rights. Replacing negative with positive feeling rules leads to self-transformation and feeds into a distinctive emotion culture among themselves. These personal and grassroots changes produce activists, who mount new claims of LGBT rights.

Self-Transformation

Before [learning about human rights], if I had some point of view, I did not dare to express my point of view, because if I said something, people might look down on me. . . . When I knew about my rights, I know that I can express my ideas, I can express my thinking. (Chan Thar, interview, May 15, 2013)

Chan Thar describes a familiar experience with self-transformation among my interviewees. They begin to relate their individual selves to society in a different way: they are not lower creatures but somebody entitled to human rights. Abandoning feeling rules rooted in stigma, inferiority, and resignation and adopting new ones based on the entitlement of queers to human rights, they gradually replace emotions of pain, self-hate, and fear with hope and confidence. They begin to exercise self-responsibility, "living well" and "changing behavior," and become LGBT activists with an amplified sense of responsibility to fight for the collective good of queers. Some report wanting to have "ambitions in their lives" or "change their way of life because they felt motivated" (field notes, VIVID outreach meeting, November 27, 2015).

Besides interview accounts, I have observed this kind of transformation over time. Yamin, whom I have known since September 2012, is an example. Earlier that year, Yamin attended her first movement workshop. From 2012 to 2014, I noticed that she appeared in feminine clothing only when she felt safe to do so, such as during a movement workshop or the international LGBT rights conference that I attended with her and other movement activists. When Yamin lived with her parents, she would stop at a friend's house to change her clothes and appearance so that they would not find out about her gender identity (Yamin, interview, March 31, 2013). Her later interviews confirmed my observations: "I had no confidence. Even when I went out, I was afraid of everything, and I didn't even dare to talk with—I didn't even dare to have phone conversation with men, or I thought that there was something wrong with me" (interview, July 8, 2015). In her 2013 interview, she said she used to wish she could be a "real woman" and believed others were entitled to treat her badly because of her gender identity. By 2016, she no longer put up with

discrimination against queer people as an accepted fact of life, instead attribut-
ing it to "society's belief" (interview, July 26, 2016). She had become a movement leader and embraced being a *trans woman* or *meinmashar* (she uses both
terms), expressing herself in feminine clothing more frequently in everyday life
and for public appearances as a movement spokesperson.[34]

A crucial aspect of the new sense of self involves improving interpersonal
relationships, especially with parents and other family members, which brings
greater social belonging and human dignity to queers. As queer Burmese who
become LGBT activists and carry around a new sense of self, their social interactions change too. The improved social interactions lead to better relationships or perceptions of better treatment and feed into constructing a better
sense of self. These changes connect their individual selves to other people,
affirming them as social beings who feel they belong to society.

Having their mothers or fathers treat them kindlier, even if just a little bit,
is often the first and rare taste of dignity for many queer Burmese in my study.
Yamin's mother, who struggles with Yamin's gender identity, had asked her to
leave many times. Since the human rights workshop in 2012, Yamin said she
had "become brave" with her mother (interview, March 31, 2013). She gave her
mother VIVID's magazines to read and tried to convince her that she could
"live a good life like this" (interview, July 8, 2015). The relationship remains
a work in progress, but it is improving, Yamin said as she showed me the text
messages on her phone with her mother midway through our conversation in
2015. In their exchange of messages, her mother called Yamin *tha the me*, literally a combination of the affectionate reference to "son" and "daughter" respectively, a possible sign of progress for somebody who did not accept that her
"son" identified as a woman.[35]

Being able to make money from LGBT activism also contributes to the
improved relationships at home. To queer Burmese, and Burmese generally,
contributing to household finances earns them respect and makes them feel
dignified, which they see as realizations of human dignity.[36] To outsiders, bas-
ing familial relationships on material contributions may seem mercenary, but
it is honest in the tough realities of Burmese life to sustain daily survival and is
consistent with LGBT activists' emphasis on fulfilling social roles, such as being
"good" children.[37]

My study identified many examples among queer Burmese who transform
their sense of self by reaping tangible benefits as LGBT activists that help improve their familial relationships. With a few exceptions, most people in the

movement are not local elites. They have limited formal education and professional experiences and come from families of peasants, fishing folk, shopkeepers, and factory workers. Kyaw Kyaw had felt what it was like to be poor and unable to support his parents and siblings. He had crammed himself onto a boat with other migrants and left for Thailand in search of better prospects. Originally a migrant laborer, he became a part-time grassroots organizer for queer Burmese in Ranong and worked his way up in the LGBT movement. Elaborating on how he was providing his mother and sister a "middle-class life" these days (their father no longer lives with them), Kyaw Kyaw said he sent money home and built a house for them in the village. "Now I can support my mother more than my [straight] brothers can. I even said this to my mother, 'I am not like your other sons. . . . I am *lein thu* [homosexual], but I am responsible and I take care of you'" (interview, June 27, 2015).

At the grassroots level, most activists do not have fully paid positions, unlike their national-level counterparts; nevertheless, some movement projects provide stipends that subsidize or replace their meager income. For instance, the movement implemented in a few locations a human rights documentation program that pays modest stipends to LGBT activists who work for it. Win Sein, a *tomboy*, used to work at a local market, waiting on customers and carrying heavy goods. After he joined the program, he quit the odd jobs because the stipend he now earned was more than he could make at the market (Win Sein, interview, July 2, 2015). Even where grassroots activists receive no direct financial reward, being part of the movement cultivates local patronage, which boosts their personal prestige and social status (MacLean 2004; Taylor 2009; Keeler 2016). If they obtain funding for movement events or projects, as local patrons, they bring beneficiaries in their hometowns income, business, and work, and garner loyalty and respect for themselves in return.[38] Grassroots organizers whose social networks benefit from HIV/AIDS programs can further strengthen those patronage ties through their affiliations with the LGBT movement. For others who did not already enjoy those benefits, such as lesbians, LGBT activism enables them to create rudimentary forms of patronage. For example, Aung Aung's leadership of the human rights documentation program in his town enables him to bring in other lesbians to work for the program and receive stipends.

Furthermore, joining the movement increases social prestige. Being able to travel frequently to Yangon and other cities for movement meetings and other activities is a source of envy and pride for residents in rural areas and small towns. In these places, it is still a big deal to travel even to Yangon, where most may never have the opportunity to visit, much less live. My social media account is filled with updates from activists who share generous quantities of their photos traveling to and from LGBT movement activities held in Burmese cities or abroad.[39]

Regardless of whether they directly receive financial rewards or indirectly benefit, queer Burmese affiliated with LGBT activism report having gained social standing in their hometowns. That means they receive better treatment, which translates into feelings of belonging and greater dignity. Khin Kyine, who left her village to make a living in Ranong, Thailand, started out as a "house maid" and then a seafood factory worker. Since joining SUNSHINE as a volunteer, she has become one of the few lesbian leaders in the movement: "My life has changed. I started out at the low-level domestic job in another country. . . . The people who are around me are happy for me for what I am now. I have status in my community" (Khin Kyine, interview, March 30, 2016). My interviews and observations also indicate similar findings among grassroots organizers such as Aung Aung and Win Sein, who became leaders of a lesbian group and human rights documentation program in their town.

Distinctive Emotion Culture

"You can see the obvious difference between how the LGBTs [in the movement] behave and how the LGBTs outside are behaving" (Ywet War, interview, August 2, 2016). This remark by Ywet War, a heterosexual, cisgender lawyer and movement ally, highlights the second important consequence of the movement's grievance transformation. The movement's feeling rules underlying self-transformation contribute to a unique emotion culture, whose adherents, LGBT activists, deal with their grievances distinctively from older queer communities.[40]

Despite recruiting through social ties among older queer communities, the LGBT movement is distinguishable from the former. A few activists, such as Zin Yaw, work as *nat kadaw*, who help humans communicate with *nat* to find out about their future, realize a wish, or change their fortunes. Others, such as Gyo Kyar, make a living doing hair and makeup. However, they treat their niche occupational worlds and LGBT activism as separate parts of their lives. They did not talk about the former in the interviews for my study unless I specifically asked them about it.[41] According to my interviews and analysis of movement documents, LGBT activists also try to engage more beauticians and *nat kadaw*, inviting them to movement workshops and IDAHO and TDoR celebrations.

However, they notice that the ones who are well known and established in these occupations, while willing to lend their names to and make public appearances at IDAHO and TDoR events, do not take up the movement's cause.

The key differences lie with the LGBT movement's emotion culture, which includes the feeling rules produced by grievance transformation. LGBT activists' interpretation of suffering and proffered solution are nothing like those of older communities. Beautician work and pageantry mimic heteronormative celebrations of female beauty, whereas in *nat* worship, *nat kadaw* enjoy respect for serving as conduits to the spirit world. Although these queer communities are dissimilar in occupational nature and origins, they are similarly distinguished from the movement based on emotion culture. They do not focus on the source of oppressive conditions, much less depict them as human rights violations. Instead, they concentrate on offering occupations in which *apwint* and *apone* have been tolerated and have even attained social standing.[42] Since the 1960s, *apwint* and *apone* have carved out niches in spirit mediumship and female beauty, being stereotyped as better suited to them than heterosexual, cisgender women are.[43] Many have managed to stay self-employed, circumventing their problems with employment discrimination. The income eases their material struggles and perhaps troubled relationships with families, either because they can provide family members with financial support in exchange for toleration (if not acceptance) or they can live independently. Doing well in the niche occupations also earns them higher social standing (also see Ho 2009). For *nat kadaw*, having close relationships with the spirits also may lessen the prejudice toward them as queer people, allowing them to redefine their inferior social status. After all, their karma cannot be so bad if they have communication channels with *nat*.[44]

Moreover, the older communities serve as sanctuaries, providing escape from the suffering that the outside world inflicts on queer Burmese. "It allows [*apone*] to dress up in female attire. That's about the only place where they can express themselves freely" (Aung Aung, interview, August 1, 2016). Aung Aung is referring specifically to *nat* festivals, but his comment can also apply to beauty pageants. Participating in beauty pageants and *nat* worship give *apwint* and *apone*—including those who do not practice the relevant trades—temporary relief from the grim realities of their everyday lives. At beauty pageants, *apwint* and *apone* dress up, bask in the spotlight, and receive favorable attention and compliments. In *nat* worship, *apwint*, *apone*, and *trans women* devotees savor love and acceptance from the spirits. They find catharsis for their anguish of losing *tha nge* lovers to heterosexual, cisgender women, especially in their veneration of Ma Ngwe Taung, a female spirit who died of unrequited love; at *nat* festivals, known to be a time and place where the usual social norms of conduct are suspended, they hook up, party, and find release for their sexual desires with relatively less judgment than otherwise (Gilbert 2016).

In contrast, the LGBT movement wants queer Burmese to appreciate their suffering as human rights violations and change their circumstances, not seek refuge from it. "[Those from older queer communities] don't really have a deeper appreciation about why many of them are stuck in this job circle. . . . They simply do not have the rights-based idea" (Khant Nyar, interview, July 29, 2016). To LGBT movement leaders like Khant Nyar, niche occupations are phenomena of the oppressive conditions that deny queer Burmese other possibilities and box them into limited stereotypes. Instead, they want queer Burmese to take action that finds them a better place in society at large. Their new feeling rules thus exhort queers to show behavior that meets societal norms, roles, and obligations rather than provide avenues of escape and release from them.[45]

New Claims

With their distinctive emotion culture, LGBT activists put forth political claims neither seen nor heard before in Myanmar, one that asserts the equal entitlement of queer Burmese to human rights—"LGBT rights" in their words. They bring to the attention of policymakers and legislators the plight and demands of a neglected social group and engage in a discourse that was once taboo. Although other Burmese activists since 2011 have increasingly spoken out about human rights in their respective areas of advocacy, the LGBT movement is the first and remains the only movement focused on queer Burmese.[46]

The most common way that movement leaders and newcomers articulate what they hope to get from human rights is to give me a list of demands similar to Htut Htut's:

> I want LGBT people to be free from discrimination from their surroundings. I want to be free from the danger of police, to be free from the discrimination of family members, like being disowned. And I want LGBT people to get equal job opportunities like other human beings . . . and get equal rights for education. (Htut Htut, interview, March 31, 2013)

I also found similar demands in the movement's reports and publications. Htut

Htut's list reflects the detailed recommendations of VIVID to the government and media released about two years after his interview. It also responds to the sociopolitical conditions of queer Burmese and ties in with the movement goals of winning social belonging and legal reform.

Since relocating their movement headquarters to Yangon in 2013, LGBT activists have brought claims for LGBT rights to Burmese politics. They openly distribute human rights publications in Myanmar. For example, in their report on Section 377 of the Penal Code, they single out the police for "perpetrating grave human rights violations" against queer Burmese and urge their government to "respect the universal principles of the UDHR." VIVID leaders also publicly call for and lobby parliamentarians about the reform of Section 377 of the Penal Code. Lawyers who are movement activists or allies represent queer Burmese persecuted by the police. Their numbers are small and their resources limited, but these lawyers attempt to alter, case by case, the way police and judges treat queer people. From 2013 to 2014, movement leaders worked with Cindy and several other lawyers to appeal all the way to the Supreme Court the sentence of an *apwint* convicted under Section 35(c) of the Police Act.[47] Although they lost the suit, it represents a high–water mark for the movement's claim making in post-transition Myanmar, the first case of its kind supported by LGBT activists and propelled by their belief that a queer person's human rights had been violated.

In addition, VIVID has implemented a human rights documentation program in three grassroots locations. Aung Aung, Win Sein, and other grassroots organizers conduct interviews with people who come to them with grievances, write up reports, and refer appropriate cases to lawyers affiliated with their movement. They often indicate on the reports that the offending acts, such as constraint on "freedom of movement" and "abuse," are "damage to dignity" in the report column for "human rights violation" (LGBT Movement Human Rights Documentation Report, February 2015).[48] Although their claims of violations probably do not amount to any formal legal action, they demonstrate that LGBT activists have started to make rights-based claims for a group of people in a society not used to their assertiveness and their demands to be treated with dignity.

. . .

In this chapter, we saw the three salient features of human rights practice as a way of life. The processes of grievance transformation make and remake emotions that perpetuate LGBT activists' human rights practice. LGBT activists creatively engage cultural schemas and resources to develop emotional fealty to human rights, drawing from common experiences, religious beliefs, and social norms that support the movement's cause and sidelining the ones disadvantageous to it. Their unique interpretation, centered around dignity, social belonging, and responsibility, regards human rights as a collective good to be collectively achieved. The recursive processes of grievance transformation lead to three interrelated outcomes—self-transformation, distinctive emotion culture, and new political claims (for a new claimant)—that demonstrate how human rights practice have the potential to influence formal institutions of law and politics from the bottom up.

However, there is more to why and how LGBT activists stay with the movement and carry on its practice of human rights. Besides being emotionally bound to human rights, they are affectionately tied to one another as a result of community building, another crucial component of human rights practice as a way of life. Next, we look at this other set of recursive social processes, which (re)constitute emotions as well as interpersonal relationships and contribute to the production of the three interrelated outcomes.

Chapter 4

Building Community

Emotional Bonds Among Activists

After listening to Tun Tun's speech about uniting and standing up for their rights, Tin Hla and his companions lit candles, placed them on the lake, and let them float away under the evening sky. Everyone was somber, taking a moment to remember queer Burmese who died from violence committed against them because of their gender identity. Then Tin Hla joined other REGAL members, carrying a cake onto the stage: REGAL is five years old! The crowd broke into song, "Happy Birthday," and cut the cake. *Apwint, apone, gay* men, *trans women,* and lesbians milled around, chatting with friends from the movement. (Field notes, Yangon, November 20, 2015)

SOON AFTER BRAVING the perils of attending a human rights workshop in Chiang Mai, meeting Tun Tun for the first time, and fooling customs officers to sneak home human rights paraphernalia in his suitcase, Tin Hla started calling himself *gay*. Two years later, he became a leader of REGAL, an LGBT group open to all queer Burmese regardless of how they identify themselves. He runs activities such as the TDoR event and REGAL party described and trains new grassroots organizers, inculcating them into the movement's human rights practice.

Tin Hla's adoption of *gay* as his identity, REGAL's inclusive membership, and the social interactions that take place during its activities demonstrate the third set of processes at work in the human rights practice as a way of life: those of community building. They engender emotions that germinate affective ties, another essential ingredient to sustain the dedication of people like Tin Hla.

That is, while grievance transformation develops emotional commitment to human rights, community building forges emotional bonds among those who commit to their practice, forming a community of LGBT activists. The bonds sprout in part from the affinity of sharing the collective marker of LGBT and in part from the social interactions involved in making sense of and putting human rights into action together.

Community building complements grievance transformation by contributing to the three interrelated outcomes. LGBT activists blend Burmese understandings of gender and sexuality into the meanings of LGBT identities, and relate them to the three core meanings of human rights—dignity, social belonging, and responsibility—enhancing their characterization of human rights as a collective good that requires collective action to attain. By associating the adoption of LGBT identities with having greater dignity, they fortify the self-transformation of queer Burmese. The affinities of being LGBT and the affective ties developed from participating in human rights practice shape an inclusive form of queer bonding, the second fundamental element of their distinctive emotion culture. As a community with a redefined sense of self and unique emotion culture, they represent a new claimant of LGBT Burmese and shoulder the responsibility of demanding their human rights in Myanmar.

Fostering a New Collective Identity

"LGBT is an identity." Emblazoned on T-shirts, displayed on posters, and splashed across banners, the theme for IDAHO 2014 says it all. It embodies why LGBT activists, since their movement's founding, have constructed a collective identity of LGBT. Their efforts at collective identity construction are integral to their human rights practice for reasons intimately tied to their appreciation of queer conditions and the meanings they give to human rights.

Countering Derogatory Burmese Terms

LGBT activists encourage newcomers to their movement to adopt sexual and gender identities represented by "LGBT"—lesbian, gay, bisexual, and transgender—believing that those identities counter derogatory Burmese references and help change the way queer people feel about themselves. National leaders and grassroots organizers in my study consistently express little concern for the foreign origins of LGBT.[1] More vital to them, LGBT identity terms personify dignity, an essential meaning in their understanding of human rights. Their cultivation of these self-identifiers complements grievance transformation, which aims to change the queer Burmese sense of self and replace their negative feeling rules with positive ones.

Movement leaders as well as grassroots organizers associate certain Burmese words with the queer suffering of insult and abuse described in Chapter 3, characterizing them as symbols of oppression and prejudice: "The terms we are using in our culture are very negative, very offensive . . . we have been suffering from the terms like *achauk*" (Pyae Soe, interview, February 21, 2013). *Achauk*, most commonly referring to *apwint*, literally means something dry, and is believed to connote the physical quality of having anal sex with *apwint*. *Gandu*, the word that provoked Pyae Soe into a fight with his classmate in Chapter 2, supposedly refers to the anus or buttocks and is also a vulgar reference to *apwint*. *Baw pyar* literally means "flat balls" and refers to *tomboys*, presumably in denigration of their lack of male sexual organs.[2] Many more words invariably poke fun at queers' sexual organs or stir up disgust about their sex life:[3] "They suggest that you are not capable of anything, you are good-for-nothing people. But the new terms [LGBT], they don't have that feeling" (Zwe Naung, interview, February 20, 2013).

The difference is the "feeling of the words" (Thiha Aung, interview, November 14, 2014). LGBT identities sound better than these Burmese terms because they do not refer graphically to their sexual conduct or organs. Thiha Aung, a grassroots organizer from northern Myanmar, gives a typical explanation: "'LGBT'" is "more polite," whereas "local words are crude and not pleasing to the ear." It is the most common comparison that interviewees bring up when asked if and why they prefer "LGBT" over the longstanding Burmese terms.

The feeling of the words matters profoundly to LGBT activists' quest to transform the queer Burmese sense of self through human rights. The Yogyakarta Principles, to which they refer for the application of human rights to queer persons, uses "LGBT" in the preamble, connoting the meaning that queers are as worthy of human rights as anyone else. This connotation supports grievance transformation processes, meant to displace feeling rules that breed self-hatred, fear, and shame and instill new ones to inspire hope and confidence. For LGBT activists, cultivating LGBT identities can help change how queer Burmese relate themselves to the rest of society, not as inferior, deviant beings but as people who, like everybody else, deserve to be treated with dignity.

The effort of cultivating LGBT identities is a conscious one. Most interviewees said they were unfamiliar with and understood little about these terms or the corresponding understandings of sexuality and gender. Movement pioneers Seng Naw, Kyaw Kyaw, and Pyae Soe found out about LGBT identities only after meeting Tun Tun. Under military rule, access to outside information and the Internet was limited, a situation that remains so for parts of the country even today.[4]

Therefore, LGBT activists usually begin from scratch to cultivate new identities among movement newcomers. First, they introduce and explain the acronym, LGBT. They spell out the term represented by each letter. They explain the difference between sexuality and gender identity and what each word in the acronym represents. Then they ask participants to talk about their sexual attractions or gender identities and discuss whether any of the LGBT identities apply to them. Such workshop interactions are consistent with the trainer's guidelines in an early LGBT module that Seng Naw first persuaded Tun Tun to incorporate into the human rights training manual of JUSTICE, VIVID's parent organization. In one version of the manual, trainers were instructed to explain, "Lesbian = *a myo tha mee chin chit thu*" (a female who loves another female) and so on. Alongside "LGBT," activists introduce *lein tu chit thu* ("those who love the same sex"), a Burmese term they claim was coined by Tun Tun and Seng Naw and is used interchangeably to refer to "homosexual" and "LGBT."

Outside the workshops, LGBT activists cultivate the use of LGBT identity terms among themselves, and with allies, government officials, politicians, and donors. They refer to "lesbian," "gay," "bisexual," and "transgender" in their movement meetings, internal correspondence, and VIVID's magazines, as well as during IDAHO, TDoR, and other public events. They link the acronym to their movement's symbol for human rights, the rainbow flag, which appears prominently at movement activities, at public events, and on its paraphernalia. For instance, they distributed IDAHO 2014 T-shirts, banners, and posters printed with "LGBT is an identity," together with stickers depicting the rainbow flag, to ten towns and cities where celebrations were held. In other years, grassroots organizers have also displayed at their IDAHO events banners and posters with "LGBT" or "lesbian, gay, bisexual, and transgender."

Interviewees, however, do not adopt LGBT identities based on internationally accepted definitions wholesale and instead apply them in ways influenced by Burmese notions of sexuality and gender. Movement leaders do not enforce them either. I noticed—and VIVID leaders confirmed in interviews—that they let fellow activists choose whatever LGBT identity they want.[5]

Consequently, LGBT activists produce varied and unique meanings of LGBT identities with their human rights practice. LGBT terms have different connotations to different people and are employed differently, even changing over time for the same person. Some *apwint* decide they are *transgender* or *trans women* or prefer to call themselves *gay*. Others, like Yamin, used to be *apone* and considered themselves *gay*, because even though they internally identified as female and were attracted to partners who were designated male at birth, they were still outwardly masculine presenting; later, when they became *apwint* and openly expressed their gender identity, they switched over to *trans woman, transgender*, or *T.G.* Among *tomboys*, some consider themselves "lesbians," but others—the ones most inclined to call themselves *trans men*—limit "lesbian" to feminine-presenting women who have relationships with them, people I describe as *lesbians* (with italics). A few interviewees, like Htut Htut, simply refer to themselves as "LGBT," seeing the entire acronym as representing their non-gender-conforming, nonheteronormative selves. The result perhaps echoes that of "dubbing" in Indonesia (Boellstorff 2005), where local queers also reinterpret identity terms like "gay" and "lesbian" to produce localized meanings of the imported words.

Creating Political Unity

This is just for political concern. . . . But in our LGBT community, we are different. (Seng Naw, interview, April 25, 2013*)

LGBT activists believe that the collective marker of LGBT, by nurturing feelings of affinity, politically unites the diverse population of queer Burmese. They regard the LGBT rubric as accepting, rather than threatening, their diversity, because it embraces queer Burmese based not on their specific gender or sexuality but a shared understanding of human rights in the form of their movement's practice. Put another way, somebody who simply takes on an LGBT identity label but does not partake in the movement's practice would not be deemed a member of their community, which consists of LGBT activists—people who assume the responsibility to fight for the human rights of queer Burmese.

Activists of the LGBT movement express dissatisfaction with longstanding Burmese terms and English loan words for failing to encompass the wide spectrum of sexualities and gender identities. Each familiar Burmese term refers to a particular sexual orientation or gender identity, regardless of whether it is pejorative (*achauk*), neutral (*apwint, apone*), or mixed in the nature of its connotation (*meinmashar, yaukkashar*).[6] Although the English loan term of "men who have sex with men" (MSM), found in HIV/AIDS parlance predating the LGBT movement, is broader and includes *apwint, apone*, and *homo*, among others, it is still a classification based on the sexual conduct of those who were assigned male at birth.[7] Queer persons who were deemed female at birth are excluded from the MSM umbrella; if they are masculine presenting, they are usually considered *tomboys* or *yaukkashar*.

Moreover, the familiar terms embody heterosexually gendered notions of sex and relationships. They recognize sexual attraction between a male- and a female-identified person but offer little space for those attracted to people with the same sexual orientation and gender identity (Chua and Gilbert 2016; Gilbert 2016). *Apwint* and *apone* are understood to be attracted to masculine-presenting, heterosexual men, *tha nge*; I was told that *apwint* and *apone* could also partner up, but when I asked whether two *apwint* could get together romantically or sexually, I was told it would be unlikely, and my question was often greeted with amusement. Similarly, among queers who are assigned female at birth, the prototypical pairing is that of a *tomboy* or *yaukkashar* with a feminine-presenting woman. Couples who are both feminine-presenting women do exist—and I managed to interview a few—but *tomboys* or *yaukkashar* cannot imagine each other as possible sexual or romantic partners. Some *lesbians* cannot or will not imagine being with somebody who looks like them (feminine-presenting), because they regard their masculine-presenting partners as "men," who assume the "man's role" of initiating courtship and providing for her material needs.[8] Such gendered notions of relationships and sexuality also exist in neighboring societies like Thailand (Jackson 2000; Sinnott 2004), Indonesia (Boellstorff 2005; Blackwood 2010), and the Philippines (Garcia 2009).

On the other hand, "'LGBT' can cover the whole group. It's a complete word for us" (Tin Hla, interview, May 15, 2013). Again, national activists and grassroots organizers in my study are little bothered by the foreign origin of "LGBT" or its potential to threaten queer diversity. To them, the collective marker is broad enough to embrace their diversity, and possibly stimulate feelings of affinity among all kinds of queer people regardless of their sexual orientation, gender identities, or assigned sex at birth. Crucially, it includes queers who cannot or do not want to fit themselves within local identities, primarily because those terms adhere to heterosexually gendered notions of sex and relationships. It gives these queers a place of belonging, affirming they are not invisible among the marginalized. For the same reason, LGBT activists sometimes use the Burmese alternative of *lein tu chit thu*. The phrase more accurately connotes "homosexual" or "same sex," but interviewees generally accept its wider application to a similar range of diversity as "LGBT."

Riding on the embodiment of greater inclusivity in "LGBT," activists try to overcome internal prejudices among queers who are demarcated along Burmese identifiers. For example, some *apwint* harbor prejudices against *apone* and masculine-presenting *gay* men. They see the two as leading easier lives by being able to "pass" as heterosexual, cisgender men, whereas they bear the brunt of ostracism. Meanwhile, some *gay* men are known to distance themselves from *apwint*, for fear that they would be lumped together and ridiculed. According to Myanmar's social hierarchy, *gay* men could be ranked "higher" than *apwint* and *apone*; even though they also have sexual relations with people assigned male at birth, like *tha nge* do with *apwint* and *apone*—they are perceived to have not "degraded" themselves into women and their inferior sexual roles. Pyae Soe admitted to me that his mother could accept he was *gay* but would not have been able to do so easily if he were a *trans woman* or *apwint*.[9] Another common division lies between lesbians, on the one hand, and *apwint* and *apone*, on the other. According to interviewees, the former stereotypes the latter as criminal and sexual deviants, just like others in their society have been conditioned to do so. Those abused by patriarchs and other men are also suspicious of *apwint* and *apone*, perceiving them to enjoy male privilege by virtue of their male designation at birth.[10]

Having treated "LGBT" as the embodiment of dignity, LGBT activists build on its intimate association with their human rights practice to construct a politically united type of queer belonging, an LGBT community of activists. They hold out "LGBT" as a composition of people who similarly appreciate queer suffering as human rights violations and embrace feeling rules that motivate collective responsibility to work for human rights. LGBT activists urge their community members to be unified in their practice of human rights as a way of life though they are varied in their sexuality and gender.

To construct this collective identity, LGBT activists routinely designate sessions at movement meetings and workshops to discuss the differences in sexuality and gender among them and to air their internal biases. During the discussions, they remind everyone of the nature and sources of their grievances, that is, human rights violations caused by prejudicial social norms, laws, and state actors and others around them (an exercise that also forms part of grievance transformation). Subsequently, they ask everyone to come up with ideas for bridging their divides, discussions that form part of the brainstorming sessions for strategic action.

While the proposed solutions are quite predictable, such as encouraging more collaboration between *gay* men and lesbians (field notes, movement meeting, March 1–2, 2015), they illustrate the deliberate efforts at building the collective identity of LGBT. One of the first activities to encourage lesbians and *trans women* to socialize together was a soccer match held in conjunction with IDAHO 2009 in Ranong: Khin Kyine led the lesbian team in blue jerseys to a crushing 6–0 victory against their opponents in yellow jerseys (Khin Kyine, interview, February 23, 2013; photos provided by Khin Kyine and SUNSHINE). Thiha Aung carried on the tradition of soccer matches, leading lesbians in a 2–0 victory against *trans women* at an IDAHO 2016 grassroots celebration. Another example is REGAL, the grassroots organization founded by Cho Cho and headed by Tin Hla for the LGBT "family" in the Yangon Region (Cho Cho, interview, May 15, 2013). Movement leaders also put activists of diverse sexualities and genders into situations in which they have to interact and cooperate with one another. They include participation in human rights workshops and movement-wide strategy meetings, as well as the organizing of such public events as IDAHO, TDoR, and exhibitions.

Forging Affective Ties

Besides constructing a collective identity of LGBT, community-building processes forge affective ties among activists. The ties are informed by their shared practice, further underscoring the point that mere adoption of LGBT labels does not count as inclusion in their community. As recruits and seasoned activists practice human rights together, they inevitably interact with one another. The interactions produce emotions separate from those brought into the movement from formation processes or constituted as part of grievance transformation, though they may occur at the same event or activity. Rather, they remake emotions affiliated with the other two sets of processes and turn them into affective ties that provide mutual support and encouragement to fight together or induce people to stay with the movement despite the hardships and risks.

Bonding over Fear and Anxiety of Getting Caught

Camaraderie emerges from LGBT activists' shared apprehension about "security concerns" or "security reasons." Up to the early 2010s, as we learned in Chapter 2, grassroots organizers feared getting caught and punished by the military government for being affiliated with human rights activism or possessing the movement's paraphernalia. Interviewees admitted that in those early days of the movement, some of them did not dare bring contraband into the country.

Although fear and anxiety already play their part in constituting formation processes, they are remade through community-building processes when newcomers and activists realize they harbor similar fears and anxieties and bond together to cope with these unsettling feelings. For example, grassroots organizers used to travel in groups back and forth across the border to Thailand to participate in movement activities. As a group, they mustered courage and collected themselves as they dealt with checkpoint officials who questioned them about traveling overseas or rummaged through their suitcases in which they had stuffed human rights publications. In 2009, during a VIVID workshop, participants reported seeing somebody secretly taking photographs of their activities. Nobody could confirm what was going on, and panic broke out. The participants based inside Myanmar wanted to stop the workshop, worried that the government was spying on them. To calm everyone, Seng Naw renamed the workshop to something innocuous about consultancy, designed a new banner for the workshop, and asked all the participants to take photos in front of it (Seng Naw, interview, April 25, 2013*). Having to deal with everyone's fears, devising strategies together, and caring for one another in those early days, Seng Naw, Pyae Soe, and Zwe Naung also became family. "The three of us are brothers," Zwe Naung said (interview, February 20, 2013).

LGBT activists also build camaraderie when they share these experiences of fear and coping with fear at workshops and movement meetings. Seasoned activists and newcomers learn from one another about the challenges of ensuring their safety, discuss their experiences, and come up with coping strategies. According to internal minutes and reports of the movement, as well as my interviews, they exchange news about the plight of human rights activists in Myanmar, vent their concerns, and allay one another's fears with words of encouragement and advice.

Bonding Over Queer Suffering

People got very, very emotional, telling their stories . . . it was really, really
powerful. (Sandy, interview, May 5, 2013*)

The resource person was crying. The interpreter was also crying. (Cho Cho,
interview, May 15, 2013)

And, in an amazing moment, [Tun Tun] came in and [one of the participants]
who had started crying, apologized to the group, because it's a huge loss of face to
cry. . . . [Tun Tun] said, "We all have to thank you, because you let yourself cry for
things that we've all experienced." (Sandy, interview, May 5, 2013*)

Sandy and Cho Cho's separate descriptions of the same incident at a VIVID workshop illustrate how LGBT activists develop solidarity from their recounting of queer suffering. Emotions of pain, despair, and fear in their lives appear in grievance transformation, where they are summoned to create resonance for human rights. And then, through community-building processes, they are remade into affective ties. These emotions not only connect activists and recruits as people with shared grievances but also bring them closer by providing mutual support—the feeling that they are not alone. We know from Chapter 3 that LGBT activists encourage workshop participants to talk about their experiences with discrimination, depict them as human rights violations, and reattribute the blame to the state, society, and prejudicial norms. Crying during those social interactions is common, perhaps even cathartic. Participants open up, finally having a safe space and finding the courage to talk about what they have endured all of their lives. Confirming the same incident that Sandy and Cho Cho described, Tun Tun said, "Sharing the courage and the strength among the team . . . that's why we are working as a group. The kind of understanding, sympathy, even sharing tears, happens a lot" (Tun Tun, interview, May 14, 2013*).

This type of solidarity is also about feeling that they are in the fight together, binding them through collective action and common goals of winning human rights for queer Burmese—in other words, the movement's practice. The affective tie coexists with the motivation produced by grievance transformation to assume collective responsibility. In Chapter 3, Char Thar cried after learning about human rights in Chiang Mai in 2011 for two reasons: rejoicing for himself, knowing that queer folks like him nevertheless deserved dignity, and feeling sorry that many fellow queer Burmese did not know that. The latter reason is related to the empathy aroused by grievance transformation processes, but empathy also simultaneously relates Chan Thar to LGBT activists who already feel the same and are already trying to bring change. Drawn into the movement's fight, Char Thar's first act of LGBT activism was to smuggle VIVID's human rights publications across the border back to Myanmar. He later joined REGAL, Tin Hla's grassroots organization.

Besides workshops and movement meetings, this type of solidarity is cultivated at IDAHO and TDoR. At these annual gatherings, movement leaders remind the audience about human rights violations committed against queers. Then they redirect the emotions of suffering toward a call for collective action. For example, at TDoR 2015 in Yangon, Tun Tun said, "There are lives of *T.G.* who are lost because of their identity and we are here to pay respect and remember them. . . . We have to try to get the acceptance of society and we have to build up capacity to improve our lives." Afterward, he urged fellow queers to "work in unison to achieve our goal" (field notes, November 20, 2015).

The movement paraphernalia that Chan Thar and other grassroots organizers brought home also help build solidarity. VIVID's magazine features articles about the human rights conditions of queers and interviews with activists who talk about their personal struggles and why they got involved with the movement. Packed into suitcases, wedged between *longyi* (sarong), and traveling along dusty roads in old buses and cars, VIVID's magazines, posters, and flyers bring the message to queer Burmese in small towns and villages that they are not alone: a queer community called "LGBT," represented by such symbols as the rainbow flag, is trying to improve their lives. For some people, reading the magazine kindled their first connection with the movement. Zin Yaw is one example. He came across VIVID's magazines in his town, started reading them, and one day boarded a bus to Yangon to meet VIVID's leaders (Zin Yaw, interview, June 11, 2014, and August 3, 2016).

Bonding Over Trust, Affection, and Respect

At workshops, meetings, and public events, newcomers, leaders, and grassroots organizers socialize and get to know one another, generating feelings of trust, affection, and respect that strengthen interpersonal relationships among them. These community-building processes often overlap with the ones that foster camaraderie and solidarity discussed in the preceding sections, as well as with the processes of grievance transformation. For example, at the 2015 TDoR event described at the opening of this chapter, after grieving together about queer suffering during the candlelight ceremony, they switched into party mode when they celebrated REGAL's birthday with song and cake.

Making friends is just as important to community building as the deliberate construction of an LGBT collective identity and the bonding over fear, anxiety, and queer suffering. On the surface, friends and fellowship have nothing to do with human rights practice, seemingly incidental to grievance transformation. After all, people usually have to interact to get things done in a social movement. But it is not simply the ideals of human rights, heart-stirring motivations, or the commonalities of being LGBT that encourage this group of people to come together. Some activists may not care as much about such things as they care about the trust, affection, and respect for other people in the movement—the stuff that makes people stay together, put up with one another, get through the tough times, and even take risks.

While many interviewees said they joined the movement because they were motivated to fight for the human rights of queer people, my observations and interviews suggest they are also attracted to the movement community because they made friends and enjoyed one another's company. For a typical workshop or movement meeting, grassroots organizers around the country travel in small groups by bus to and from the venue and stay together at the same hotel arranged by VIVID. On the first day, they are usually excited to see one another since the previous gathering weeks or months ago. Gossip and small talk ripple through the room: who is falling out with whom, what they are wearing, and what they are going to do at the end of the day. To kick off proceedings or stimulate everyone after lunch, the leader usually asks attendees to take part in icebreakers, the sort typically played at organizational retreats and camps. The icebreakers frequently turn into mutual teasing and sexually explicit jokes, particularly among *apwint* and *trans women.*

During the substantive proceedings, small group discussions compel people who do not usually socialize, such as lesbians and *apwint*, to huddle and work together. The serious exchanges are interrupted by silly jokes, more teasing, and the occasional improvised skit that distracts and sends everyone into fits of laughter. From time to time, arguments break out and heated debates ensue. At rehearsals or behind the scenes preparing for musical and drama performances at IDAHO, TDoR, and other public events, they also squabble and tease one another as they try to get on with the plan for the day. Back at the workshops and meetings, occasionally the proceedings are sidetracked by personal emergencies. In the middle of the March 2015 movement meeting, Gyo Kyar suddenly cried out in dismay. She needed to rush home to deal with an emergency with a wedding job (for her beautician business), but she could not change her bus ticket. The meeting came to a standstill as others got on their phones to resolve Gyo Kyar's crisis (field notes, movement meeting, March 1–2, 2015). At the end of a workshop or meeting day, just as I saw on my first trip to Chiang Mai, longtime movement participants and newcomers head out in small groups. They go shopping, have dinner, grab a beer, or head to popular nightspots.

What is more, the community is bound together by love and respect for Tun Tun. Since the LGBT movement's early days, Tun Tun has been the inspiration for many others who joined him. Seng Naw, Kyaw Kyaw, and Pyae Soe's journeys into the movement exemplify his influence. They and other LGBT activists refer to Tun Tun with the prefix of *Sayar* (teacher). On social media, my interviewees often reminisce about their first meetings with their *Sayar* and post photographs of their first meetings in Chiang Mai, usually in front of a movement event banner. To most LGBT activists whom I interviewed, Tun Tun is a hero, a student leader of the '88 generation, and a human rights activist who dared to come out openly about his sexuality. Since relocating the LGBT movement's headquarters to Yangon, Khant Nyar and other VIVID leaders have been running its daily operations, whereas Tun Tun has increasingly busied himself with other human rights issues. Nonetheless, Tun Tun told me, the LGBT movement remains special to him. He still goes to its workshops, meetings, IDAHO, and other public events, usually to give motivational speeches at the beginning. He energizes the audience with his words, cracks them up with his jokes, and brings tears to their eyes with the story about his boyfriend in the rebel army (field notes, January 28–30, 2016).

Dropping Out and Weak Emotional Bonds

The cases of people who leave the movement or go no further than participating in a few of its human rights workshops accentuate the importance of affective ties to community building. With some recruits, LGBT activists' efforts at community building fail. The initial ties from the formation processes that got these people recruited were insufficient to sustain their engagement. Neither were the ideals of human rights, which *did* resonate with them, nor LGBT identities, which some of them even adopted for themselves. Among interviewees, the people who stopped being LGBT activists (former LGBT activists) and those who did not join the movement (dropouts) lack emotional bonds to its activists or have stronger attachments to other communities.

Htut Htut, a former LGBT activist, felt that his affection for the movement's community was unreciprocated. I first met him at the September 2012 workshop in Chiang Mai. Tun Tun had invited promising grassroots organizers like him to return for advocacy training. Htut Htut participated enthusiastically in the workshop. He joked and had fun with his peers. In Chapter 3, I quoted him from our 2013 interview on what he wanted to achieve with human rights. He spoke passionately about the movement and at length about how much Tun Tun valued his potential as an LGBT activist. Two years later, when I noticed Htut Htut's absence, I tracked him down and persuaded him to do a reinterview. Htut Htut said he had stopped volunteering as a grassroots organizer. He had tried to apply for a job with VIVID, he told me, but was rejected several times and given generic reasons about his unsuitability. Although Htut Htut tried to act nonchalantly, he revealed in the interview, "Sometimes I have emotional feelings seeing the people who work for rights in the movement, because I had been working with the group for quite some time as a volunteer . . . so it's hard to understand, and also there are one or two people whom I cannot understand, but I think that *Sayar* [Tun Tun] didn't look out for me" (Htut Htut, interview, July 4, 2015). From my separate conversations with Khant Nyar, I infer that Htut Htut and Khant Nyar probably also have personal issues between them. Htut Htut could have continued to volunteer for the movement as a grassroots organizer, but he dropped out, feeling that Tun Tun, his idol, no longer cared about him (though it was more likely that Tun Tun had relinquished VIVID's daily responsibilities to Khant Nyar) and feeling unwanted by Khant Nyar and perhaps others who had assumed leadership positions in the movement.

The problem of lesbians who used to be LGBT activists or who dropped out is related to weak emotional bonds as well. Lesbians leave the movement after failing to experience strong fellowship with activists in the movement. Like other recruits, they were initially curious enough to brave the same risks to answer the recruitment calls; in fact, they had to overcome additional hurdles that hinder women's ability to travel and participate in movement activities (see Chapter 2). Through grievance transformation, they grew attracted to the promise of human rights. However, they eventually dropped out. Since its founding, the movement has been dominated by activists designated male at birth, especially *trans women, apwint*, and *apone*. Regardless of the varying degrees to which this majority self-identifies as female, they socialize differently from lesbians, who do not enjoy male privilege in Burmese society. At meetings and workshops, this majority is generally more outspoken. They often converse in their own slang and about topics lesbians find inaccessible and inappropriate for women (including those who self-identify as *trans men*). For example, at the September 2012 workshop, the discussion strayed to "eating oranges" (queer slang for having sex with monks).[11] "[They] speak openly about what they did the night before. . . . The lesbians cannot take [this kind of] behavior and over time they feel isolated" (Cho Cho, interview, November 13, 2014). While LGBT activists try to transcend these differences with the efforts explained earlier in this chapter, the difficulty remains. Cho Cho notices that some lesbians show up, initially feeling drawn to the movement, but drift away after a few gatherings, feeling they do not fit in with the majority. The poorer retention of lesbians due to their weaker emotional bonds is a manifestation of the movement's persistent gender divide, which I examine in Chapter 5.

Others dropped out because of stronger affective ties to other communities, including queer communities coalesced around niche occupations. Moe Saing, who attended VIVID's workshops twice in Chiang Mai, said he was inspired by the movement's human rights practice and wanted to get involved, but he was not invited to subsequent activities. He felt unwelcome because he did not work in the "NGO field" (Moe Saing, interview, October 14, 2013). While most LGBT activists do work or volunteer for nonprofit organizations, his emphasis on this connection reveals the importance of emotional bonds. Moe Saing is not part of the "NGO field," because he is more connected to another community. He admitted that he was, in any case, too busy providing training to beauty pageant contestants and aspiring models. Moe Saing probably came across as uncommitted to the movement, which would have discouraged LGBT activists from engaging him further. This conclusion is consistent with the opinions of movement leaders, who perceive dropouts to be more strongly attached to other communities.

Community Building and the Interrelated Outcomes of Human Rights Practice as a Way of Life

Hand in hand with grievance transformation, community building shows how human rights practice starting with personal change has the potential to accumulate broader impact. Community building encourages the adoption of LGBT identities, an integral part of achieving self-transformation. It shapes an inclusive means of queer bonding for those who share the LGBT marker and the affective ties of practicing human rights as a way of life—the second key component of their movement's distinctive emotion culture. The new sense of self and emotion culture give shape to a political community of LGBT activists who advocate for the human rights of a new claimant in Burmese politics: LGBT people of Myanmar.

New Identity and Self-Transformation

Queer Burmese who join the movement and adopt LGBT identities—some with their own twist—feel that the new identity terms affirm who they truly are and relieve them of familiar prejudices and abuse. While a small number of people knew about LGBT identities before coming into contact with the movement, the importance is not merely about the adoption of a new self-label. The significance of adopting LGBT identities lies with its association with LGBT activists' human rights practice, especially their efforts to achieve self-transformation, so that queer Burmese can feel as worthy of human dignity as anybody else.

"The terms of LGBT are not giving negative effect to anyone . . . the same way like LGBT rights" (Maung Maung, interview, May 14, 2013). Maung Maung is one among many interviewees who joined the movement and whose subsequent self-transformation comes with self-identifying as *gay*. Another example is Aung Aung, who used to call himself a *tomboy*. After spending time with the movement, he felt more authentic as a *trans man*:

> I started using this English word, because I believe it fully respects my gender identity and my existence as a whole. At first, I could not find a word that was good enough to describe myself when I was young. As you know, many people would call me things like *yaukkashar, baw pyar*, or *achauk*. Those terms are all meant to discriminate or make fun of us. . . . I want to be respected as a person for my identity. (Aung Aung, interview, August 1, 2016)

The self-transformative aspect of LGBT identities is the most important to cisgender interviewees attracted to people with the same assigned sex at birth as theirs. Because the longstanding Burmese terms connote heterosexual and gendered notions of relationships between a man and a woman, this group of queers felt they were outcasts, not even belonging to the traditionally "deviant" groups of *apwint* and *apone*. They were confused, at a loss for words to ascribe to themselves. Such was Pyae Soe's experience in Chapter 2, where we read about his time in Phuket and journey into the movement. "Before [JUSTICE], I didn't know the term *gay*, but I knew I was attracted to guys since young. In my community, if one was attracted to a guy, one had to be a girl" (Pyae Soe, interview, July 3, 2015). But Pyae Soe did not want to identify as a woman. Although queers from bigger towns and cities may find out about and adopt the English loan word of *homo* or *tomboy*, the same cannot be said of those in villages and remote towns, places where Pyae Soe and many others in the LGBT movement come from.[12] Pyae Soe's confusion followed by relief and affirmation after realizing that he has an identity to which he belongs appears in other interviewees' stories. For instance, Min Min and Naing Lin decided they were better identified as *gay* rather than *meinmashar* or *apwint* after joining the movement.[13] Before learning about LGBT identities from the movement's human rights workshop, Nyan Lin, a *trans man*, also "did not have the language to call myself" (interview, June 28, 2015).[14]

New Ways of Bonding and Distinctive Emotion Culture

The affinities of a collective LGBT identity and the affective ties amount to a more encompassing form of queer bonding, an essential element of LGBT activists' distinctive emotion culture. The inclusive ties connect queer Burmese of different sexualities and gender identities based on their being part of LGBT and the shared human rights practice that informs it. They also bring queers together based on the camaraderie, solidarity, and fellowship cultivated among themselves as they come together through formation processes and engage in grievance transformation processes.

For LGBT activists, the inclusive form of bonding sets their queer community apart. Even though they have limited success at realizing it (see Chapter 5), their efforts nevertheless demonstrate its significance to them. "Whether you are . . . *apwint* or *apone* or you may be varied, we have to stick together and work in unison to achieve our goal" (Tun Tun, field notes, November 20, 2015). Tun Tun's speech at the TDoR 2015 celebration is yet another example of the emphasis they place on uniting diverse queers. Earlier, I recounted LGBT activists' efforts to bridge the divides, getting them to air prejudices against one another, name their common sources of grievances, and come up with solutions. In addition, according to my observations and interviews, friendships strike up between queers who in the past would not have thought they could be friends. Thiha Aung, a *tomboy*, did not socialize with *apwint* in the past. Yet after joining the movement, Thiha Aung became friends with Thein Gi, an *apwint*. The two come from the same town in northern Myanmar, so they have gotten to know each other as they travel together to and from Yangon to movement activities (interviews: Thiha Aung, November 14, 2014, and Thein Gi, November 14, 2014).

This form of queer bonding and the mere effort at achieving it stand out in Myanmar. Whereas LGBT activists use the collective marker of LGBT to unite a broad spectrum of people with different sexualities and gender identities, older queer communities tend to keep to their own kind. Communities built around niche occupations, for instance, favor queers who were assigned male at birth and identify as being female in gender. Stereotyped as well suited to be *nat kadaw*, *apwint*, *apone*, and *trans women* gain power and influence if they succeed in the occupation. Such opportunities, however, barely exist for lesbians, especially *tomboys* and *trans men*.[15] Similarly, the celebration of heteronormative female beauty by occupations in hair, makeup, and pageantry represents the complete opposite of what *tomboys* and *trans men* epitomize. The membership of communities revolving around the occupational niches or their supporters inadvertently alienates and "does little to help advance the cause of lesbians and *tomboys*" (Zin Yaw, interview, August 3, 2016).

Observant LGBT activists, such as Zin Yaw, point out that the longer-standing queer communities do not aim to unite queer Burmese or reach out to queers who differ from them in sexuality or gender.[16] In fact, certain well-known *apwint* from those communities reject queers who were designated male at birth and are attracted to men, but do not identify as female in gender. On a televised program featuring viewpoints from LGBT activists and famous *apwint* beauticians about the challenges of queer Burmese, one of the *apwint* beauticians said, "We ourselves cannot accept *gays* and *homos*, because if a male loves another male, that's naturally because he has the mind of a female. But a relationship between two well-built muscled men with moustache cannot possibly involve love" (TV program, October 30, 2016).[17] In contrast, LGBT activists attempt to overcome this very kind of prejudice among queer Burmese.

Moreover, the inclusive manner of queer bonding is new in Myanmar because it arises from emotions that LGBT activists generate and experience when practicing human rights. The bonds are anchored in their diagnosis of queer suffering as human rights violations and their claims for human rights as its solution. Unlike the LGBT movement, older queer communities deal with suffering by providing refuge in alternative familial kinships anchored in occupational niches. For instance, established *nat kadaw* and beauticians act like mother figures whose relationships lead vertically downward to apprentices and followers;[18] they provide mentorship and professional connections to younger members in the same trade, helping them become self-employed and alleviate their individual struggles with material needs and social standing (Gilbert 2016). Those kinships, even lesbians' informal social networks that do not coalesce around a particular trade, offer their own comforts and benefits. Hence, some movement dropouts, such as Moe Saing, feel emotionally rewarded in and more attached to such older communities. However, those bonds are not built on emotions shared in taking collective action together, much less in jointly practicing human rights.[19]

New Claimant

The strains of a familiar song, "See Lone Chin Twet Tha Chin Ta Pote" (Song for Unity) started playing, and seven queer performers began to dance, dressed in the traditional attire of Myanmar's seven officially recognized ethnic minorities. Behind them, two rainbow flags draped each side of the stage. As the song and dance reached its climatic end, another traditionally attired queer dancer carried Myanmar's national flag onto stage and led the performers in the finale. (Field notes, IDAHO, Yangon, May 2013)

Represented by a community of activists—people who transform their sense of self, have their own collective identity, and connect to a distinctive emotion culture (feeling rules created by grievance transformation and inclusive queer bonding by community building)—a collective claimant of LGBT steps onto the Burmese political stage. Inside their country, LGBT activists, the representative and advocate of this new claimant, champion their human rights, LGBT rights for LGBT people. Internationally going by the name of "LGBT," these activists access opportunities to funding and other assistance.

The Song for Unity dance visually illustrates the manner in which this new claimant projects itself to Burmese media, public, politicians, and government—as LGBT people who are part of Myanmar's diverse population but are nevertheless united in their claims for human rights in the country they all call home. In televised discussions about the sociopolitical conditions of queers, media reports about employment discrimination, and news coverage on IDAHO, LGBT activists describe their movement as "LGBT." In 2013, following Mandalay police officers' arrest and alleged abuse of queer persons in their custody,[20] LGBT activists carried out a "signature campaign," inviting members of the public to sign a petition to the Myanmar National Human Rights Commission and President Thein Sein to ask them "to condemn the human rights abuse of Police force, Mandalay division, and to ask for justice and free of discrimination on LGBT people."[21] On the petition, they describe their movement as "working for LGBT people." In June 2015, during a specially arranged meeting with members of Parliament, Khant Nyar introduced himself and his team as representing the "LGBT" movement; the politicians, from NLD, the military-backed USDP, and other smaller parties, adopted the language that Khant Nyar used in his introductory remarks, also referring to them as "LGBT" (field notes, June 11, 2015). After the NLD took power in 2016, LGBT activists continued to project "LGBT" as a political claimant whenever they spoke to parliamentarians behind the scenes or engaged in public dialogue with Aung San Suu Kyi (media report, January 1, 2017).

Looking outward, being an LGBT claimant connects the movement to other LGBT movements and human rights movements around the world. "There are so many people who are like us in other countries," Zin Yaw realized after reading VIVID's magazines for the first time (interview, June 11, 2014). As early as the movement's founding days, their IDAHO events have disseminated information about the discrimination of LGBT persons not only in Myanmar but also elsewhere, going as far back as the Nazi persecution of homosexual persons during World War II. VIVID's magazine also contains information about the conditions of LGBT people and their human rights advances in other countries. During the 2014 ASEAN Civil Society Conference/ASEAN People's Forum held in Yangon, an annual conference of nonprofit and grassroots organizations from the ten member states of the Association of Southeast Asian Nations (ASEAN), LGBT activists participated in the coalition that fights for the inclusion of sexual and gender minorities in the ASEAN Human Rights Declaration.[22]

More than a "we are not alone," feel-good sensation, the international affiliation attracts money and other forms of assistance, benefits that scholars find among groups whose claims are successfully recognized as human rights. The LGBT movement's organizations rely on international donors, especially European and, to a lesser degree, North American establishments. On their grant applications and reports, VIVID and grassroots organizations such as REGAL represent themselves as the human rights claimant known as LGBT. The international connection is becoming even timelier with the influx of foreign government aid and international agencies into Myanmar since 2011. The movement increasingly attracts attention from international donors and uses their expanded funding to launch new initiatives, such as the human rights documentation program described in Chapter 3 and more training workshops for lawyers and other allies.

. . .

This chapter continued to explore the three principal features of human rights practice as a way of life. Community-building processes elicit feelings of affinity, camaraderie, solidarity, and fellowship, affections that bind people together as LGBT activists; make it appealing for them stay with the movement; and sustain the practice itself. The processes contribute to the three outcomes of self-transformation, distinctive emotion culture and new claims and claimant by emphasizing LGBT identities as an embodiment of dignity, offering a form of bonding inclusive of all queer Burmese, and creating an LGBT activist community. They reinforce the outcomes' interrelated nature, as they further highlight the potential to influence formal institutions of law and politics starting from personal and grassroots changes.

Nonetheless, human rights practice as a way of life is far from perfect. Up to this point, I have mainly addressed its strengths: that it can inspire a marginalized group of people to take up collective action and yield meaningful outcomes for them. But we did catch glimpses of its limitations in this chapter when recruits left or dropped out, not having developed strong enough emotional ties to the movement community. Chapter 5 looks at the practice's flaws and limitations more extensively and then, accounting for both its strengths and shortcomings, considers the power and prospects of human rights.

Chapter 5

Faults, Fault Lines, and the Complexities of Agency

Tin Hla's life seems to have taken a better turn since becoming an LGBT activist. He had left the sheltered existence of the Yangon barracks in search of livelihood as a twenty-year-old. After hustling for wages from one town to the next for more than a decade, he returned to Yangon still looking for "survival." He met Cho Cho, went to Chiang Mai to see Tun Tun, discovered a word, *gay*, that made him feel good about himself, joined the LGBT movement, and quit the mattress shop to work for REGAL. He has friends in the movement and a mentor in Tun Tun. He speaks to the media about LGBT rights and educates queer Burmese about their rights. One Sunday, dressed in traditional Burman attire in front of friends, activists, and relatives, Tin Hla married his boyfriend, the man with whom he had fallen in love on his travels along the banks of the Ayeyarwady.[1] (Interview, June 26, 2015)

THE TALE OF TIN HLA the LGBT activist, and the larger story of human rights practice as a way of life nevertheless has run into bumpy moments and insistent troubles. After all, humans are its protagonists, and their agency is powerful yet limited. The individual and collective agencies of LGBT activists are complex. Fluid and multiple, they are capable of challenging sociopolitical forces, but they are also shaped by those forces. On that account, so are the emotions and interpersonal relationships constituting and constituted by their practice and the very practice itself.

Formation, grievance transformation, and community-building processes thus unfold depending on the social positions and the interactions of human agents involved. Power dynamics, differences, and divides among LGBT activists result in varying degrees of self-transformation and adoption of their distinctive emotion culture. Their ability to make LGBT rights claims is also hampered by deeply set norms, beliefs, and distribution of power, and hierarchy in Burmese society.

Because the faults and fault lines arise from the social processes of human rights practice and the agency behind it, they also critically inform our appreciation for the power and prospects of human rights to stimulate collective action and social change, the broader conclusion of this book. They are just as vital as the enthusiasm and optimism encountered in previous chapters. Together, the positive outcomes and shortcomings indicate that human rights practice as a way of life is far from overtaking the old and entrenched—other modes of feeling, interacting, and knowing already existing in Burmese society. Instead, with human rights, LGBT activists offer an alternative way of life alongside others.

Social Positions, Interests, and Needs: Variations in Self-Transformation and Emotion Culture

LGBT activists' social positions affect their interests and needs, their interactions with one another, and ultimately the processes of human rights practice. They came into contact with the movement, answered its recruitment calls, and joined the cause with preexisting social positions, self-understandings and interpersonal relationships. These are formed by existing norms, beliefs, power, and hierarchy, which they do not and cannot simply leave at the proverbial door. They vary in not only gender and sexuality, but also such demographics as class, education, and geographical origin. Accordingly, their emotions and interpersonal relationships emerge in different ways from the movement's human rights practice, leading to divergent degrees of self-transformation and adoption of emotion culture.

Internal Contestations
"Less partying! More messaging!"
"But it's our culture!" (Field notes, LGBT movement meeting, May 11, 2013)

When LGBT activists met in Yangon to discuss their preparations for IDAHO 2013, tension bubbled up between VIVID's leader, Khant Nyar, and grassroots organizers. Khant Nyar beseeched grassroots organizers not to spend VIVID's funds on fashion shows and beauty pageants, which typically feature *apwint* in elaborate feminine costumes—what he meant by "partying." Grassroots organizers responded that such events were part of the culture of queer Burmese, especially *apwint* (field notes, LGBT movement meeting, May 11, 2013).

The incident, a contestation between national and grassroots activists, illustrates variations in the application of new feeling rules produced by grievance transformation. LGBT activists engage in grievance transformation processes to help queer Burmese understand their conditions as human rights violations and believe they deserve the dignity promised by human rights. They craft new feeling rules to overcome self-hatred, shame, and fear of being queer and instill a greater sense of self-worth, optimism, and confidence. These freshly cultivated norms make up an essential ingredient of an emotion culture distinct from older queer communities, whose feeling rules are not based on human rights (see Chapter 3). Among themselves, however, LGBT activists are not equally committed to the movement's feeling rules. Some maintain stronger attachments to emotion cultures nurtured by more established queer communities.

Variations in the adoption of new feeling rules appear most starkly in the contestations between national and grassroots activists because of the power dynamics between them and their struggles with the realities of life in Burmese society. The movement's national leaders at VIVID set its agenda, hold grants from and reports to international funders, and control the purse strings. They regard tactics based on the *apwint* "culture" of fashion shows and pageants as detracting from grievance transformation. However, VIVID needs activists who are connected to queer populations at the grassroots to mobilize them and implement the movement's programs. The grassroots organizers, who are usually more enthusiastic than the national leaders about fashion shows and pageants, often behave opportunistically to fight for personal prestige, patronage, and every day "survival" or livelihood.

In the incident described above, national and grassroots activists reached a compromise following a passionate debate. For IDAHO 2013, grassroots organizers assured Khant Nyar they would emphasize "messaging" amid the performances already planned (field notes, LGBT movement meeting, May 11, 2013). From 2014 onward, they did not spend VIVID's funds on fashion shows or pageants, though they were allowed to use them for such performances as action songs and skits that incorporated messages about IDAHO, LGBT identities, and human rights. In Khant Nyar's words, this was "self-imposed discipline" to ensure "advocacy work instead of these fun activities" (interview, July 26, 2016).[2]

To Khant Nyar, fashion shows and pageantry uphold feeling rules that the movement is trying to displace, for he considers those activities to perpetuate *apwint* stereotypes of being frivolous and interested only in their appearance.

While occupations in female beauty and fashion offer a livelihood and their concomitant queer communities serve as sanctuaries, he is worried that they relegate queers to a narrow slice of Burmese society rather than seek belonging for them in society at large. Khant Nyar also has a background different from that of his predecessor, Seng Naw, as well as Tun Tun. He was born and raised in a Yangon family of professionals and civil servants. He took over Seng Naw's position at VIVID having accumulated extensive working experience with international NGOs and the United Nations. Compared to most of the other LGBT activists, Khant Nyar in these respects is a local NGO elite. In contrast, Seng Naw hailed from Kachin State and a family with ties to the Kachin Independence Army; Tun Tun, despite his military family background, was a 1988 student protest leader, a rebel soldier, and a dissident. Seng Naw and Tun Tun relate more to the grassroots, having organized migrants and dissidents in the borderlands for years. When they were in charge of IDAHO, they planned "fashion shows" in Ranong and Chiang Mai in 2009–2010 and let organizers put up theirs in 2012 in Sagaing and Mandalay Region (IDAHO reports and event schedules, VIVID).

Grassroots organizers also have different biographies from Khant Nyar. They generally have less formal education and fluency in English. They agree that human rights messaging is important, but it is "too boring" on its own to keep the attention of residents, queer and otherwise, in their towns and villages (field notes, LGBT movement meeting, May 11, 2013).[3] Despite the movement's efforts at creating a new emotion culture, grassroots organizers remain drawn to the older queer communities, whether to work in them or use their services. They enjoy the pageantry and worry less about the effect of reinforcing feeling rules rejected by the movement. For them, these events are quintessential forms of *apwint* self-expression.

Like the grassroots organizers, Khant Nyar's VIVID colleagues originate from rural areas and small towns. They seem more sympathetic than Khant Nyar, perhaps even enthusiastic, about model shows and beauty contests. In fact, it was awkward to ask Khant Nyar about this subject in the presence of other VIVID activists and vice versa. Yamin, for instance, has participated in pageants, and I have noticed Pyae Soe eagerly offering advice, both solicited and unsolicited, about her outfits and stage walk. Since joining the LGBT movement and rising through the ranks, however, the other VIVID activists have transformed their lives, turning into urban dwellers who can provide their parents and siblings back home with middle-class comforts (see Chapter 3). They are committed to the movement's human rights practice and follow Khant Nyar's lead. So although they seem personally more enthusiastic than he is about the traditional pageantry of *apwint* expression, they tend to keep those aspects of their lives separate from the movement, a point I revisit later in this chapter.

Besides differences in class and urban-rural geography, sociopolitical conditions concerned with patronage and daily survival are at work in the internal contestations over the movement's feeling rules. Together, the demographic differences and the struggles of daily life, demonstrate why grassroots organizers are eager to stage fashion shows and pageants, quite apart from their genuine enthusiasm about them. In Chapter 3, I noted that participating in the LGBT movement brought grassroots organizers opportunities to develop their local patronage ties and improve their social status. The pursuit of patronage is linked to concerns with daily survival, which affects grassroots organizers more than national leaders at VIVID and often encourages opportunism in Myanmar (Skidmore 2004). The concerns with survival extend to providing for their families, which is tied to their self-worth. Hence, it is understandable that entrepreneurial grassroots organizers vie for opportunities to get as much VIVID funding as possible to stage events, accumulate and distribute resources to satisfy both theirs and their beneficiaries' need for survival, and boost their own social status as patrons, even though doing so may divert them from the movement's feeling rules.[4]

Opportunities from the LGBT movement to enhance personal patronage are scarce and therefore precious to grassroots organizers. Only LGBT activists who work for VIVID receive full-time salaries. With the exception of REGAL, grassroots organizing is voluntary.[5] VIVID every now and then gives out small stipends from one-off funding of specific programs. Grassroots organizers who also serve HIV/AIDS NGOs or community-based organizations—which come with their own dynamics of patronage and contestations—may be able to incorporate the LGBT movement's messaging into their paid work. Most of the time, though, they need to seek other means of survival. That is why staging fashion shows and pageants is attractive: they allow grassroots organizers to do something for the movement while simultaneously taking care of their personal needs and interests.

Although the contestations and disparities in feeling rule adoption suggest that grassroots organizers are less committed than national leaders to human rights practice as a way of life, it does not mean grassroots organizers are insincere about their involvement. My analysis in earlier chapters strongly indicates that their emotional fealty to human rights is genuine and their bonds to one another heartfelt. They join the movement willingly, pushed by their desires to escape pain, fear, and despair and pulled by affections toward movement leaders. They stay because practicing human rights, engaging in grievance transformation and community-building processes, makes them feel better about themselves and gives them new ways to find social belonging among other queers and in the larger Burmese society.

But in Myanmar, as it is in other places, activists do not come with the same social positions. They have plural but coexisting interests, both selfish and altruistic. They try to tend to all of them, though not always managing with balance or success.

Multiple Identities and Belongings

Besides the feeling rules, LGBT activists diverge in their commitments to the movement's LGBT identities and manner of queer bonding, and they negotiate them with other identities and queer communities, changing as their social positions shift with the interactions. Through community-building processes, the activists construct individual and collective LGBT identities to complement queer self-transformation and create an inclusive political front based on their affinity with LGBT and shared human rights practice. Nonetheless, they do not sweep away the older queer communities from which they set their movement's apart. Those communities, which coalesce around niche occupations and informal social networks, continue to endure with their own emotion cultures and in fact maintain their appeal to many interviewees. Moreover, LGBT activists live in a society with negative feeling rules that ferment prejudice and queer suffering. The movement's LGBT identities thus exist alongside familiar terms, such as *achauk*, which interviewees say they want to displace. They exhibit lack of a consistent self (Keeler 2016), fluidly and strategically moving in and out of communities and identities (Gilbert 2013) and switching identity terms, pronouns, and demeanor as they go along.

LGBT activists are more likely to talk about "LGBT" and the respective identities it represents at human rights workshops and movement meetings; sessions with international funders, allies, officials, or politicians; or media events. Movement leaders are the most inclined toward "LGBT," but they do not enforce its consistent use. Grassroots organizers agree that "LGBT" and *lein tu chit thu* are affirmative and conducive to political cohesion, and they adopt LGBT identities for themselves, but they admit to falling back to familiar local terms when mobilizing their constituents back home. "'LGBT' needs translation for the local language. It is very difficult" (Zarni Mann, interview, May 10, 2013*); "In order to give message to the people, if I use formal language, sometimes it's not very easy for normal people to understand. So I just say *achauk* . . . instead of saying *lein tu chit thu*—it's big words" (Swe Lin Aung, interview, March 29, 2013). As Zarni and Swe Lin Aung said, having to explain "LGBT" or *lein tu chit thu* to nonurban, non-English-speaking Burmese hinders effective communication at the grassroots. Even movement leaders turn to the local terms for these same practical reasons.

Personally, LGBT activists maintain multiple identity terms, preserving older self-references at the same time as they remold their queer sense of self with the new. Outside the movement or even during break times between movement workshops and meetings, they often slide back to Burmese terms to refer to themselves or those around them. The variations hint at (but do not definitively suggest) a demarcation along a combination of class, urban-rural divide, and education that influences the internal contestations already noted. In casual conversation, grassroots organizers and VIVID activists who come from small towns and villages sometimes use the Burmese words that they said were derogatory in their interviews with me. For instance, it is common for *apwint* to call themselves or others *achauk*, intending it as a term of endearment. At home in the north, even though Min Min identifies as *gay*, he usually resorts to *meinmashar* to explain himself to others (Min Min, interview, July 7, 2015). But somebody like Khant Nyar probably does not, given his English-speaking background and having self-identified as a *gay* man before joining the movement. Sint Sint, who also has an overseas Western education and comes from a middle-class Yangon family, prefers to call herself *gay* or "lesbian." However, she modifies her self-identification depending on the other party. She keeps her hair short and usually wears T-shirts, shirts, and pants—a masculine-presenting look associated with *tomboys* (but some *tomboys* and *trans men* opt for the traditional men's *longyi* [sarong]). Although she does not relate to being a *tomboy*, if the other person "has no knowledge of LGBT," she would use *tomboy* to describe herself (Sint Sint, interview, July 1, 2014*).

The fluidity of self-identity labels indicates something deeper. When they move from one identity to another, LGBT activists leave one community to enter another community or Burmese society at large, and they behave according to the corresponding emotion culture. The feeling rules and ways of queer bonding over there influence the manner they conduct themselves and interact with others. In Chapter 3, Ywet War, a heterosexual, cisgender activist, observed that LGBT people from the movement "behaved" differently from queer folks "outside" (interview, August 2, 2016). What Ywet War did not point out was that LGBT activists conduct themselves differently when they are not in activist mode as well. For example, while on a road trip to visit grassroots organizers, Yamin and a REGAL activist gossiped about *tha nge* in queer slang inappropriate for movement meetings and workshops or formal conversations with politicians and allies. When they arrived at their destination and started their discussion with fellow activists, they returned from the social world of informal *apwint* networks to the movement's LGBT community, assuming the demeanor of movement leaders whose conduct comports with their notion of *eain dre theit khar* (dignified behavior and moral character) (field notes, June 11, 2014). As another example, at a March 2016 movement workshop held at a beachside hotel, *trans women* and lesbians got along amicably and joked with one another during the workshop. However, at the end of the day when they went to the beach to play and swim, they moved out of the community bound by its collective LGBT identity and human rights practice and reentered the informal social networks coalesced around specific queer subjectivities: lesbians hung out together and socialized separately from *trans women* (field notes, March 28–30, 2016).

One particular identity or emotion culture is no less authentic than the others that LGBT activists simultaneously possess or relate to as they negotiate the new, the old, and the seemingly contradictory. The interviewees in my study practice human rights and embody its emotion culture and identities when they are immersed in the LGBT community. But they also go to *nat* festivals and let loose there, earn a living as a beautician or *nat kadaw*, and participate in beauty pageants. All of them, of course, concurrently have to deal with the rest of society still imbued with feeling rules that breed prejudice and inflict queer suffering.

Zin Yaw is an example of an LGBT activist who constantly negotiates multiple identities and corresponding modes of feeling, knowing, and interacting. Zin Yaw describes himself as *gay*. During interviews in 2014 and 2016, he dressed in typical male attire, a shirt and men's *longyi*, and referred to himself in the male first-person pronoun of *kyun taw*. At movement activities and his shop, he dresses in similar fashion. But as a *nat kadaw* who was assigned male at birth, Zin Yaw may be regarded by others as *apwint*. When he performs his role as a *nat kadaw*, he appears as a woman and takes on a feminine role (Zin Yaw, interview, August 3, 2016). At home, Zin Yaw is husband to a heterosexual, cis-gender woman. When he was younger, his family arranged the marriage for him, believing it would "correct" his sexuality or gender identity (interview, June 11, 2014). Zin Yaw remains with his wife, though she does not like his "*gay* friends." He usually keeps his three worlds separate: the marriage that meets heteronor-mative norms in his society, the world of *nat* worship, and the LGBT movement. Occasionally, however, he inhabits two or more of them at the same time, for example, when his friends visit his marital home to hire his wife to sew their *nat kadaw* attire for them (interview, August 3, 2016).

As another example, Yamin sheds the role of *transgender* beauty contestant and morphs into an LGBT activist, and vice versa, all the while handling the de-mands of being a child to a mother who is adjusting to her gender identity. As an LGBT activist and *trans woman*, Yamin usually refers to herself as *kyun ma*, the female "I," but when she interacts with her mother, her gender identity becomes more muddled. Perhaps it is a reflection of their work-in-progress relationship. In Chapter 3, I noted that Yamin reported that her mother was gradually accepting her gender identity as a *trans woman*. However, her mother sometimes still refers to Yamin as *min*, a male form of "you" that elders often use toward a younger person,[6] or calls her *tha the me*, literally "son-daughter."[7] When Yamin speaks on the phone with her mother, sometimes she converses with words that indicate her female gender, such as *shint*, a polite end-of-speech word a younger female person uses toward an elder,[8] but sometimes she calls herself *kyun taw*, the male version of "I" (field notes, July 25–August 6, 2016). In those moments, Yamin shifts from being the confident *trans woman* and LGBT activist to being the child whose mother is still trying to get used to her as the daughter who was a "son" in her eyes.[9]

Gender Divide

Although lesbians' recruitment has improved since the movement's early years, LGBT activists constantly struggle with their retention, a problem that dimin-ishes their creation of inclusive queer bonding, the other essential ingredient of the movement's emotion culture. Lesbians not only face social prejudices against them as queers but also sexism in a highly patriarchal society that hin-ders their participation and leadership in the LGBT movement. When lesbians leave the movement, it loses people who can rise to leadership positions and better organize lesbians. Although community-building processes produce a more all-encompassing group based on being LGBT and shared human rights practice, gender dynamics in the LGBT movement inadvertently favors those who were deemed male at birth. Since the movement's founding, *trans women*, *apwint*, *apone*, and *gay* men have dominated in numbers and in leadership.

At most, lesbians make up one-quarter of activists, and few occupy leadership positions. The regulars are usually the few who participate in VIVID or serve as grassroots representatives. The rest "come and go" (Khin Kyine, interview, February 23, 2013). When the movement first emerged, its pioneers had little success recruiting lesbians, having relied on HIV/AIDS ties that connected to informal social networks among *apwint* and other queers who were assigned male at birth. Eventually they managed to bring in lesbians through these social ties (see Chapter 2). Over the years, VIVID has increased efforts to recruit and incorporate lesbians into the movement, setting aside funding for lesbian-specific programs. However, the difficulties of retaining lesbians linger. By 2014, lesbians from BRIGHT no longer participated in the movement's meetings. At REGAL, Cho Cho and Tin Hla lamented that lesbians seemed disinterested, dropping out to concentrate on their romantic relationships or livelihoods.

Rather than lacking resonance with human rights, the challenges with lesbians' retention have more to do with norms in Burmese society that disadvantage women. Lesbians who were LGBT activists or dropouts did respond positively to human rights and believed that their realization would improve lives. Consistent with my findings on grievance transformation processes generally, these interviewees developed emotional fealty to human rights, describing their first encounters with those rights as empowering and inspiring them to join the movement. They were also attracted to LGBT identities. For some lesbians, however, the promise of human rights was inadequate to surmount gendered norms.

Control over the physical movement of those designated female at birth is one obstacle. "They have the events in the evening. . . . So, the parents—they won't allow the girls to go out. . . . Some people, the family, send someone to escort them" (Pa Dauk, interview, May 9, 2013). Parents, elder brothers, or uncles frequently prohibit lesbians from going out at night or require them to be accompanied. They do not consider the time appropriate for women, or they worry about sexual assault, common in Burmese society, where victim blaming and distrust of law enforcement are widespread. Lesbians risk being punished by elders or revealing their sexuality or activism to their families if they are unprepared to be escorted by male members of the family. Zin Yaw observed that it would be "neither appropriate for them [lesbians] to be seen hanging out all the time with us [*apwint, apone, trans women,* and *gay* men], who are 'biological' males" (Zin Yaw, interview, August 3, 2016), meaning that the latter in the eyes of other people around them are "men" who have no familial connection to these lesbians.

Yet movement events are often scheduled based on the preferences of *gay* men, *trans women, apwint,* and *apone* and account less for lesbians' needs and challenges. Unlike lesbians, queers assigned male at birth have fewer qualms about going out at night and face less familial constraint because of the male privilege with which they are born (including *apwint* and *trans women*). Pa Dauk's statement came from our conversation about the number of lesbians involved in IDAHO. When I brought up the concern to VIVID's leaders, most of whom were assigned male at birth, they genuinely seemed to realize for the first time that it was a problem. In response, they said they would offer "taxi vouchers" to lesbians. It is not apparent, though, if that solution fully addresses the problem, since traveling in a taxi can also be unsafe (Kean, Toe Wai Aung, and Hammond 2015) and an alternative (free) mode of transportation may not change parents' minds about restricting their lesbian children's freedom.

Other lesbians in my study gave up LGBT activism because of pressure to fulfill family obligations. Those who live with their parents are expected to contribute financially or care for somebody in the parental household, often in unspoken bargain for quiet toleration. Pa Dauk, for example, makes money for her parents as a jewelry trader. Her parents know that she is a lesbian, but they have let her be. "The situation, however, could change if I were not the bread-winner" (Pa Dauk, interview, May 9, 2013). Nyan Lin, a *trans man*, was eager to become an activist when we first met in September 2012 in Chiang Mai. He was invited to the movement's human rights workshops after meeting Pa Dauk and Shwe Wah through a mutual friend, another *tomboy.* Almost three years later when I reinterviewed him, the thirty-year-old said he had to give up that ambition and "listen to the family." Nyan Lin is financially dependent on the family. He helps out at home and looks after his mother's food stall. When LGBT activists invited him to a five-day follow-up workshop on leadership skills, "I could attend one day and could not attend the rest due to work. So . . . [they] did not invite me to other events anymore" (Nyan Lin, interview, June 28, 2015). When we met for the reinterview in 2015, Nyan Lin had taken on the responsibility of caring full time for his late sister's infant daughter.

Other lesbians cannot spend time on LGBT activism because they need to make a living. They are often lesbians who live independently with their partners to escape family pressure. Some families push lesbians into hetero-sexual marriages. Others force lesbian couples to break up under the threat of violence or expulsion from home. The gravity of choosing between one's partner and parental household must be understood in the context of Burmese society, where unmarried adult women usually live with their parents and are expected to obey them. Lesbians who leave their parental homes in defiance often struggle financially. Although they have their own social networks, they lack the occupational niches of *apwint*, *apone*, and *trans women* and have to struggle with livelihood, perhaps more so than many other Burmese people, if they are cut off from their parental households and face discriminatory pay and hiring practices against women. The LGBT movement's ad hoc funding for grassroots programs and the opportunities that it occasionally opens up for local patronage have benefited lesbians but to a lesser extent. In fact, for those programs and opportunities to benefit lesbians, they need strong leaders at the grassroots to hold fellow lesbian activists together, such as Aung Aung and Win Sein's network of lesbians. Yet it is lesbian leadership that the movement lacks.

Furthermore, lesbians leave the movement because of gendered disadvan-tages in professional experiences, leading to mismatches of expectations between them and movement leaders. The problem arose prominently among BRIGHT activists. Shwe Wah vented her frustration about being asked by VIVID leaders to revise BRIGHT's grant proposal multiple times and volunteer at movement events. Pa Dauk, another BRIGHT leader, repeatedly complained in my follow-up interview that BRIGHT activists were expected to participate in local move-ment events without any daily allowance (which Burmese NGOs usually provide only for out-of-town participation). Their complaints may seem trivial and petty, but they signal gendered disadvantages. Shwe Wah, Pa Dauk, and other BRIGHT activists have little NGO experience, whereas lesbians who represent women's rights groups or other NGOs stay silent about their sexuality and do not speak up for women as lesbians (more on that later in this chapter). They are therefore unfamiliar with the requirements and expectations of grant writing, budgeting, and advocacy. In their conversations with me, Shwe Wah and Pa Dauk also re-vealed their lack of appreciation for organizing work. This type of work requires time-consuming and patient cultivation of grassroots support and does not im-mediately reap tangible results, unlike the charity work they are used to perform-ing in their neighborhoods. In contrast, many LGBT activists designated male at birth are affiliated with HIV/AIDS organizations and enter the movement with valuable experience with NGOs as employees or volunteers.

The dominance of queers who were assigned male at birth inevitably buttresses male privilege in the LGBT movement community. The processes of constructing LGBT identities and emotional bonding have replaced distrust and apprehension with some degree of cohesion, solidarity, camaraderie, and friendship between them and lesbians. However, newly recruited lesbians often feel uncomfortable at movement events, which are typically dominated by queers assigned male at birth. Lesbians and other LGBT activists in my study, like Cho Cho, notice that new lesbian activists often feel they do not belong and end up with weaker emotional bonds to the movement community. It does not matter that *trans women* or *apwint* identify with the female gender. They speak in their own slang and commonly refer to sexual intercourse and male sexual organs in their conversations.[10] In the earlier example about Yamin and a REGAL activist, it is quite typical of their conversation about *tha nge* to make explicit references to having sex. This type of social interaction, however, is not something that lesbians, including those who identify as *tomboys* or *trans men* (and heterosexual, cisgender women like my Burmese assistants for that matter), are used to engaging in or even feel appropriate being around. Lesbians do have their own banter about romantic interests and courtships, but the movement may not seem like the place for them. Despite the emotional appeal of human rights, some lesbians eventually distance themselves from the LGBT movement community, preferring to stay in their tightly knit circles of lesbians at home.

Legacies, Norms, and Fissures: Deficiencies in Claims and Claimant

Apart from variations in LGBT activists' self-transformation and emotion culture, sociopolitical conditions hamper their ability to produce new claims and claimant, that is, LGBT rights for LGBT Burmese. Notwithstanding the hope and confidence that human rights practice has inspired in them, LGBT activists are introducing a new mode of feeling, knowing, and interacting in a place where the state remains a major violator of human rights. They are asking people to let go of norms and beliefs that have legitimized and regulated who possesses power and privilege and what is right or wrong for generations. Even they themselves are not spared from the biases and fissures.

Structural Legacies

Human rights claims, the LGBT movement's and beyond, are far from conquering the endemic abuse of power, corruption, and arbitrary rule, problems with the Burmese state that remain unresolved. Since 2011, the USDP and NLD governments have released political prisoners, permitted the return of exiles, and implemented legal reforms relating to such civil-political liberties as press, association, and assembly. Although older laws and newly enacted legislation still restrict civil-political freedoms, overall, activists in my study interpret the political developments positively and perceive less fear and control over human rights activism than in the past. The LGBT movement's activities inside the country so far have not encountered direct state repression. Its activists have even engaged the NLD government on human rights violations regarding queer Burmese.[11] Nonetheless, the structural legacies pose challenges at the frontline for the movement.

In practical terms, the structural legacies most directly affect the LGBT movement at the grassroots level. "High-level government has changed. . . . The lower and midlevel still keep their old practices" (Cho Cho, field notes, March 29, 2013). As Cho Cho reminded fellow activists during a discussion about post-2011 political developments, the national government's already limited reforms are slow to trickle down to towns, villages, and other grassroots locations where the movement is expanding. Although the situation varies from place to place, grassroots organizers commonly express difficulty dealing with local authorities.

"Police do not understand human rights" (field notes, VIVID Outreach Meeting, November 27, 2015). LGBT activists are concerned that local bureaucrats and police still do not care about anybody's rights, including those of queer Burmese, the "deviants" in their society. In the meeting quoted above, *apwint* living in a township on Yangon's outskirts reported to movement leaders that the police ignored their objections when they reminded arresting officers of their rights. In Mandalay, LGBT activists who organized IDAHO and TDoR reported encountering local officials who obstructed their work on the grounds of preserving "culture" in Myanmar's last royal capital. LGBT activists usually hold their public events in privately owned spaces, such as hotels and parks operated by private entities (they ostensibly seem like public spaces); nevertheless, in case local authorities cause trouble, organizers in several towns, including Mandalay, apply for permits or seek tacit consent from them anyway.

Corruption, widespread across law enforcement, contributes to the local constraints. In the earlier example about the Yangon township, police there disregard *apwint* demands for rights and even proper legal process because they are also motivated by bribes. As discussed in Chapter 3, being a vulnerable social group makes queers, especially *apwint*, easy police targets. A lawyer volunteering for the LGBT movement said, "The police will arrest them, threaten with 30(d) [the notorious in-the-shadows law], then their friends or families will come and have to get them out with bribes. That's what the police plan for" (field notes, VIVID outreach meeting, November 27, 2015). The problem of corruption extends to movement organizing work. One year in Mandalay, activists had to pay bribes to several authorities to obtain permission for IDAHO and TDoR (Htut Htut, interview, March 31, 2013). In his town, Nay Win used to avoid trouble with local authorities, because "when we do events, I give them free services—food and room arrangements" (interview, May 13, 2013).

Arbitrary rule, characterized by personal power in Myanmar (Steinberg 1992; MacLean 2004), compounds the local constraints. According to interviews and field observations, when activists in my study talk about handling local authorities, they consistently emphasize "good relations" as key to successful grassroots mobilization. Mandalay activists who bribed local authorities to organize IDAHO and TDoR concurrently stressed maintaining good connections with officials (interviews: Wunna, May 9, 2013, and Htut Htut, March 31, 2013). Nay Win, quoted above as having bribed local authorities, in the same breath explained his actions as being about keeping a "close relationship with local authorities" (interview, May 13, 2013). When I first spoke to Swe Lin Aung in 2013, he worried about the future of IDAHO and TDoR celebrations in his town because the official with whom he had had a "good relationship" was transferring to another place, and he was uncertain whether the successor would strike a similar "understanding" with him (interview, March 29, 2013). While friendly relations smooth dealings with local authorities, they reveal the problematic influence of personal power. Movement activists cannot count on respect for civil-political liberties, human rights, or even rules and procedure, but have to deal with the whims and fancies of local authorities.

Prejudices Among Allies

The prejudices against queers as deviants who deserve their ill plight run deep not only among police and other perpetrators but also politicians, lawyers, and other human rights activists with whom LGBT activists are trying to strengthen alliances. Tun Tun acknowledges that the prejudices prevent them from gaining public support from any "famous religious leader" (field notes, January 30, 2016)—that is, apart from local monks and nuns who perform prayer rituals during movement events. Among their allies, the prejudices usually do not express themselves in direct discriminatory actions but fester in reluctance and inaction, bubbling occasionally to the surface. They are understandably tricky for LGBT activists to tackle because they have to avoid damaging hard-earned alliances.

The political allies of the movement hesitate to initiate action perhaps because they are cautious that legal reform or simply standing up for queer Burmese would be an unpopular move in light of ingrained prejudices or because they harbor the same biases. Even if they are sympathetic, the prevalence of such bigotry may have colored their perception of the LGBT movement's importance and influenced them to relegate its claims to the bottom of a long list of pressing issues confronting their government. In a June 2015 meeting with various political parties (see Chapter 4), representatives of the military-backed USDP questioned the morality of "LGBT people" in front of movement activists and expressed reluctance toward legally protecting such a "minority" (field notes, June 11, 2015). Generally NLD representatives verbalized more support at the meeting and on other occasions. So far, however, NLD has not taken any concrete legislative steps or clear public stand on LGBT rights, even though VIVID leaders said they had been quietly lobbying the party to reform Section 377. In a public dialogue with Aung San Suu Kyi, an LGBT activist asked that discriminatory laws against queer Burmese be abolished. The NLD leader did not directly address the activist's call for legal reform. Instead, she replied that laws alone could not eliminate discrimination and that "society's values" would have to be "altered" through education, for which both the government and society are responsible (media report, January 1, 2017).

Among lawyers, LGBT activists have secured some staunch allies, such as Cindy and Ywet War, but they have yet to win widespread support in the profession. Since 2014, LGBT activists have been expanding their movement alliances to the legal profession, recruiting lawyers to special workshops to educate them about LGBT issues and discuss Section 377's reform.[12] VIVID leaders spoke optimistically to me about their progress in this area. A few enthusiastic lawyers recruited from these workshops have offered their assistance; Khant Nyar pointed out to me his "very supportive" uncle (field notes, lawyers' workshop, May 15, 2016*), a lawyer who attended several of the special workshops. The supportive lawyers help LGBT activists draft legal reform proposals that they hope NLD legislators will sponsor one day. According to my interviews and field observations, however, the larger pool of lawyers to whom the movement reaches out are noncommittal at best.

Despite LGBT activists' educational efforts, most of these lawyers cling to the common prejudices. They empathize with the problems of police abuse and other forms of discrimination, but they seem reluctant to regard LGBT people as human rights claimants (field notes, lawyers' workshop, May 15, 2014). At the first lawyers' workshop in 2014, three lawyers who expressed such conservative views (out of roughly twenty-five) on the first day did not show up the following day (field notes, lawyers' workshop, May 16, 2014). At another workshop, after a weekend of discussions about discrimination against queer Burmese and decriminalization campaigns in other countries, one lawyer who had attended the movement's prior trainings turned to Moora, my assistant who was sitting next to me, and said to her in Burmese, "It should not be this way. If my children become like this, I will not be happy or be able to accept it" (field notes, lawyers' workshop, May 15, 2016).

For similar reasons, LGBT activists have difficulty with women's rights activists. Since their movement's inception, they have used interpersonal relationships to build alliances with their counterparts in Burmese women's rights, first in Thailand and then in Myanmar. Leading up to the 2015 national elections, REGAL partnered with a prominent women's rights group to carry out voter education and registration. Cho Cho also tries to gain inroads with national coordinating bodies for women's rights activists, convincing them to let LGBT activists help organize and participate in their high-profile events. For instance, at a national women's rights convention, Cho Cho and REGAL members highlighted lesbian discrimination and asked questions about what could be done (Cho Cho, interview, November 13, 2014). They did not receive any direct answer. In fact, before LGBT activists initiated contact, women's rights activists had paid little attention to lesbians or queer Burmese generally.

According to women's rights activists interviewed for my study, their organizations are concerned that foregrounding queer sexuality would taint their credibility and jeopardize their agenda, already an uphill battle in Myanmar (interviews: Ma Aye, October 16, 2014, and Su Su, October 23, 2014).[13] Women's rights activists who are sympathetic or lesbian stay reticent to avoid conflict or to protect themselves (Su Su, interview, October 23, 2014). From time to time, their groups allude to lesbians, but they concentrate on their organization's broader agenda, such as domestic violence, reproductive rights, and sexual health, to maintain the moral legitimacy of representing heterosexual, cisgender women. Their agenda would cover lesbians as women, but women's rights activists do not highlight the compounded plight of lesbians as queer Burmese.[14]

Furthermore, some women's rights leaders hold the common prejudices and regard queer women as going against nature or Burmese culture (interviews: Ma Aye, October 16, 2014; Su Su, October 23, 2014; Myat Lay, November 2, 2014; and Myintzu, November 6, 2014). The most eye-opening interview was with a newly elected NLD member of Parliament who headed a prominent women's rights organization. She acknowledged that queer Burmese did not have a choice in being "like this," that they deserved human rights, and that Section 377 potentially violated human rights. However, at the end of the interview, she said rather candidly that such laws were "unnecessary as parents . . . have to understand their children's behavior, give counseling to them, talk to them nicely, and try to correct them so that they can change back to straight" (interview, January 25, 2016). My interpretation of the interview is that she, as well as other allies interviewed or observed, could be persuaded to believe in human rights for queer Burmese, but the tug of entrenched beliefs is so strong that she could not help but feel there was something nevertheless wrong and it would be better if they could just suppress their queerness.

Behavior and Gender Norms

LGBT activists are likely unaware of how much gender norms, which regulate behavior, insidiously influence the scope of their human rights practice, limiting their imagination of what they should and should not do or question. Perhaps they tacitly and uncritically endorse heteronormative biases, and even disempower queers by requiring that they comply with standards of socially appropriate behavior. As a result, they possibly reaffirm the social hierarchy that subordinates queer Burmese in the first place.

The most notable example is the call for "change behavior" in grievance transformation. The approach brings their human rights practice in line with norms regulating conduct, including the behavior and roles of women (applied by LGBT activists to *apwint*). In Chapter 3, I discussed why it would be understandable for them to do so. Faced with widespread prejudices, LGBT activists stress the importance of conducting oneself with *eain dre theit khar* (dignified behavior and moral character) and "changing behavior" in hopes that queer Burmese can more easily win social belonging and greater human dignity. However, the implication is that queers should otherwise conform and not "misbehave" if they want others to overlook, even accept, their queerness. Hence, they may attract criticisms of promoting "homonormativity" (Duggan 2003),[15] because by seeking inclusion, they possibly end up sustaining rather than challenging heteronormative norms in their society that control sexual and gender expression.

The potentially disempowering nature of restrained behavior contrasts sharply with the world of *nat* worship, from which the movement distinguishes its emotion culture. Indeed, *nat* worship offers a queer community with little room for lesbians (see Chapter 4). Nonetheless, it is potentially liberating for queers designated male at birth, such as *apwint*, *apone*, and *trans women*, who can find belonging there. Other than opportunities for queer *nat kadaw* to amass influence and redefine their social status, and therefore resist Buddhist notions of bad karma against them (see Chapter 3), participating in *nat* worship gives queers license to be disinhibited. Queer devotees openly express and receive their love for and from the spirits they follow, and they immerse themselves passionately in *nat* festivals, an "ecstatic place" of queer belonging (Gilbert 2016, 203). Rituals and worship aside, attendees at *nat* festivals party, drink, and enjoy sexual encounters.[16] The world of *nat* worship is a time and place where queers feel that they can suspend the behavioral standards of Burmese society and temporarily free themselves of heteronormative restraint and modesty, the boxes that LGBT activists entreat them to fit into.[17]

The entrenched and unquestioned nature of heteronormative norms extends to other aspects of LGBT activists' claims. One powerful example concerns access to Buddhist temples. In Myanmar, women are commonly barred from sacred places such as the highest level of a pagoda. They are not allowed to place the lower halves of their bodies above Buddha's statue, because female genitalia are considered "unclean."[18] During movement workshops, after learning that human rights entitle everyone to equal treatment, participants sometimes ask whether the prohibition applies to *apwint*, who identify as female.

Zin Yaw captures the essence of two views that LGBT activists in my study, save for rare exceptions, usually take: "The concept of equality in human rights . . . does not mean that we should go against the traditional Buddhist restrictions against women going up to the most sacred places of the pagodas" (interview, August 3, 2016).[19] Both views leave unquestioned the misogynistic nature of the prohibition and treat it as a social practice to be followed out of respect for their religion. The first reasserts male privilege for *apwint*: The prohibition should not apply to *apwint*, since they were assigned male at birth. Zin Yaw, for example, was upset when he visited a temple wearing long hair and earrings and was barred from entering areas out-of-bounds to women (interview, August 3, 2016). The second is related to the first and accepts heteronormative male privilege: *Apwint* should not go to temples in female appearance and expect to be treated with male privilege and demand access to places from which women are prohibited. "In Buddhism, women are not allowed to go to certain places in the pagoda. So *transgender* persons are also not allowed if they dress as a woman" (Pyae Soe, interview, January 29, 2016). Hence, after talking about his personal encounter, Zin Yaw added:

> As a concession to traditional Buddhist views . . . you may want to wear as *apwint* [express yourself openly in the female gender], but when you go to pagodas, it is only right that you dress up as *apone* [appear masculine in dressing]. In that way, society will be more accepting of you (interview, August 3, 2016).

Burman and Buddhist Privilege

While it is true that this entire LGBT movement is supposed to be all-inclusive . . . I would say that it is still a rather distant dream. (Yamin, interview, July 26, 2016)

In spite of their best intentions to create a united political front with the collective marker of LGBT, movement activists mold a claimant who lacks transcendence in one respect. Just as Burmese politics and society grant privilege to Burmans and Buddhists, so does their human rights practice. The LGBT movement emerged, expanded, and recruited activists by relying on social ties. Its activists draw on local norms to make human rights resonate with queer Burmese and motivate them to join the fight for human rights. Yet relying on social ties and local norms renders their human rights practice Buddhist-centric, inadvertently producing their collective claimant of LGBT as Burman. Scholars have long observed that Burmese identity is essentially Buddhist (Lehman 1987; Brac de la Perrière 2009a). Furthermore, Buddhism in Myanmar is Burmanized, dominated by Burman interpretations, despite the fact that ethnic minorities practice Buddhism with their own variations (Walton 2017a; also see Schober 2011). A Buddhist-centric human rights practice thus corresponds to a Burman-dominated identity. Analogous to the allegation that political reforms mainly benefit Burmans and Burman-centered activism (Walton 2013), the movement aids mostly Burmans, who are mostly Buddhists, while lacking in both self-awareness of its privilege and the ability to assist non-Burman, non-Buddhist queers.

The majority of LGBT activists in my study self-identify as Burman and Buddhist. Few self-identify as an ethnic or religious minority. The only prominent LGBT activist who was non-Burman and non-Buddhist was Seng Naw, a Kachin Christian, who left the movement in 2012 due to poor health and passed away in 2015. Cindy, the heterosexual, cisgender lawyer, is Chin Christian. A couple of grassroots organizers are Karen but identify as Buddhists. The Kachin state representative thus far is a Burman and Buddhist. I interviewed two Muslim grassroots organizers, but one of them left around 2014 because he had become too busy with his full-time job. Another Muslim grassroots organizer died before I had a chance to interview him. Khant Nyar confirmed that the movement did not conduct outreach targeting Muslims (Khant Nyar, interview, December 1, 2015*) or any other minority religious group.

LGBT activists' self-identification is revealing because it strongly reflects Burman privilege. Historically, people living in Myanmar have adopted Burman identity for politically strategic reasons (Walton 2013). Many of my interviewees who self-identify as Burman actually have multiethnic descent, for example, one parent is Mon, Shan, South Asian, Chinese, or mixed. However, I would find out about their multiethnic descent only when I asked about their parents; when they were simply asked about their *lu myo* (race or ethnicity), they would say *Bamar*.[20] Some even stressed their *Bamar* identity after telling me about their parents, who are either non-Burman or have a multiethnic background. Tin Hla described his father as "part Karen, mixed blood," but he "only sees [himself] as a Buddhist Burman" (interview, August 2, 2016). One movement leader said his mother was half Mon and half Burman, but he regarded himself as Burman. Another said he was Burman, but when he talked about his family, it turned out that his father has Arakan, Burman, and South Asian parentage. This person told me that his paternal great-grandfather migrated from India. Then he stressed that it was northern India and that his great-grandfather had fair skin, which he emphasized on various other occasions. I took his emphasis on fair skin to imply his family is different from darker-skinned South Asians, such as the persecuted Rohingya or others who are derogatorily called *kala* in Myanmar.[21] One grassroots organizer who described his father as Hindu and "a bit mixed" nevertheless replied that he was "pure Burman" (though he also regards himself as a "Hindu-Buddhist," after his father and mother, respectively).

The centricity of Buddhism comes with an inadvertent lack of self-awareness of its privilege. I was struck by my experiences with trying to find interviewees who are religious minorities (names are not necessarily indicative). When I asked informants already included in my study, a few offered suggestions, saying so-and-so was Muslim or Hindu. But subsequently I would find out from the interviews with the suggested individuals that they are actually Buddhist.[22] I can only surmise that my informants presumed they were Muslim or Hindu because they have darker skin, compared to most Burmans, and supposedly South Asian features.

The dominance of self-identified Burmans and Buddhists can be traced to the movement's recruitment and expansion method of relying on preexisting social ties, which are primarily Burman and Buddhist. Seng Naw's case is unusual, connected to Tun Tun's early days of traveling among pro-democracy activists as well as ethnic rebel strongholds. Ever since, the movement has mainly relied on professional ties to HIV/AIDS NGOs and social networks among queer Burmese. Parts of the country known to be populated by ethnic minorities or demarcated as conflict zones are largely outside its coverage. When I asked VIVID whether there were plans to reach such places as Arakan State, where the movement had not yet established a grassroots presence, Khant Nyar said that because they relied on interpersonal ties to initiate recruitment, they would be able to reach only Buddhists in Arakan and not religious minorities such as Muslims, who are "segregated" (interview, December 1, 2015*). When Yamin visited Chin State in March 2016 to explore whether the movement could extend its reach there, she "realized how heavily the entire community was influenced by Christianity, which is why I believe it would be more difficult for us—who are largely Buddhists—and our trainings—which often refer to Buddhist teachings—to venture into that community" (interview, July 26, 2016).[23]

Along with the lack of self-awareness of Burman and Buddhist privilege is the lack of ability to address the unique challenges of queer people who are neither. Yamin rightly observed that their human rights practice mainly engages Buddhism. Pyae Soe, who is in charge of the movement's human rights training programs, said they usually tried to avoid addressing questions about how to reconcile one's sexuality with other religions, such as Christianity and Islam, because they did not know how and did not have fellow activists who could. "I don't have much experience with Christian people," he admitted rather candidly in front of Moora, my Karen Christian assistant (interview, December 12, 2015). Khin Kyine, who also trains new activists, replied tentatively that she would just ask religious minorities to consult materials and experts from their own religions (interview, August 5, 2016). In any case, Khant Nyar believed the challenge would seldom arise, because they mainly reach out to Buddhists (if not Burmans) (interview, December 12, 2015), a phenomenon that arguably self-perpetuates their movement's Burman and Buddhist privilege.

Agency and Human Rights as an Alternative Way of Life

The faults and fault lines of LGBT activists' practice may call to mind the common pitfalls of human rights, especially their tendency to reproduce inequalities in the local context and failure to achieve social change. The contestations between national and grassroots activists possibly reflect local elitism at work. The gender divide and Burman and Buddhist centricity marginalize queer constituents who are non-Burman and non-Buddhist, embodying yet more power dynamics at work. Meanwhile, the enduring existence of local patronage, older queer identities and communities, structural legacies of abuse, corruption, and arbitrary rule, and ingrained prejudices and norms exemplify the ineffectual side of human rights practice.

Yet engaging in overlapping and recursive social processes, LGBT activists are able to yield positive results with human rights while maintaining their own sensibilities about who they are and what they value. By creating emotional fealty to human rights and affective ties among themselves, they make human rights resonate with local populations and inspire collective action. Their unique interpretations counter concerns that human rights impose Western notions of morality or identity. And their interrelated outcomes of self-transformation, distinctive emotion culture, and new claims and claimant of LGBT rights for LGBT people in Myanmar reveal the potential of human rights practice to build momentum from the personal and grassroots to target formal institutional change.

Put differently, we are looking at the complexities of human agency. In Chapters 2 to 4, agency enabled LGBT activists to carry out human rights practice. Here, it constrains them. As elaborated in Chapter 1, agency is presupposed by the availability, nature, and rootedness of cultural schemas and resources, which compose structures exerting sociopolitical influence. LGBT activists draw a wealth of innovation from these schemas and resources to bring human rights to life, but in doing so, they simultaneously erect walls circumscribing their imagination and ability.

Together, the apparently contradictory findings of the previous chapters and this one give a more complex answer about the power and prospects of human rights: LGBT activists' human rights practice shapes an alternative way of life that exists alongside others. Human rights generate some potent effects, but they are not a dominant power. The faults and fault lines, ironically, indicate that LGBT activists' practice does not come anywhere close to being the only game in town. Sociopolitical forces with far longer histories in Myanmar are at work, entrenching older modes of feeling, interacting, and knowing in Burmese society.

They do not simply give way to the newcomer, human rights, notwithstanding the latter's international backing and recent surge in political legitimacy.

LGBT activists juggle human rights practice and other ways of life, each with its self-understandings, emotion cultures, and communities of belonging, moving in and out of them when it is strategic, beyond their control, or desirable to do so. They not only fight for the new, human rights, but also battle (sometimes to no avail) the old that has made them who they are and their society what it is. They try to live up to the LGBT movement's practice and achieve its goals of self-acceptance, social belonging, and legal reform. But at times, some of them act out of personal interests to survive or thrive. Or they disagree with and distance themselves from one another because they are simply different people, with dissimilar sexualities, genders, family backgrounds, education, work experience, and social networks. In a society where personhood is fluid and multiple, shifting according to time, place, and people, sometimes they are LGBT activists in the movement, queers by another name in another queer community, or daughter, son, wife, husband, or "deviant" in the eyes of others in their society. Finally, they have to deal with and sometimes surrender to larger sociopolitical forces, which threaten to diminish their movement's claims and claimant.

· · ·

This chapter took the sheen off human rights practice as a way of life and exposed its flaws and limitations. Formation, grievance transformation, and community-building processes play out unevenly, leading to disparate degrees of self-transformation, adoption of its distinctive emotion culture, and creation of groundbreaking claims and claimant for Burmese politics. The internal contestations, navigation of multiple identities, gender divide, recalcitrant state actors, and enduring norms and privilege are part and parcel of the story of human rights practice as a way of life. They are connected to the hopefulness, confidence, and promising outcomes by agency, the wellspring of human rights practice.

Combined, the strengths and weaknesses make it no straightforward task to conclude that human rights are the panacea for queer Burmese or, conversely, pointless or hurtful to them, a marginalized population in an underdeveloped country. They present a meaningful but flawed alternative. What then can we learn from the LGBT movement's human rights practice as a way of life? In the Conclusion, I look back at the concept's principal features and contributions and ahead to its broader lessons.

Conclusion

Even if [human rights] were a Western idea, there is no reason why we shouldn't adopt them if they help improve our way of life. After all, our army is making use of grenades and artillery invented by the West instead of traditional weapons, like spears or knives. (Tin Hla, interview, August 2, 2016)

T IN HLA, the boy who watched from the barracks in 1988, learned about human rights from Tun Tun, the Rangoon University student marching down the streets outside. But when Tin Hla and Tun Tun appeared in the events first described in the Introduction, the two would not meet until twenty years later. How they crossed paths, how Tun Tun founded the LGBT movement, and how Tin Hla became an LGBT activist form the book's centerpiece, a story about human rights, about how a group of people put them into action, and about how human rights matter.

As this story about the trials and fortunes of human rights draws to a close, Tin Hla's words capture the spirit of the Conclusion. When asked about the Westernness of human rights, Tin Hla referred to a poignant example from his life and for his country, describing the Burmese military's weapons as inventions of the West.[1] The military, wielding its "Western weapons," fabricated a way of life filled with violence and suffering. Human rights, while also seemingly Western in origin, offer a hopeful alternative, an improved way of life. They hearten queer folks like him to live more authentically as queer—people who love their queer self and can find social belonging and thus human dignity. The origins of the alternative do not matter to Tin Hla. Wherever it hails from, an alternative inevitably gets entangled with the sociolegal conditions and political struggles of the place. Western weapons become the tools of violence and fear. To Tin Hla, it is what people do with an alternative, whether it is a physical instrument, an idea, or a legal document.

Human rights became an alternative way of life for Tin Hla, Tun Tun, and many others we have gotten to know in this book because of practice—a mode in which human rights are made sense of and put into action—and the driving force behind it, their agency. Tin Hla, Tun Tun, and their compatriots adapt human rights to their local conditions and produce their own meanings and identities. They defy fearful conditions, come together, and speak up for LGBT rights. Flawed and limited, their human rights practice coexists and sometimes contends with other ways of life in Burmese society.

I learned about LGBT activists' accomplishments and frustrations by studying human rights empirically, treating their meanings, implementation, and consequences as social facts to be investigated. This approach is part of a line of research that shifts the conversation about human rights from normative and juridical discussions in the abstract to empirically grounded questions and answers of how human rights travel and become active (or not) in social life. Etched with the memory that human rights arose from struggles over arrangements of social relations and power, this approach accepts that they are neither innately good nor bad, powerful nor weak (Roberts 2015). It is open to human rights as a potential redress for suffering—the physical, the emotional, and more—and, conversely, their possible impotence, irrelevance, and even harm.

And so I conclude with the intellectual premises with which I started this book, the social nature and empirical study of human rights. We have looked at queer lives in Myanmar beyond the visually dazzling celebrity of those viewed as trans in the eyes of Western travelers. We have learned much about queer conditions and LGBT rights in a society faraway from the Western democracies whose LGBT rights movements have occupied the most scholarly attention on the subject.

However, this book is more than all of that, for the story is ultimately about how human rights matter. It is important to take stock of the central concept, human rights practice as a way of life—how it has informed human rights scholarship as well as the sociolegal study of rights and social movements and our understanding of the potential of human rights to advance collective action and attain social progress. It is also imperative to reflect on what the emotional and relational emphases of the concept tell us about the empirical study of human rights.

The Three Salient Features and Contributions to Scholarship

From the starting premise that human rights are social in nature and ripe for empirical study, I anchored the book in my fieldwork on the LGBT movement in Myanmar. Simultaneously I read and drew from a wide range of literature, including the multidisciplinary study of human rights, sociolegal scholarship, social movements research, sociology, anthropology, and law school writings about law and emotions. I was then able to devise the concept of human rights practice as a way of life to place a theoretical framework around my findings from the field. As I told the story about LGBT activists in Myanmar, I highlighted, step by step, three salient features of the concept, each with its original contribution to the study of human rights and sociolegal scholarship on rights and social movements.

According to this concept, when human rights are put into action, they are social processes constituted by and constituting emotions and interpersonal relationships. Human rights are not mere substance; they are constantly recursive, overlapping processes. For the LGBT movement, I discerned three sets of processes: formation, grievance transformation, and community building. They are animated by emotions and interpersonal relationships, the heart and soul of political action. More than conduits, instruments, and triggers, emotions and relationships embody all aspects of human rights practice, such as adaptations of the substantive meanings of human rights, their circulation and implementation, and outcomes.

Guided by the conceptual framework of human rights practice as a way of life, I painted a living, breathing portrait of human rights as experienced by activists from the birth of their movement to its maturity.[2] With close attention to individual, social, and cultural factors, I traced the emergence of a movement from the stories of its founders, leaders, and newcomers, accentuating the roles of emotions and interpersonal ties—not just in the abstract but grounded in the particulars of their lives and experiences. I documented how human rights practice grew out of their feelings and relationships fused with cultural schemas and resources in their society, as well as legal and political ideas, and, in turn, how the practice created emotional fealty to rights and bonds among activists strong enough to perpetuate it. I demonstrated, through common feelings and social ties as much as reason and ideas, that the aspirations of a few can be communicated to others, and scattered individuals and groups can coalesce around collective goals. I did not take for granted the meaning of dignity, though it is generally considered a universal essence of human rights. To understand the meanings of human rights, I looked at my empirical findings. I treated the meanings not as juridical norms or ideology but as socially situated, constructed by the movement through a practice that melds the international and foreign with the local—much of which formal law or political theories would probably not recognize as human rights per se.

Yet this kind of bottom-up practice is fundamental to movement building, bringing people together, and rallying them to claim human rights. From the emotional fealty and bonds, I showed how social change could grow out of the self-transformation of individuals and lay the foundation for reaching legal reform and other formal institutional goals from the ground up. Through processes imbued with emotions and relationships, human rights became integrated into individual subjectivities, acting as a common currency to forge a political community across disparate people. The processes generated profound meanings of human rights that altered the queer Burmese sense of self into feeling worthy of human rights and feeling responsible for achieving them. By assuming responsibility, they became activists of the movement, a community that champions rights claims new to their society. As LGBT activists, they obtained greater dignity and social belonging, for it is part of self-transformation to adopt the movement's distinctive emotion culture, unique meanings of feeling and bonding based on their interpretation of human rights. They kept on affirming their newly acquired sense of self as they continued to make sense of and act on human rights, and so they kept on sustaining movement and practice.

Although I found inspiration from the many disciplines I have noted, the concept of human rights practice as a way of life is unique. Whereas existing human rights studies acknowledge the social nature of human rights, I went further to articulate empirically the theoretical link between human rights and collective action in the form of overlapping, recursive social processes. I took this book beyond a recent wave of scholarship dealing with the "vernacularization" of human rights in domestic contexts (Merry 2006; Levitt and Merry 2009) and the process-oriented approach in sociolegal studies of rights and social movements whose focus has been mainly domestic civil-political rights (McCann 2006; Cummings 2017). I incorporated into my concept important strands of social movement theory about culturally constructed emotions and social ties and extended them to human rights movements. Other studies on rights-based movements may refer to emotions or ties, such as solidarity, at a scholarly distance or in generalities, but few, if any, demonstrate them empirically with a grounding in such personal stories of people whom we have come to know through my telling, and perhaps have grown to admire, like, or dislike.[3]

The interrelated nature of the three outcomes, showing the potential of human rights to challenge formal political institutions from the ground up, offers another original contribution. I extended to human rights movements insights about the connection among movement outcomes and their mutual impact over time. My analysis more than affirms the significance of cultural effects in social movements studies, or sociolegal scholarship's observations about the indirect consequences of rights away from courtroom victories.[4] I detailed empirically how the social processes of human rights practice lead to self-transformation, the production of a distinctive emotion culture, and the making of new claims and claimant and how one outcome feeds into the other, from the personal to the grassroots collective to political claim making. Even more important, I explained how each outcome arises from emotions and interpersonal relationships that are made and remade by the processes of practice.

Broader Lessons on Resonance and Collective Action

The lived experiences of activists, particularly the emotions and interpersonal relationships involved in the processes of collective action, are key to gauging whether human rights practice as a way of life bears any relevance to the study of other movements in Myanmar or elsewhere. One may suggest that the LGBT movement enjoys an opportune moment due to Myanmar's recent political transition and benefits from the enthusiasm of international organizations and foreign governments in funding anything related to human rights in Myanmar. One may also speculate that their conditions are especially suited for this type of analysis, since the extremes of their political oppression and the nature of their suffering lend themselves to heightened emotions.

Where the particularities of the LGBT movement are concerned, human rights practice as a way of life probably cannot travel very far. Certainly the sociopolitical conditions of Myanmar and the lived experiences of queer Burmese are contextualized and peculiar to them. LGBT activists contended with as well as selectively made use of cultural schemas and resources particular to their society to adapt human rights.

What can travel well is the concept's emphasis on process, emotions, and interpersonal relationships. The feelings, ties, and interactions of the LGBT movement in Myanmar of course are culturally specific. The same feelings and ties are unlikely going to be relevant in the same manner for another movement, nor are the processes going to unfold in similar fashion. However, the existence of such phenomena in social life is common. At times, feelings and relationships, or their expressions, may be suppressed. At other times, there may be an obligation to possess or display them. But they do exist. The controls and regulations are forms of interaction, resulting in processes that vary according to the social positions of the people involved and the norms, beliefs, and distribution of power, and hierarchy of that place.

These features of human rights practice as a way of life—process, emotions, and relationships—suggest that the promise of human rights thrives on collective agency that keeps on "making rights real" (Epp 2009). Emotional fealty to human rights and affective ties among movement activists, leading to self-transformation and emotion culture, supply and strengthen normative commitments (Emirbayer and Goodwin 1994), which sustain the LGBT movement and its human rights practice. Such passions and desires do not happen by chance. Grief and suffering are a necessary source of motivation, but they are insufficient for group action; activists have to do something about those feelings to change the course for a group (Gould 2002). People may fortuitously come into contact. Lucky breaks in politics or formal law may help. We saw in this book, however, they usually require hard work together. Often activists also need to create opportunity (Polletta 2004) so that the hard work can take place. The hard work and creativity represent collective emotional labor (Whittier 2001) or emotion work (Gould 2009), the conscious and deliberate cultivation of emotions and relationships to build and innovate social movements together, even under difficult and perilous circumstances.

This type of collective agency often needs local activists, who are pushed and pulled by social ties and emotions, who also know how to foster and reshape them, and who astutely fuse cultural schemas and resources from their society with human rights norms set out in legal documents and treaties.[5] Hence, contrary to criticisms that human rights lack cultural resonance, LGBT activists in this book develop fealty to human rights. Their new feeling rules recuperate their self-worth and give them hope and confidence so that they dare to dream of a future with less suffering and instill in them a sense of responsibility to pursue it. To maintain passion and increase confidence, movement leaders follow up with further training to improve activists' advocacy skills and proficiencies at grant writing and organizational planning. Pursuing human rights together, they turn into new people: they are now activists. By empirically detailing how individuals connect to activism and collectively fight for rights (McCann 2017; McCann and March 1996; Lovell 2012), this book's findings thus vary from the empirical study of northern Thais in another predominantly Theravada Buddhist society (Engel and Engel 2010). The research subjects there view the pursuit of rights as selfish, materialistic, and against Buddhist teachings. The findings also vary from those about the failure of human rights education to inspire collective resistance among marginalized populations (Englund 2006; Massoud 2013; compare Holzer 2013, 2015). Instead, the critical role of activists and their concerted exercise of agency bring this book closer to studies that focus on collective action or social movements, such as women's rights movements in Africa (Tripp 2004; Ferree and Tripp 2006), Thai activists and cause lawyers (Munger 2014, 2015), and other Burmese activists (Dale 2011; Holzmeyer 2009).[6]

Importantly, this type of collective emotion labor has to be able to transform people so that they persevere in the hard work.[7] Burmese LGBT activists eventually identified with the movement because of their collective emotional labor for the movement community and whom they had become as a result (LGBT activists). The work accomplishes much more than raising the awareness of target populations and affirming them with abstract knowledge of human rights. Therefore, rather than feeling a disconnect, or alienation, between national or international NGOs and grassroots constituents (see, e.g., Massoud 2013; Englund 2006), affective ties flourish among LGBT activists within the national and grassroots levels and between them. Swidler (2013) observed that human rights NGOs in Malawi fared poorly compared to organizations of axial religions, because the latter gave Malawians a community that provided material and spiritual support and reaffirmed their new identities as they too took part in converting others to their religion. In this book, LGBT activists acquired an identity that made them feel connected to one another, and they relished newfound belonging as they spread human rights according to the movement's emotion culture.

Love, Agency, and the Empirical Study of Human Rights

Throughout this story about human rights practice as a way of life, the nature of agency to enable as well as inhibit is undeniable. It is why the practice coexists in Burmese society as an alternative, instead of dominating, among other modes of knowing, feeling, and interacting. I looked closely at my findings and realistically conceded that LGBT activists' processes of human rights practice were imperfect. They changed lives and Burmese politics for the better, but they also lost disaffected participants and struggled with shortcomings.

I appreciated these circumstances for the multiplicity of humanity, the consequence of having fluid and complex agency. When we study human rights empirically, we cannot expect neat juxtapositions, such as global-local or powerful-powerless, when the time comes for us to evaluate human rights. It depends. It depends on the sociopolitical conditions of a place, and it depends on how the local practitioners of human rights deal with the cultural schemas and resources that compose them. It also depends on perspective—the activists', their opponents', or the researcher's. Is the proverbial glass half full or half empty? "It depends" is often an answer that sociolegal scholars arrive at. Defending this answer, Kurasawa (2007) "refuses to play a game of intellectual blackmail" (200) in which one feels compelled to take sides about human rights. He describes human rights as "contingent and perilous" (201), social struggles to be evaluated based on who is using them, for what purpose, and how they do it, a view that resonates with my interpretation of Tin Hla's words at the start of the Conclusion and the very premises of this book.

For me, however, rather than standing up to "intellectual blackmail," giving an answer of "it depends" is to have intellectual backbone to commit to the empirically subjective with love. The commitment does not ignore the failings of those we study or lavish them with undue admiration and praise. It is to commit to telling as well as possible how rights become active in social life and to telling an oft-messy tale with compassion for humanity. This telling includes the complexities, contradictions, and—critically, as I have learned from human rights practice as a way of life—emotions and relationships, the pain and joy, fears and desires, longings and loathings that nourish our human fullness. It means respecting the dignity of those who protest the unjust and demand their wrongs be put right. To be compassionate is to respect dignity, for "protestors are you and me" (Jasper 2014, 186).

Therefore, I was first and foremost driven by the empirical realities of LGBT activists in my study. I tried to show compassion to the devotion they developed for human rights, and the attachments they developed for one another as they put human rights into action together. Most of all, I tried to be compassionate about their subjectivities, the agency that ran throughout their practice, though flawed and disappointing as they sometimes turned out to be.

Queer suffering was their prime source of motivation. In the stories of Burmese LGBT activists, Buddhist karmic logic and social hierarchy support one another and contribute to the shame, self-hatred, and fear of being queer. So they try to displace these norms and beliefs, create more positive rules, and construct a more inclusive form of queer bonding. As Tripp (2004) observed about women's rights movements in Africa, the fact that they challenged customary practices and rules "shows how seriously they regard these systems as impediments to their advancement" (16).

Why human rights? Surely other solutions exist in their society. For instance, occupations in spirit mediumship and female fashion and beauty serve as alternatives for some queer Burmese. In some respects, they are perhaps more empowering than the movement's method, which urges responsibility and adherence to society's standards of behavior. However, the communities revolving around occupational niches largely exclude lesbians, who are not endowed at birth with male privilege. They have their own regulation of affect and kinship, as well as sexuality and gender. Human rights practice as a way of life and these other alternatives all possess their own internal logics and disciplining effects. All of them are shaped by interactions with the sociopolitical conditions of a given context. All of them can be empowering or disempowering, liberating or constraining.

Therefore, the more pertinent concern for me was how human rights matter to the people who choose to practice them. To Tin Hla, Tun Tun, and other activists in this book, human rights offer a counterdiscourse for the marginalized. They see in human rights not the embodiment of oppressive foreign power coming ashore to spread its vision of morality but salvation that could liberate them from their suffering. Writing about the history of the Kachin, Sadan (2013) argues that Christianity was "not considered a legacy of colonial brain-washing but rather as a liberating force of mind, body and spirit that invigorates their struggle against the overwhelming claims of Burmese state-sponsored Theravada Buddhism and thus of Burmanization in the postcolonial state" (8). Tin Hla, Tun Tun, and their fellow activists do not reject established queer communities and their remedies. They straddle multiple worlds. But they do not romanticize the traditional and local as the solution to queer suffering. They fell in love with something different: human rights.

In spite of their flaws, LGBT activists at least aspire toward the best of human rights, hoping they will win dignity and belonging and forge unity in a society wracked by fissures and prejudices. Just as Currier (2012) learned about Namibia and South Africa, embracing human rights and LGBT vocabulary saved some queer people from self-hate, fear, and hopelessness. Parsing through the contentious history of the UDHR, Roberts (2015) reminds us that it was anticolonial states, many of them smaller and non-Western, that insisted on the universality of human rights because for those living under colonial rule, they were "emancipatory and held great hope" (126).[8] In the American context, Williams (1991) points out the emotional command that civil-political rights had over African Americans. They were willing to fight hard, even die, for rights; although rights have failed and will continue to fail to do everything they are supposed to do, they bring hope, strength, and the promise of a collective good (also see Crenshaw 1988; Matsuda 1989).

With powerful emotions, queer Burmese bring to bear on a core aspect of their suffering: that regardless of bad karma from past lives, they can and should change their destiny together. They mustered extraordinary courage to found and join an initially obscure movement. They exhibit innovation to make sense and make use of human rights. They weave friendships and fellowships with one another. Certainly some of them may have taken into consideration the potential of human rights to attract donor money and affiliation with the movement to enhance personal benefits; nonetheless, they knowingly make those decisions based on their assessment of human rights' value to them. Whatever the motivation—and they have multiple—they pursue human rights pushed and pulled by desires and longings to "improve [their] way of life," to quote Tin Hla from the beginning of this chapter.

Out of human rights, LGBT activists fashion a way of living more authentically as queer people. They believe it helps them feel freer to live this life as queer and love themselves for it, while being able to find belonging and thus the dignity they are so often denied. Although they still maintain their multiple selves, the new way of life empowers them to inhabit those selves with their queerness and express it in whatever self they project at a given moment, be it activist, lover, or child.

In the Burmese context, this way of life is a radical one. While it is not radical in the revolutionary sense of toppling regimes or eradicating structures, it challenges deeply rooted beliefs and the social hierarchy and organization of relations founded on them. It has the audacity to transform the norms of feeling that apply to a certain kind of people—how others ought to feel about them and how they ought to feel about themselves. The very pursuit of this way of life is groundbreaking in itself.[9] LGBT activists dared to dream about achieving it and dared to pursue it from a time when they should not even have heard, spoken or come within reach of human rights, not without the fear and the imagination of physical and mental anguish. In a place where fear once reigned supreme, the promise of this way of life emboldens them to resist fear where it strikes first and strikes potently—in the heart.

. . .

I have a commitment. I believe in human rights. I will never give up. I believe in doing the right thing, and the right thing will win. (Tun Tun, interview, December 1, 2015*)

In 2012, Tun Tun finally returned to his homeland and reunited with his mother, who had to publicly disown him two decades ago. He did not know when that day would come, if at all. He did not know when, if ever, he could speak about human rights openly in his country. Under the leadership of a democracy icon once revered by many, his country remains riddled with armed conflict, poverty, corruption, and abuse of power. Yet Tun Tun still clings to human rights after almost three decades. With sheer courage and tenacity, he led a fledgling movement into an exciting time in their country.

The potential pitfalls of human rights may or may not materialize for the LGBT movement. The structural legacies, ingrained norms and hierarchy, and Burman privilege that trouble its practice may shift over time. They may not. In this exciting time of politics, Myanmar is in a state of flux, so making any accurate prediction for the future of human rights and the LGBT movement is difficult. However, we do know this: in less than ten years, a group of ordinary Burmese have overcome barriers and defied the odds to give voice to queer people in their country. As Tun Tun's successors persevere, reaching for the goals of queer self-empowerment, social belonging, and legal reform, they will keep on negotiating their own terms with human rights, including the place human rights occupy in their hearts and in their lives.

The man who started it all made the tough choice of becoming a human rights activist. Tun Tun could have chosen a different path. In the interview above, he said he had the chance to move on, settle down in another country, and visit Myanmar only on occasion. He did not.

Tun Tun's passion, anger followed by political disaffection, pushed him to take up arms and then human rights activism, all of which he could not have imagined when he entered Rangoon University to study English literature. His choices in the moments of bloodshed and tears of 1988 kindled the LGBT movement and the fervor of others to take up human rights and strive for a new life together. From the hillsides to the deltas, across rivers, and into villages and small towns, his pursuit touched the hearts and forever changed the lives of Seng Naw, Pyae Soe, Zwe Naung, Kyaw Kyaw, Tin Hla, and many more, binding them to one another. Human rights may not get what they want all the time or everything they wish for. But then hardly anything in their lives has ever done that. Though at times defective, often far from omnipotent, and frequently vilified, human rights are worth fighting for, because, for them, human rights are worth living by.

Appendix

Fieldwork and Methods

My journey studying the Burmese LGBT movement and its human rights practice began where it originated. On the first day of my fieldwork in September 2012, I walked into what would become a familiar sight for the next few years of my life: a movement workshop. In 2012, the movement's national organization, VIVID, was still based in Chiang Mai, Thailand. The workshop, described in Chapter 1, was taking place in a conference room of a hotel in downtown Chiang Mai. The participants were Burmese migrants living in Thailand and grassroots organizers from different towns in Myanmar. Tun Tun was leading the workshop; Khant Nyar was assisting him; Tin Hla was mingling with other workshop participants; and Pyae Soe and Zwe Naung were busy in the back of the room, sorting through papers and magazines and typing on their laptops.

The most enduring observation on my first day was the social phenomenon right before my eyes, and I asked myself, how did these people end up together in this room talking about human rights and LGBT identities? The deceptively simple query motivated me to develop the three questions behind this book—How did the movement emerge? How do its activists make sense of human rights and put them into action? What are the implications of their human rights practice?—and carry out my qualitative fieldwork from September 2012 to April 2017.

As the movement and the number of those involved grew, my research morphed with them, and gradually I conceived of the movement's development, strategy, and tactics as the practice of human rights as a way of life. Over the course of four and a half years, I tracked the movement from its original base in Chiang Mai to its relocation to Yangon and its expansion across Myanmar. I conducted several hundred hours of semistructured interviews and reinterviews with 125 informants from the movement leadership, grassroots locations, and other organizations, as well as observations of movement events, meetings, workshops, international conference participation, road trips, and office routines. I collected and analyzed photographs, videos, movement documents, media reports, publications from other NGOs, and legal documents.

Fieldwork and Analysis

To answer the three motivating questions, I focused my qualitative data and analysis on LGBT activists, their organizations, social groups within the movement (such as lesbians and *trans women*), and the movement as a whole. I treated each interviewee, organization, and social group as separate units of analysis embodying the movement's practice and, in turn, each unit as forming part of a bigger one, such as individual activists in relation to the social group of lesbians or a movement organization. Then I analyzed all of them as comprising the practice overall. Therefore, I was able to discern the broad contours and contents of the practice, particularly the three outcomes, the infused meanings of human rights and identities, and the faults and fault lines. At the same time, I could parse out the details, such as the variations among individuals and social groups, their interpersonal relationships with families and other queer communities, and how the outcomes, limitations, or flaws of the practice play out among them.

I did not directly ask interviewees whether emotions or interpersonal relationships mattered to their movement or human rights trainings. I did ask how they felt about specific events, issues, or struggles or certain interactions with certain people, and I made observations about emotions and social ties. But the processual nature of their practice and the place of emotions and interpersonal relationships emerged much later from my data analysis, which was also informed by my reading of various bodies of literature regarding the intersection of emotions or interpersonal relationships with law, rights, or social movements.

I was mindful of my position as a researcher: I am not a Burmese person, much less a queer Burmese. I am an outsider, somebody less aware of the issues affecting my interviewees. I know little of the language and understand that even with translation, some expressions—as in any other language—have their specific connotations. Moreover, emotions are culturally specific (Geertz 1973; Rosaldo 1984; Lutz 1988; Thoits 1989; Boellstorff and Lindquist 2004), and so are interpersonal relationships, which are permeated with emotions.

Bearing these issues in mind, my approach was to conduct the study constantly remembering that it was far more crucial for a good researcher to be open, honest, deeply interested in the research subjects, and committed to accurately and adequately representing their experiences (Corbin-Dwyer and Buckle 2009), which I hope I have done to the best of my ability in this book. I did not imagine myself as a native of the research context and then try to figure out what I thought in their shoes; rather, I searched out and analyzed symbolic forms, such as words, images, institutions, and behaviors (Geertz 1984). I embraced who I was, an outsider, and the benefits that status had to offer. For instance, I asked what might have been obvious or stupid questions to so-called insiders—about such topics as karmic beliefs, *eain dre theit khar*, and local sexual and gender identity terms. I probably noticed things and drew conclusions that insiders might have overlooked due to shared understandings or the taken-for-granted nature of life around them (Hayfield and Huxley 2015)—for instance, about gender divides in the movement, the predominance of queers designated male at birth in the movement, and its Buddhist-centricity and Burman privilege.

Furthermore, my experiences in the field eventually made me realize the blurry lines between so-called insider and outsider. One can be an insider *and* outsider, or shades of them at the same time (Hayfield and Huxley 2015), perhaps echoing the study's findings on the plurality of personhood. An encounter early in my fieldwork was particularly poignant. The first assistant, whom I let go after the first week of research in September 2012, was a Burmese person, but when I asked her to interpret the conversations at the workshop, she kept insisting to me that she could not understand what they were saying. When I asked her to simply give me the literal translation of the words, she told me they were talking about going to the monastery to "eat oranges" (queer slang for having sex with monks). She was either truly ignorant of queer slang, which is rather unique, or she was using naiveté to shield her discomfort. However, when I heard the literal translation, I understood the meaning right away, and I was not uncomfortable about the subject matter. Perhaps it is because I had conducted research on LGBT activism in other contexts and was used to the cultural subversions of queer slang. Looking back, I often wondered: In that moment, who was more of the outsider—the Burmese translator or me?

The insider-outsider status is blurry for my assistants too. Moora and Khine Khine, the two assistants whom I eventually hired, are Burmese, but they are outsiders in relation to the movement by several counts. Moora is Karen Christian, and Khine Khine is Burmese Chinese (recall that the movement is predominantly Burman). Both are heterosexual, cisgender women. In addition, they are university educated, speak English fluently, and originate from urban Yangon, unlike many of the LGBT activists.

Getting Started and Gaining Access

I began in September 2012 with a two-week trip to get a sense of the lay of land for the movement and figure out how to gain further access to its activists.[1] From the news report on IDAHO celebrations earlier that year, I knew there was a Chiang Mai connection. I managed to locate JUSTICE and VIVID on the Internet and contacted Tun Tun by email to arrange a visit. My plan was to go to Chiang Mai for one week and find out how much Tun Tun and the others at JUSTICE and VIVID were willing to assist me in my research.

Not yet knowing VIVID's recruitment methods and connections to grassroots organizers based in Myanmar, I also had a plan B for the trip. I started with what I know from my other research, that is, queer organizing sometimes occurs within the ambit of HIV/AIDS NGO work, often allowed even by authoritarian governments to limited extent (Chua 2014; Chua and Hildebrandt 2014). Through a colleague, I found a Burmese in Singapore who used to work for an international HIV/AIDS organization in Myanmar. He agreed to an interview and set up appointments with Burmese staff from HIV/AIDS NGOs and grassroots organizations in Yangon and Mandalay for the second half of my September 2012 trip. Starting at two disparate points of entry—or so I thought—later helped me appreciate the LGBT movement's emotion culture, especially its distinctiveness from that of other queer communities.

After the first field trip, I figured out the links between Chiang Mai and the grassroots organizers in Myanmar, as well as with other Thai towns popular with Burmese migrants along the Myanmar-Thailand border. I asked Tun Tun and VIVID activists how they located the workshop participants. I also learned about the southern base in Ranong and their other base for conducting workshops in Mae Sot. I began to extend my fieldwork—while still paying attention to events and interviewees in Chiang Mai—to Ranong, Mae Sot, and then Yangon and Mandalay. After VIVID was relocated to Yangon in March 2013, I completely shifted my attention toward Myanmar and expanded my coverage to other Burmese locations.

During the course of my fieldwork, I had to split my time between my responsibilities in Singapore and research time in Thailand (the earlier part of 2013 only) and Myanmar. I was a pretenure faculty member at the National University of Singapore at the time, so I carried a full-time teaching load during semesters without any sabbatical leave. Fortunately, Singapore is a bit less than three hours by direct flight from Chiang Mai or Yangon. I took frequent trips in between teaching days and other obligations on campus. These frequent trips during term time from 2013 to 2016 lasted about five to seven days each. During the longer vacation period in June and July, I went on visits of about a month each time.

For the rest of the time that I was unable to spend personally in the field, I was fortunate that my two assistants could do so and that they stuck with me all these years. Given the social prejudices against queers, suitable assistants were crucial to interviewees' safety and the project's success. Through a colleague, I found Moora, an English-language teacher and experienced interpreter based in Yangon. We had good rapport right away, and Moora was comfortable with the subject matter. After the first few days working together, I decided she was a good colleague. The other assistant, Khine Khine, was a Burmese student studying at my institution. She approached me out of the blue in late 2013 to ask if she could work as my assistant. Like Moora, she struck up a good rapport with me and understood the research. With Moora and Khine Khine, I was able to collect more observations and follow-up interviews when I was not able to do so personally. Sometimes they picked up documents or other materials from informants on my behalf. The two went above and beyond merely translating words from one language into another. They were extra sets of eyes and ears for me. They provided background knowledge that gave meaning and context to interviewees' words and picked up verbal and nonverbal cues that provided insight into their responses, behaviors, and body language (Fujii 2013).

The multiyear nature of the fieldwork, with two regular assistants, was also conducive for establishing trust and good relations with interviewees over time. They were increasingly more willing to talk about their personal lives, details that informed my findings on self-transformation. The ongoing nature of the project also made it easier to approach *tomboys* and *trans men*, who initially seemed aloof and even intimidating. After my assistants and I got to know them at movement events and from the interviews, I realized they were rather shy and usually kept to their circle of *tomboys* and *trans men*. Once they felt more comfortable with us, especially with Moora, interviewing them was much easier.

Overall, informants were willing to talk to me and to grant access to their organizations. I am well aware that foreign scholars often encounter caution and fear among their Burmese informants (see, e.g., Skidmore 2004; Dale 2011).[2] Although my field-work began after the post-2011 political changes, the early days of transition under the USDP government were still uneasy, and scrutiny and surveillance have persisted, especially over politically sensitive issues. I do not have any definitive explanation for my experiences, but I have often considered several reasons. Maybe I came across as less distant compared to a researcher visibly identified as Western, being somebody who grew up in Malaysia and lives in Singapore, two of Myanmar's Southeast Asian neighbors. Maybe it was the subject matter. I have learned from my other research that activists working on queer issues are often willing to talk and assist, perhaps because their work had not received much scholarly attention previously. Maybe a certain degree of *anade* was also at work. It is possible that some interviewees acceded to my requests because they did not want to cause me discomfort and did not want to say no to me.[3] Maybe it had something to do with my appearance. I am heavily and visibly tattooed, and perhaps many interviewees had not previously met women like me. I was frequently asked about my tattoos or requested to take photographs with them (to which I obliged).

Interviews and Interviewees

I developed my pool of interviewees in three main ways. I asked people who had become my interviewees for suggestions, met people during observations in the field, and identified them from movement documents, such as workshop attendance records and minutes of meetings. I started with a list of about twenty to thirty people I wanted to interview or reinterview from the September 2012 trip to Chiang Mai, Yangon, and Mandalay and expanded my list from there.

Finding and interviewing informants entailed being flexible and adapting my plans in response to unanticipated circumstances. Because I relied on introductions and social ties, sometimes I ended up getting the unexpected. In Chapter 5, I wrote about asking informants to suggest people who are non-Buddhist. But during the actual interviews, I would find out that these people were Buddhist after all, and they were probably stereotyped by my informants as non-Buddhist because of their darker, South Asian–looking features (associated with being Muslim or Hindu). My assistants and I did not feel comfortable asking these potential interviewees directly over the phone about their religion. We conducted those interviews anyway. I treated the interviews as providing yet more valuable data, and in fact I was able to learn about their experiences as ethnic minorities (though not religious minorities). The experience of being led to these interviewees also ended up as part of the analysis on the movement's Burman and Buddhist-centricity.

Out of the 125 interviewees, 81 are or were LGBT activists—people who organized movement events, implemented its programs, or carried out advocacy work at the grassroots or national level, or represented the movement as a national or grassroots spokesperson. With a few exceptions, most of them started out as recruits who attended JUSTICE (early days) or VIVID's human rights workshops. If they took up LGBT activism but eventually left the movement, they counted as former LGBT activists; if they did not, they counted as "dropouts," people who turned away from the movement after

attending a few human rights workshops. I included former activists and three dropouts (these were harder to locate) to understand their decisions; as it turned out, they
were important to the analysis on community building. The 41 interviewees who were
non-LGBT activists included NGO staff, women's rights activists, political activists, and
human rights lawyers. They assisted the movement, understand Burmese queer issues,
or know about doing activism in Myanmar.

The LGBT activists in my study form a diverse spectrum of people. Being an "LGBT
activist" does not indicate the person's sexuality or gender identity, though most former
and current LGBT activists in this study are queer: twenty-three are lesbians, five are
heterosexual, cisgender persons, and the rest identify with one or more of the Burmese
terms or LGBT terms relevant to queers assigned male at birth. The majority of them
practice Buddhism, the dominant religion in Myanmar. Others identify as Muslim or
Christian. Besides Burmans, there are people of Karen, Kachin, Chin, Shan, Chinese
and South Asian ethnicities. However, if I were to take the activists' self-identifications
at face value (when in fact, as I noted in Chapter 5, many of them have multiethnic
descent), ethnic and religious minorities are arguably underrepresented, reflecting the
Buddhist-centric and Burman-dominated nature of the movement examined in Chapter 5. Altogether, the activists come from the twenty Burmese locations indicated in
Figure 1, which cover not only major Burmese cities but also smaller towns and rural
areas. Their interviews took place at movement events where they met me or one of my
assistants or places to which we traveled: Yangon, Mandalay, Dawei, Pyay, Bago, Ranong, Mae Sot, Chiang Mai, and Bangkok. They also come from a range of income levels
and occupations. Besides the few who work full time for the movement, they are staff
and part timers for other NGOs, shopkeepers, small business owners, factory workers,
daily wage laborers, beauticians, *nat kadaw*, students, and lawyers.

The initial interviews and reinterviews usually lasted between one and two hours;
a few went on for as long as three to four hours, with lunch or tea breaks in between.
Follow-ups (shorter conversations) and some first-time interviews were briefer, between
twenty and thirty minutes. There were also countless short conversations throughout
the years at movement activities and events being observed, some with me and others
with my assistants.

Most of the time, I kept my questions simple, asking for descriptive answers. These
kinds of questions got people talking much more easily and elicited empirical details
useful for my own analysis. For first-time interviews, I asked how they initially came
into contact with the movement ("how" usually led to why they became LGBT activists),
which events and activities they started attending, what they did and were then doing
for the movement, what they learned or gained from the movement, what difficulties
they had, and what it was like to be queer in Myanmar. With interviewees who were
non-LGBT activists, I modified the questions to find out whether and how they worked
on queer issues and their views on queer sexualities and gender identities. I also asked
interviewees to talk about their views on human rights. This was the least descriptive
type of question asked, and I had to try different variations of the question in the same
conversation. When I asked directly what human rights meant to them, I commonly

received the response that they meant "dignity" and that queer people were equally entitled to the same human rights. Though such answers seemed predictable and rather canned, I did not dismiss them. Eventually, along with observational and documentary data, I figured out their deeper meaning: the important realization and insistence that queer people are not "lower" than other humans due to bad karma. However, I also asked what they wanted to achieve with human rights, a question that encouraged more elaborative answers. Their hopes for human rights generally corresponded to pain, fear, and despair caused by queer suffering; the answers told me a lot about how they understood and made sense of human rights and about their replacement of negative with positive feeling rules. I also asked what they would like me to call them in terms of their sexual or gender identity and asked them why. At first, I worried that such questions would be too personal or offensive, but my interviewees seemed to react well and even appreciated my curiosity; a few enthusiastically illustrated their explanations with gestures and actions. I used the answers to find out what LGBT identity terms meant to them and why they adopted a particular term for themselves and why they changed their choices (if they did).

From these interviews, I eventually distilled the relevance of emotions and social ties, the interaction with Buddhism, and their notions of dignity and responsibility. These findings emerged when I analyzed them together with follow-ups (shorter conversations of twenty to thirty minutes), reinterviews (longer), and the other data. I conducted follow-ups and reinterviews when I developed new insights in my analysis and wanted to verify them with interviewees or get their views on new developments in the field.

Reinterviews and follow-ups with lesbians and informants who left or dropped out from the movement contributed significantly to the findings on emotional bonds and the movement's internal gender divide. With lesbians, I conducted the follow-ups and reinterviews specifically about their exceptional challenges after realizing that they displayed an important empirical pattern. With dropouts, I contacted people who were interviewed earlier in the study or appeared in earlier movement records but were no longer present at later activities. These follow-ups and reinterviews required a bit of tact. I explained that I wanted to learn about their experiences with the movement, even though they were no longer active. Most of them were willing to give me some time. I usually inquired about how they had been since leaving the movement and then gently asked why they left.

Another type of reinterview, which I dubbed the "long interview" with my assistants, asked informants' for lengthier narratives about their childhood, biological family, the place where they grew up, their adulthood, and their struggles in life (not necessarily related to being queer). Most of these reinterviews took place in 2015; Tin Hla's story about his childhood came from a reinterview, supplemented by an earlier interview and later follow-ups. For some interviewees' narratives, such as Tun Tun's, I drew from multiple interviews over the years. I decided to conduct long interviews at a juncture when I was unsure where I could go next with the project. I had written what I wanted to say in article length about the movement (Chua 2015, 2016), but I was not entirely satisfied with those theoretical framings in hindsight. Nor did I want to wrap up the project, because I felt strongly that there was more I could do with it. I decided to take a chance and conduct a series of long interviews with a purposive sample of national and grass-roots activists and see where they took me.

The long interviews reenergized my study and encouraged me to analyze the place of emotions in LGBT activists' human rights practice much more closely. Social ties were already present in my earlier theoretical framing, but the combination with emotions made them much more prominent. The long interviews became key to my analysis on the emotions of suffering and why the meanings of human rights stem from feeling their absence in their lives (human rights violations). They were also crucial to the findings on self-transformation, especially how practicing human rights changed their sense of self and how such changes connected social belonging to dignity. The findings from the long interviews prompted me to go back and reanalyze earlier interviews with other informants and conduct follow-ups.

I verified the interview data in a variety of ways. Many of the personal accounts could not be checked against any other source, so as the fieldwork continued, I verified them by talking to the same interviewees over and over about the same topics, using the passage of time to check their narratives. Where their stories intersected with major political developments or news events, such as the 1988 uprising, the 2007 protests, and the 2008 Cyclone Nargis, I read secondary literature to see if their stories were generally consistent with scholarly writings or journalists' reports. With some stories, I was able to cross-check against interviews with other informants whose names came up in the narratives. I also verified the interviews using other types of data. In particular, I was able to corroborate accounts of recruitment, crucial to formation processes, by referring to VIVID's minutes of meetings, workshop records, and travel expense reports.[4] I also checked raw video footage shot by VIVID at various events and photographs, especially those taken in front of event banners displaying dates and venue names.

Most of the time, I could verify the interview data using one or more of these approaches. Usually the inaccuracies came from misremembering the dates or locations of events. I decided to discount the interview data from particular informants, at least the factual aspect, on only a few occasions—for instance, if the facts simply did not corroborate when checked against other interviewees' narratives. I also made such rare decisions to discount certain interviews based on personalities. Having known the participants over the years and after discussing the matter with my assistants, we decided who was most likely to have given a more reliable account.

When it came to interview data concerning informants' views on human rights and LGBT identities—rather than about factual details—I was cautious that interviewees might have felt compelled to say what they thought I wanted to hear as an English-speaking foreigner. They might have wanted to convey the impression of being modern by giving favorable views on human rights or LGBT identities.[5] To address this concern, I complemented the interview data with observations described in the following section. Furthermore, the consistency of responses across interviewees and over time bolstered my confidence in the validity of my findings. In any case, it is possible that interviewees increasingly approved of human rights and LGBT identities as they became more involved with the movement and interacted more intensely with other LGBT activists, the result of the social processes of human rights practice. Moreover, I did not rely only on the answers directly regarding their views on human rights; I considered the descriptive answers on how they got involved with the movement and so on, from which I also discerned the relevance of emotions and interpersonal relationships to the meanings of human rights and their appeal to interviewees.

Informants usually appeared rather reticent in the interviews about other queer communities, save for saying they had social ties to such and such groups of people who put them in touch with the movement, or alluding to their niche occupations. Maybe they did not consider the information as being relevant to our conversations about the movement or human rights. To address such reticence, in follow-ups or reinterviews, I asked them specifically about other queer communities. In addition, I treated the reticence itself as data, consistent with their desire to create a distinctive emotion culture, and their interviews as indicative of their having entered the LGBT movement world and assumed the social position of LGBT activist when talking to me. I also read secondary literature to gain a better understanding of other queer communities to supplement and verify my findings regarding the differences in emotion culture.

About 80 percent of the interviews were conducted in Burmese with the aid of interpretation and the rest in English (marked with an asterisk in this book).[6] I briefed my two assistants: They were not to translate into English queer Burmese identity terms such as *apwint* and *apone*. I conducted most of the interviews in person. When Moora and Khine Khine carried out a small number of them on their own, those were usually interview types with which they were familiar, that is, we had done similar interviews together. After the interviews, we discussed what each other thought of them, the consistency of the stories compared to other interviews, and what I might not have comprehended. I benefited incredibly from Moora and Khine Khine's insights during our long hours in the field together.

Observations

The types and number of observations expanded with my access to the field and pool of interviewees. I kept in touch with interviewees regarding upcoming activities and planned ahead to go personally or ask one of my assistants if I could not fit the dates into my work schedule. The observations started with workshops and movement meetings and then extended to daily office interactions at VIVID, road trips to visit grassroots organizers or other meetings, public events like press conferences and IDAHO commemorations, international conference participation, and discussions with allies.

As I knew more and more LGBT activists, it became easier and more comfortable to ask whether my assistants or I could join their road trips or observe office routines. I put Moora and Khine Khine to the task of hanging out with activists on the road or at VIVID's office. Typically I arranged for them to provide language assistance or (in Khine Khine's case) basic legal research that LGBT activists sorely needed. I briefed both of them clearly that they had to make it known they were there to observe what people said and did, even though they were helping out.

I paid attention to the substantive content of the observed events and activities. I examined how people talked about human rights, explained the meanings of human rights to newcomers, referred to international instruments like UDHR, and the manner in which they used LGBT identities. These observations provided corroboration for interview data that formed my analysis on the emotions of suffering, karmic beliefs and responsibility, feeling rules, and thus the emotional fealty cultivated toward human rights. They also provided data on the analysis concerned with emotional bonding over shared suffering, collective struggles, and fear.

In addition, I paid attention to social interactions during the substantive proceedings, break times, mealtimes, and conversations and interactions not part of the substantive content relating to activism or human rights. I took note of what people said and did before, in between, during, and after an event, learning that they chatted about *nat* festivals and beauty pageants and used the derogatory word *achauk* as a term of endearment for one another. Moora and Khine Khine closely interpreted these casual conversations for me. As they grew more comfortable with the movement community, they took it upon themselves to gossip with the activists and find out what else was going on in their lives, what they were doing, and who was getting along or falling out with whom. Again, the participants at meetings and workshops knew they were helping to conduct research. The observations of social interactions became significant to the analysis on the emotional bonds of friendship and fellowship. I learned about other parts of their lives and other interests, such as beauty pageants, that they were reticent about in the interviews. I also learned more about their personalities and interpersonal relationships with one another, which helped me better understand what they said in interviews.

Regardless of whether I was personally at the observed activity, I made sure I had detailed notes not only on the substantive proceedings but also the other interactions. I trained Moora and Khine Khine to understand the latter's importance. We debriefed each other about the observations and discussed our notes. Analyzing the observations of substantive proceedings and nonsubstantive interactions, I arrived at the construction of a distinctive emotion culture. I noticed the unique features of their movement community and identities and, at the same time, their navigation in and out of them. These findings led to the analysis on variations in the frequency and use of LGBT identities and thus the unstable and variable nature of their practice.

Documents, Photographs, and Videos

I collected and analyzed photographs, videos, movement publications, movement organizations' internal documents, publications by other organizations, media reports, legislation, executive directives, and court documents. The main purpose was to supplement and complement the other two sources of data. They were also particularly important for discerning the outcome of new claims and claimant. Moora and Khine Khine organized the documents and translated many of them (similarly following the translation guidelines on identity terms). For the purposes of checking time lines and participation in movement events that took place before my research began, I reviewed all of the relevant documents. For the analysis of patterns such as human rights meanings, the use of LGBT identities, and how human rights workshops were conducted, I randomly sampled about 25 percent of the movement documents collected. I counted the number of documents for each type, whether they were publications meant for public consumption, reports and proposals for international donors, minutes of meetings, training materials, and correspondence between movement organizations or activists; then I numbered each document in each category randomly and used a "virtual dice" program to sample 25 percent from each category. I also analyzed all publications by other organizations, media reports, and legal documents that I had purposively sampled.

I obtained photographs from interviewees. I befriended many of the interviewees on social media—if they were connected to the Internet—and gained access to generous quantities of photographs posted online. A few participants showed me paper photographs, and I got their permission to photograph the images using my smartphone. VIVID activists let me copy their event photographs onto thumb drives and bring them home. The photographs were the most helpful for verifying accounts of movement participation.

VIVID activists provided the video footage of many of their workshops, meetings, and celebrations, including skits, discussion, and rehearsals. I used the video for the same verification purposes as the photographs, as well as to observe the emotional bonds of friendship and fellowship between them. The videos dated as far back as 2009. VIVID used to edit some of the footage into short clips and distributed them on CDs. But I was able to obtain the dozens of hours of continuous, unedited raw footage. During my first trip in September 2012, I had noticed video cameras. It was obviously not yet appropriate to ask about videos right away, so I waited for several months to do so. After VIVID activists told me they had thirty-five mini-DV tapes of raw footage, I managed to persuade them—and the cameraman who worked for JUSTICE—to let me borrow the tapes to convert into digital format. When I returned the original tapes, I gave them a copy of the digital format as well.

The movement documents comprise publications for public consumption and internal documentation including minutes, workshop attendance records, travel expense reports, training materials, documentation of human rights violations, and grant applications and reports. Publications like magazines and posters were easy to obtain. For the internal documentation, I relied on VIVID activists' generosity. I periodically asked them for documents, which they willingly supplied. Grassroots organizers kept fewer records, probably due to the lack of organizational structure and formal education, which discouraged them from keeping written records. Khant Nyar lamented about the difficulty of getting grassroots organizers to turn in written reports, and when they did, the submissions were often handwritten. Most of the grassroots records actually came from VIVID's files.

Because my fieldwork started in 2012, I wanted to construct a reliable account of the earlier years of the movement other than depending on interview data (and also to verify the interviews themselves). VIVID kept only a few computer files related to the earlier days. Khant Nyar was kind enough to make an entire copy of his office's hard drive and pass it to me in 2013, but those files did not cover the years when Seng Naw was in charge, from the mid-2000s until 2012.

I found two solutions. In February 2013, when VIVID activists were packing up to relocate from Chiang Mai to Yangon, I visited their office and got their permission to go through their trash. On previous visits, I had noticed old files and papers lying around the office. When I learned they were packing up for the move, I knew I had a good opportunity to go dumpster diving. Using my smartphone, I photographed whatever documents seemed relevant. Those documents turned out to be valuable records of attendance, travel expense reports, and minutes for verifying interview data and for analysis that led to similar empirical patterns. The other solution was Seng Naw's old laptop, which he had brought home to Kachin State. Pyae Soe and Zwe Naung told me that Seng Naw kept most of his work files on the laptop. After I finally located and interviewed Seng Naw, I asked him about the laptop.[7] He still had it and still kept everything related to the LGBT movement on it. I convinced Seng Naw to let me look at the files. With his permission, I copied everything from his hard drive to save time (that alone was more than a day's work). The files from Seng Naw's laptop filled the void of the founding years. They helped me analyze early recruitment patterns, especially on the importance of pre-existing social ties, and thus verify the interview data as well. I also noticed patterns on queer suffering and the depiction of suffering in their lives as human rights violations.

In addition, I collected media reports, publications from other NGOs, relevant legislation, executive directives, judgments, and legal briefs from a variety of sources. Khine Khine monitored media reports for me. Interviewees and other contacts periodically sent me news reports. I asked for other relevant NGO publications, such as those on women's rights, from various interviewees. The lawyer informants supplied court judgments and legal briefs (court documents are not readily available in Myanmar). I obtained relevant legislation and executive directives from websites, lawyers, and roadside stalls in Yangon.

Notes

Note on Language

1. Burmese Buddhism is Burman-centric in content and in the academic study of it, whereas research on ethnic minorities' practices of Buddhism and their influences on Burmese Buddhism pales in comparison (Walton 2017a). The Buddhist- and Burman-centric nature of the LGBT movement is an issue considered in Chapter 5.

2. For example, Spiro (1967) considers *nat* worship to be distinct from Buddhism in Myanmar; for other discussions of *nat* worship and its place in Burmese Buddhism or Burmese society, see, e.g., Nash (1966), Brac de la Perrière (2005, 2009a, 2009b), Lehman (1987), Keyes (1983a), and Schober (2004). Different kinds of *nat* command different degrees of jurisdiction, ranging from the local to the regional. Arguably the most famous *nat* are the Thirty-Seven Lords, who are arranged into a formal cult with which *nat kadaw* are affiliated. These *nat* were humans who died violent or wrongful deaths, causing them to linger in this world as spirits (Lehman 1987). The founder of the first Burmese dynasty supposedly tried to ban *nat* cults, but without much success, and subsequently subordinated cultic *nat* figures into a pantheon under Buddhism (Brac de la Perrière 2005).

3. I use these terms with the understanding that they are contested. For example, opponents of the military dictatorship rejected "Myanmar." See Farrelly (2014) on the hope that habitual footnoting on the use of "Myanmar" will be discontinued in the near future.

4. The movement does not cover intersex people. Intersex issues are relatively unknown in Myanmar, and I do not know of any Burmese movement concerned with the rights of intersex people.

List of Terms

1. *Apwint* commonly take hormone replacement drugs, largely imported from China, though body modification using pharmaceuticals is not essential to becoming and being *apwint*. Only a small number of *apwint* have undergone gender reassignment surgery overseas. The cost is prohibitive to most *apwint*, and such procedures are not known to be available in Myanmar at the time of this book (Chua and Gilbert 2016).

2. My interviewees are uncertain about the origins of *gandu*, though a few of them suspect it has Indian origins. There is such a slang word in Hindi that refers to "ass" (buttocks) or "anus," or to a person as stupid or idiotic. Gilbert (2016) describes the word as being derived from the Hindi slang for "anus." It is, however, inconclusive as to whether *gandu* and the Hindi slang are indeed the same word, or how *gandu* came to be understood by queer Burmese as an insult.

3. My interviewees have varying explanations, but they consistently stress the reversal of sexual roles between *apwint* and *tha nge*. Some say it is a word play on *inga lan*, which means the reversal of sexual organs. One interviewee said *ingahlan* is also sometimes pronounced like "England" to refer to the *apwint* in the role-reversal scenario, so that the word sounds gentler. Gilbert (2016) defines *ingahlan* as referring to the *tha nge* who becomes the penetrated partner, and he also notes the word play on *inga lan*. Keeler (2017) describes *ingahlan* as a hilarious homonym for the Burmese pronunciation of "England," punning on the Burmese words for "member" and "reversal" to refer to males who take both sexual positions.

4. My use of "lesbian" is inspired by Wieringa and Blackwood (1999), who note that "lesbian" remains the sole signifier distinguishing female/women's same-sex eroticism from men's. Therefore, "lesbian" in my use is intended to distinguish the same-sex eroticism of those assigned female from those assigned male at birth, particularly in a society where by virtue of being the former is associated with having lesser merit or good karma, and thus inferior in status. Furthermore, in Myanmar, *tomboys* and *trans men*'s identification with masculine qualities not only varies in degree but also cannot be entirely equated with being female-to-male transgender as we know it in Western or so-called international parlance.

5. See note 2 in "Note on Language" on *nat* worship. Regarding the ranks and succession of *nat kadaw*, see Brac de la Perrière (2009b). According to my study and Gilbert (2016), *apwint* who are *nat kadaw* are allowed to marry only female spirits, such as Ma Ngwe Taung. They connect to male spirits in other roles such as that of a sister or daughter (Gilbert 2016). This point contradicts older research, which claims generally that *achauk* marry spirits to alleviate their social status (Coleman, Colgan, and Gooren 1992).

6. Some of the relationships with *tha nge* are long term, and some are transactional in nature, with the *apwint* or *apone* providing material benefits. The relationships often come with the understanding that *tha nge* will enter into heterosexual marriages with cisgender women (or have already done so).

Introduction

1. Interviews conducted in English are marked with an asterisk.

2. The estimated number of deaths has ranged from 3,000 to as high as 10,000, the former being the commonly cited figure these days (Steinberg 2010).

3. The military-backed party, the Union Solidarity and Development Party (USDP), won the 2010 elections amid allegations of fraud and intimidation (Prasse-Freeman 2012).

4. The number of grassroots locations is based on VIVID's calculation as of June

2017. At the time, VIVID also reported having a movement base of almost 600 members from these locations, but the figure includes both the people who became activists and those who merely participated in movement activities.

5. Reports published by human rights organizations, such as Human Rights Watch, are numerous and widely available online.

6. The semicivilian government also allowed Aung San Suu Kyi and NLD politicians to enter parliament, tried to broker a cease-fire with insurgent groups (though fighting continues in various parts of Myanmar), and permitted political exiles to return. The relaxed controls on civil-political liberties include the abolishment of prepublication print censorship, removal of restrictions on politically sensitive websites, and enactment of laws to allow independent trade unions, peaceful assembly, and greater freedom of association.

7. These are four laws known as the Monogamy Law, Religious Conversion Law, Myanmar Buddhist Women's Special Marriage Law, and Population Growth and Healthcare Law. For analysis of their legislative passage, see Walton, McKay, and Daw Khin Mar Mar Kyi (2015). The LGBT movement was not targeted by extreme Buddhist nationalists. Following the NLD's succession in 2015, LGBT movement leaders also believe that these extremists have waned in influence due to their apparent lack of political support (interviews: Yamin, July 26, 2016; and Khant Nyar, July 28, 2016). However, the long-term effects of increased legal regulation on sexuality remain to be seen. On extreme elements in Buddhist nationalist organizations such as Ma Ba Tha and their post-2015 developments, see Walton (2017b), Walton, Ma Khin Mar Mar Kyi and Aye Thein (2017), and Nyi Nyi Kyaw (2017).

8. The elections outcome has no impact on the constitutionally entrenched powers of the military, Tatmadaw, over 25 percent of the legislature and its control of defense, interior affairs, and border security.

9. Burmese queer history is little documented (Gilbert 2016), and the scholarship tends to focus on queer Burmese who were assigned male at birth (see, e.g., Keeler 2016; Gilbert 2013, 2016).

10. According to the 2014 census, about 89.8 percent of the population is Buddhist, 6.3 percent is Christian, 2.3 percent is Muslim, 0.5 percent is Hindu, and 0.8 percent is animist.

11. Challenges still remain, though the situation has improved as more researchers have gained access to Myanmar since 2011.

12. Coincidentally, Lefebvre (2013) interprets Henri Bergson's treatment of human rights in *The Two Sources of Morality and Religion* as a "way of life" that begins with personal transformation. He argues that Bergson envisioned human rights as a medium of self-care radiating outward to transform others. My concept of human rights practice as a way of life does not rely on Lefebvre or the philosophical works on which it is based. Rather, as will become evident throughout the book, it developed from my empirical analysis of the Burmese LGBT movement and various bodies of literature in the social sciences and law about human rights and social movements. Whether and how it is similar to or different from Lefebvre's discussion of Bergson fall outside this book's scope and aim.

Chapter 1

1. "Contemporary" human rights can be differentiated from "modern" human rights (Baxi 2002), which are usually traced to the English Magna Carta, the American Declaration of Independence, and the French Declaration of the Rights of Man and the Citizen, and are concerned exclusively with the rights of citizens (An-Na'im 2011). But see Hunt (2007), who traces the historical impact of the American and French revolutions and their declarations on the contemporary discourse, and Moyn (2010), who argues that although key human rights documents were promulgated as part of post–World War II developments, practically speaking, human rights ascended only in the 1970s, following the failure of "other utopias," such as socialism and nationalism.

2. They include the United Nations Human Rights Council's resolutions on Human Rights, Sexual Orientation and Gender Identity in 2011 and 2014, and Protection Against Violence and Discrimination Based on Sexual Orientation and Gender Identity in 2016.

3. This is despite the recognition of group and collective rights in human rights treaties drafted after the UDHR.

4. In an earlier article (Chua 2015), I conceptualized the LGBT movement's practice of human rights as "vernacular mobilization," but I have since refined my ideas and developed in this book the concept of human rights practice as a way of life.

5. Stern (2005) uses one of the case studies in Merry (2006) to examine collective action framing by translators but does not explicitly discuss vernacularization.

6. Exceptions that extensively consider the rights consciousness of predominantly Buddhist societies include Engel and Engel (2010) on northern Thais and state injury law, Munger (2014, 2015) on Thai activist lawyers, and Leve (2007) on secularism and human rights in Nepal.

7. Other recent work on law and society relations in Myanmar includes Crouch (2016) and Crouch and Lindsey (2014).

8. Some scholars draw distinctions between emotions and feelings and further categorize them. For example, sociologist Peggy Thoits describes "feelings" as encompassing both physical drive states, such as hunger, pain, and fatigue, as well as emotional states (1989), and social movements expert James Jasper offers a typology of feelings based on how long they typically last and how they are felt—bodily urges, moods, reflex emotions, affective loyalties, and moral emotions (2011). I adopt the approach in Maroney (2006) by not asserting the correctness of any particular terminology and using "emotion" as it is generally understood in the broad sense to refer to a range of phenomena that could be considered emotion, feeling, affect, or mood.

9. To be clear, the concept of interpersonal relationships in this book is not the same as analyses of "relational dynamics" found in some social movements studies (see, e.g., Morag-Levine 2003; Vanhala 2011; Alimi, Bosi, and Demetriou 2012).

10. I find this explanation of emotions, informed by studies such as Kemper (1978) and Stryker (2004), to be the most helpful for my concept of human rights practice as a way of life. The perspectives on the relational nature of emotions, however, are too many to review in this book. For works that survey the various theoretical emphases in the

field of sociology of emotions, for example, see Thoits (1989), Turner and Stets (2005), and Bericat (2016).

11. The legal academy's scholarship on law and emotions usually focuses on domestic civil-political rights, but its insights are relevant to human rights (Abrams 2011).

12. Book-length treatments considering the place of emotions by legal scholars include Bandes (1999), Nussbaum (2004), and Karstedt, Loader, and Strang (2014), and those by social movements scholars include Goodwin, Jasper, and Polletta (2001b), Goodwin and Jasper (2004), Flam and King (2005), and Gould (2009).

13. Scholars do not agree on the manner and degree to which emotions and cognition are intertwined. Solomon (2003) provides a helpful starting point with important classical and contemporary theories from biology, philosophy, psychology, and other disciplines.

14. Sewell (1992) refers to "emotional commitments" as a type of resource. Furthermore, since I treat emotions as inseparable from cognition, they can be regarded as part of knowledge, another kind of resource.

15. These social movements concepts are understood predominantly in rationalistic terms (Emirbayer and Goldberg 2005). However, a key article on collective action framing, Snow et al. (1986), does note that changing beliefs entails both the cognitive and emotional, whereas Aminzade and McAdam (2001) clarify that "cognitive liberation" in McAdam (1999b) contains important "emotional referents" (30–31), as did McAdam (1999a) in the introduction to the second edition of his seminal work (1999b).

16. Debates about the compatibility of Buddhism and human rights (see, e.g., Gowans 2006; Meinert and Zöllner 2010; Keyes 2011; Keown, Prebish, and Husted 2012; Hayward 2017; Perera 1991) lie beyond the scope of this book, which focuses on activists' practical adaptation and use of human rights. Generally LGBT activists' human rights practice may be consistent with perspectives that regard Burmese Buddhism as a "moral universe"—a conceptual framework comprising elements of the religion, with which many Burmese Buddhists organize and engage their worlds and flexibly interpret and deploy to make sense of their experiences, their actions, and ideas from outside (Walton 2017a). Therefore, significant variations exist among applications of Burmese Buddhism. For example, the military dictatorship tried to legitimize their rule with patronage to Buddhism, while pro-democracy activists adopted a competing vision to mount resistance against its oppression (Schober 2005, 2011).

17. However, law also possesses a double standard toward emotions. Some emotions are considered relevant, whereas others are dismissed (Bornstein and Weiner 2006).

18. See note 16 of this chapter on the moral universe of Burmese Buddhists.

19. Hunt (2007) argues that empathy—when people come to feel that they are fundamentally alike—is important to the "self-evident" nature of human rights. For a collection of writings on the mobilization of empathy for humanitarian action and human rights, see Wilson and Brown (2009).

20. Other queers in Myanmar do adopt LGBT identities without the movement's influence. However, they do not belong to the movement's community of activists, as its LGBT marker is intimately associated with the shared human rights practice.

21. Where analysis of collective action framing is concerned, Hunt, Benford, and Snow (1994) note that identity constructions, intended or not, occur inherently within these movement activities.

22. Snow, Zurcher, and Ekland-Olson (1986) find that people with weak or few ties to alternative social networks are more likely to accept recruitment invitations compared to those who have strong commitments elsewhere.

23. Myanmar's past and current constitutions do not contain the term *lu akwint ayay*. However, references to "fundamental rights of citizens," *mu la akwint ayay*, do appear in the 1974 version and the current constitution of 2008. Given the military government's brutality, constitutionally protected rights probably mean little to most Burmese people. The 2008 constitution also contains reference to *ya paing kwint*, which can be understood as an "entitlement" or a "conditional" legal right (Cheesman 2015) that arises due to the position of power occupied, such as that of Speaker of the Parliament.

24. The reinterpreted LGBT identities coexist with older Burmese vocabulary (see Chapter 5).

25. I do not describe the outcomes of the LGBT movement as "cultural" because of the treatment of cultural schemas in my conceptual framework, explained earlier in this chapter.

26. For discussions about "new social movements," see Melucci (1980); Laraña, Johnston, and Gusfield (1994); and Buechler (1995).

27. Here, I emphasize the self as embedded in interpersonal relationships, though I agree with Fineman (2008) that the self is also intertwined with relationships with institutions.

28. My treatment of the self in this book does not deal with complicated concepts of self in Buddhist teachings and their relationship to human rights (see note 16 of this chapter). It also differs from Houtman (1999), who writes about NLD leaders' methods of meditation and mental cultivation in the 1980s and 1990s.

29. Using the concept of "emotional habitus," Gould (2009) finds that emotions and changes to emotions are conducive to activism and effecting social change.

30. I emphasize feeling rules and bonds of shared understandings because they emerge as key empirical findings in my study. More generally, emotion cultures may include other elements, such as display rules (what sort of emotions one should or should not express), ideologies about certain emotions (such as romance), and beliefs about emotional conformity and control (Thoits 1989).

31. According to Fantasia (1988), class consciousness is shaped by "cultures of solidarity," the process and experiences of collective struggle.

32. Clemens (1996) specifically refers to the organizational forms of social movement groups, but I extrapolate her point to a movement community's emotion culture that embodies the diagnosis of and remedy for their grievances—essentially how they operate internally and relate externally to others.

33. In Chua (2016), I draw from the literature on intersecting forms of discrimination on individuals (see, e.g., Crenshaw 1989; Collins 1990; Rosenblum 2009; Best et al. 2011) to analyze their impact on lesbian activists of the LGBT movement. Also see

Hildebrandt and Chua (2017) on the political economy of lesbian (in)visibility in LGBT movements in China and Myanmar.

34. Perhaps these identities are layers of sediments with different histories (De la Dehesa 2010, citing Butler 1993).

Chapter 2

1. For a history on the 1988 demonstrations, see Steinberg (2001), Charney (2009), and Taylor (2009). To date, Myanmar remains one of the poorest countries in the world. According to Asian Ranking in 2016, Myanmar's gross domestic product per capital was $1,711.

2. The military junta had blacklisted citizens and foreigners deemed to be political threats. In 2012, the semicivilian government reportedly removed about 2,000 names. In July 2016, the NLD government announced the removal of another 607 names, though thousands more remain blacklisted (Tin Htet Paing 2016).

3. On political activism among Burmese diaspora, see Egreteau (2012). On how Burmese human rights groups operated through pragmatic arrangements with local authorities, see Lang (2002).

4. Officially, Myanmar has eight "national races"—Burman, the majority, Mon, Shan, Karen, Kayah (Karenni), Kachin, Chin, and Arakan (Rakhine)—but the military junta also claimed 135 recognized ethnic groups. Scholars question the calculation method for the latter figure and argue that the military used it to undermine the political power of the seven major ethnic categories (Gravers 2007). Relations between the state and ethnic minorities were fractured and tense even before British colonization of what is today's Myanmar, but they were exacerbated by the British destruction of traditional political, social, and cultural structures (Selth 2012; Charney 2009), their differential treatments of Burman and ethnic minorities (Walton 2013; Williams 2009), and complications during World War II (Walton 2013; Callahan 2003). The 1948 Constitution of the Union of Burma provided ethnic minority states with the right of secession after ten years from the date it took effect, but the constitution's "quasi [ethnic]-federal structure" in the meantime offered them little meaningful devolution of power (Smith 2007). Within the first decade of independence from the British, ethnic armed groups had overrun a significant portion of its territory.

5. Seng Naw used the words *gay* and *transgender* in his English-language interview with me. When I sought clarification from him, he said the people to whom he referred did not use English terms and probably used the word *achauk*. I have asked ethnic minorities whether they knew of any word in their own languages that refer to queer people; so far, I have learned that they adopted Burmese words such as *achauk*, the language of Burmans, or directly translated the meanings of those words into their languages. For more on Burmese references to queer people, see Chapter 4 and the List of Terms Related to Queer People, Queer Cultures, or the LGBT movement in Myanmar.

6. Following the arrival of American missionaries in the early 1800s, the vast majority of Kachin Christians became Baptists (Rogers 2015). Seng Naw was and has re-

mained the only prominent non-Burman, non-Buddhist leader of the LGBT movement. See Chapter 5 for my analysis of the movement's Burman- and Buddhist-centric nature.

7. According to other interviewees and my conversations with David Gilbert, Seng Naw was disinherited by elders of his family because of his sexuality. I could not verify this information with Seng Naw, because he died from a chronic illness one month before I was scheduled to visit him in 2015. He was thirty-eight years old.

8. On December 26, 2004, an earthquake of 9.1 magnitude underneath the Indian Ocean generated a tsunami that caused the death of more than 200,000 people in Indonesia, Thailand, and twelve other countries (Taylor 2014).

9. Thailand is the largest receiving country of economic migrants from Myanmar, with numbers reported as high as 2 million (Chantavanich 2012). However, recent political developments may have begun to encourage Burmese migrants to return home (Mya Mya Thet and Pholphirul 2015).

10. According to Pyae Soe, families in his village sometimes sent their children to meet the government's demands for forced labor because children could not contribute significantly to the military's projects, an act that could be interpreted as subversive. He added that his family would send him only if the assignments were short and near their home.

11. To get to Mae Sot with relative safety, undocumented migrants like Kyaw Kyaw might slip back from Ranong into Myanmar, travel inland northward to Myawaddy, and then cross over to Thailand again.

12. Being a group of Burmese migrants, many of whom were undocumented, SUN-SHINE probably would have been unable to register as a legal entity in Thailand. It would also have been harder to convince international donors to provide funding directly to it because its leaders had no prior experience with NGO administration or grant management.

13. Because the earlier grants did not cover SUNSHINE's staffing, JUSTICE hired Kyaw Kyaw in order to provide his salary under its principal fund.

14. Seng Naw had to quit the movement in 2012 due to his chronic illness. Also see note 7 of this chapter. Seng Naw was replaced by Khant Nyar, who appears in Chapters 3, 4 and 5.

15. Khant Nyar carried out the expansion and recruitment after replacing Seng Naw in September 2012.

16. HIV/AIDS activism is also significant to the emergence of LGBT movements in other authoritarian contexts, such as China and Singapore, where organizations working on HIV/AIDS issues in the name of public health are more tolerated by governments (Chua and Hildebrandt 2014).

17. One of the junta's post-1988 restrictions was Law No. 6/88, The Law Relating to Forming of Organizations. It operated in tandem with the 1908 Unlawful Associations Act, as well as other laws and executive directives. To obtain approval under Law No. 6/88, a domestic NGO or community-based organization would have to submit an application according to Form A of Directive No. 1/88. The application would be considered by the relevant township, followed by the district, state, and regional levels. The

application had to disclose the identities of the proposed organization's executive committee members, a requirement that could lead to home visits by the police to conduct background checks and interviews with family members (Thazin, interview, September 27, 2012). Faced with these legal hurdles, most domestic organizations did not register at all, risking charges pursuant to Law No. 6/88 or any other law that authorities saw fit. Under military rule, associations that had official sanctions were mostly government-organized NGOs, associations whose leadership was closely linked to or trusted by the junta, groups with health- or development-oriented goals, and village associations, funeral societies, and cultural groups considered to pose little threat to the dictatorship (South 2004; but see Kyaw Yin Hlaing 2007). After transition to semicivilian rule, the Parliament on June 25, 2014, replaced Law No. 6/88 with the Association Registration Law, which provides for voluntary registration. President Thein Sein signed the new legislation into effect on July 20, 2014. VIVID's parent organization, JUSTICE, successfully registered under the Association Registration Law in August 2016. As of April 2017, VIVID leaders have no plans to register their organization separately.

18. The first officially recorded case of HIV infection in Myanmar was in 1988 (Myanmar Ministry of Health 2011). About 190,000 people were living with HIV/AIDS there, an estimated 15,176 people had died of AIDS-related illness, and 7,000 more were newly infected in 2013 (UNAIDS 2012).

19. I photographed the pages of this document provided by an interviewee, who was employed at an international NGO at the time of our interview in 2013.

20. After 2011, HIV/AIDS NGOs and other types of organizations have been more openly discussing human rights.

21. In 2007, the community-based organizations and self-help groups started referring to themselves as the "MSM network." As of 2012, the network consisted of 115 groups. I am grateful to David Gilbert for sharing this information in a letter from the MSM network secretary dated August 14, 2013. Also see Chua and Gilbert (2016) on HIV/AIDS-related civil society in Myanmar.

22. While the new constitution provides for a presidential system of governance with a bicameral legislature, it also reflects the military's continuous influence over politics. The military (Tatmadaw) is guaranteed 25 percent of the seats in both the lower house (Pyithu Hluttaw) and upper house of Parliament (Amyotha Hluttaw). In addition, six of eleven seats on the National Defence and Security Council, the highest executive authority in Myanmar, are guaranteed to and have in fact been occupied by Tatmadaw appointees.

23. On international NGOs and local groups' provision of humanitarian aid despite the government's impediments in the aftermath of Cyclone Nargis, see South (2008) and Centre for Peace and Conflict Studies (2009).

24. Every time Cho Cho went to Chiang Mai, she would give airport authorities a different reason for her trip: she had to see her grandmother or sister who was hospitalized in Thailand or she wanted to attend the Thai water festival, for example. If she went through Myawaddy-Mae Sot, she would tell authorities she was going to Thailand to buy cosmetics (interview, May 15, 2013).

25. See Chapter 3 on the forms of oppression lesbians face as people who are queer and were designated female at birth. Also see Chua (2016).

26. In Indonesia, *waria*, who were assigned male at birth and identify with the female gender, put lesbians in touch with international discourses (Blackwood 2010).

27. Although Dar Dar also describes herself as *gay*, her chosen name is feminine and others often refer to her as "Aunty [Dar Dar]," a common way of referring respectfully to older *apwint*. See Chapter 4 on queer Burmese's reinterpretation and adoption of LGBT identities.

28. Aung Aung referred to himself as *tomboy* in earlier interviews, but he explained in a follow-up interview in August 2016 that he had changed his identity to *trans man*. See Chapter 4 on the shifting use of LGBT identities among queer Burmese.

29. Although Aung Aung uses *T.G.* to describe this family member as somebody who was assigned male at birth and identifies with the female gender, he refers to this person as "uncle."

30. The fears of participating in human rights activism also existed among Burmese living in Thailand. Most of them had family back in Myanmar or had plans to return one day.

31. In making this observation, I am keenly aware of the silence that fear may engender among Burmese people, who may suppress or deny fear as a strategy of survival under military rule (Skidmore 2003, 2004).

32. Interviewees report the gradual easing of controls at travel checkpoints and feeling less fearful of getting involved with human rights after 2011 (though it is uncertain to what extent their experiences are generalizable to other political causes).

33. JUSTICE, which applied for funding for VIVID when it was still a program under the parent organization, used the phrase, "multiplier effect," in some of its grant applications.

34. Tun Tun published three volumes of a magazine in the early 2000s. Pyae Soe and Seng Naw adopted the same name for VIVID's magazine and numbered their first issue as "volume 4" in 2008. With the assistance of Pyae Soe and Zwe Naung, I found a rare copy of volume 3, published in 2001; we could not locate the first two.

35. Without funding or resources to travel to Myanmar for filming, Pyae Soe and Seng Naw started with interviews with Burmese living in Thailand. When they obtained funding in 2012, they went to Myanmar for two weeks of filming, which sustained their output for almost one year. They also interviewed grassroots organizers who traveled from Myanmar to Thailand for workshops and meetings.

36. The Internet and social media are gradually becoming accessible and being used by LGBT activists to publicize their organizations and activities.

37. Before the enactment of the 2014 Association Registration Law (see note 17 of this chapter), Cho Cho looked for shops in Yangon willing to print their magazines despite VIVID's lack of legal registration. She tested the shops by asking for quotes to see which ones were open to negotiation. She told shopkeepers that their magazines were not for sale and they would state "free distribution in project area" on the back cover, following the practice of other NGOs in Myanmar. She showed the shopkeepers samples

of the magazine, tried to convince them that it was "not strong about politics or human rights," and struck "an understanding" with them (interview, September 23, 2013).

38. They were the IDAHO celebrations described in the news report that first sparked my interest in the movement.

Chapter 3

1. Maung Nyan and Kaung Sat attended some of these earlier trainings.

2. During the March 2013 interview, Yamin described herself as *gay* to indicate somebody who has not yet totally expressed herself outwardly as a woman. Two years later, she called herself *meinmashar* and *trans woman*, meaning she had become *apwint*, someone who openly expresses her female gender identity, including in her appearance and attire. Later in this chapter, I discuss Yamin's increased confidence about her gender identity. On the Burmese use of LGBT identity terms and changes to individuals' adoption of identity terms, see Chapter 4.

3. Emphasizing the relative standings and distribution of power within Burmese social hierarchy, Keeler (2017) argues that subordinate positions do not necessarily result in demeaning experiences, though they sometimes may be experienced as such. He applies this view to heterosexual, cisgender women, *apwint*, and *tomboys*. It is possible that people with lower social positions in Myanmar do not always feel debased. The experiences of queer Burmese, like queer people anywhere else, vary across individuals. Some of my interviewees report knowing queers who feel accepted and well treated by families and friends. However, in this book, I focus on the people who regard their experiences as demeaning or learn to do so and how they come to reexamine and change their feelings about those experiences after coming into contact with human rights activists.

4. Other explanations include spirits and the supernatural, which I discuss later in this chapter, and mundane scientific explanations (Spiro 1967; Keyes 1983a).

5. Ikeya (2005, 2011) and Than (2014) criticize the stereotypical view that Burmese women enjoy freedom and almost equal status to men.

6. Nuns in Myanmar are not fully ordained. They are expected to manage finances and undertake merit-making activities of making donations to pagodas, but their handling of monetary affairs, which is not expected of monks, is deemed to be spiritually polluting (Ikeya 2005); however, see Keeler (2017) on monks' handling of money when they are away from laypeople or among people they trust. The prohibition on women's ordainment has been successfully challenged in Sri Lanka and has stirred up controversy in Thailand (Falk 2007).

7. A year later, in his August 2016 interview, Aung Aung said he preferred to call himself *trans man*. For more on changes to the adoption of identity terms, see Chapter 4.

8. One day, the man who usually drove me to and from fieldwork locations on the outskirts of Yangon asked why I was always hanging out with *achauk*. After hearing an explanation about my research, he retorted, "Oh, they are like that because they did something wrong in their past lives."

9. Gilbert (2016) attributes the pressure to *anade*, a social norm that imposes self-

restraint in social interactions so as to avoid causing distress, discomfort, or offense to the other party.

10. The father of a Karen Christian interviewee tied his hands at night to a mango tree when he was ten years old. The mango tree was believed to be haunted, and his father wanted to "bring my braveness out" and "change me" (Saw Eh Toh, interview, May 7, 2013*). In the course of our respective fieldwork, David Gilbert (2016) and I have also heard of Kachin patrilineal rules of inheritance being used to exclude queers who were assigned male at brith from inheriting ancestral lands and to pressure those designated female into marriage in order to gain access to land.

11. But I also find varying Muslim experiences. One Muslim interviewee from Tanintharyi Region reported having an accepting family.

12. Interviewees who are *tomboys*, *lesbians*, or *trans men* report rape by brothers and other relatives. They believe they were attacked because they are not heteronormative or gender conforming. Nyan Lin, for example, was raped by cousins and a brother-in-law. "I wasn't behaving like I'm supposed to be, as a girl, so [the cousins] wanted to give me a lesson," and the brother-in-law said, "You are a girl, and you are going to get married one day, and you have to be like a girl" (Nyan Lin, interview, June 28, 2015). The movement's documentation of incidents in three different towns also regularly recorded incidents of sexual assaults of *tomboys*, *lesbians*, and *trans men*.

13. Abortion is illegal in Myanmar, except when it is carried out in "good faith" to save the woman's life under Section 312 of the Penal Code. In general, abortion is socially unacceptable in Burmese society.

14. Whereas the 1899 Rangoon Police Act covers today's Yangon Township, the 1945 Police Act extends to areas described in the Secretary of Home Department Notification Nos. 303 (March 19, 1946), 421, and 422 (May 22, 1947). The respective provisions, each providing for a maximum prison term of three months, are vaguely worded enough to empower the police to arrest without warrant anybody they deem suspicious or undesirable. Section 30(d) of the Rangoon Police Act allows for the arrest of "any person found between sunset and sunrise, within the precincts of any dwelling-house or other building whatsoever, or on board any vessel, without being able satisfactorily to account for his presence." The Police Act allows the police to arrest anybody "found between sunset and sunrise having his face covered or otherwise disguised, who is unable to give a satisfactory account of himself" under Section 35(c), or "found within the precincts of any dwelling-house other building whatsoever, or in any back-drainage space, on board any vessel, without being able satisfactorily to account for his presence therein" under Section 35(d).

15. According to lawyer interviewees and the LGBT movement's documentation, sex workers who are heterosexual, cisgender women and other vulnerable social groups experience similar patterns of persecution.

16. The Indian Penal Code, the predecessor of penal codes in other British colonies, was enacted in 1860 and first applied to Myanmar under British rule. Section 377 of the Penal Code states, "Whoever voluntarily has carnal intercourse against the order of nature with any man, woman or animal shall be punished with transportation for life, or

with imprisonment of either description for a term which may extend to ten years, and shall also be liable to fine." In 2016, when the Penal Code was amended to update its terminology, references to "transportation for life" were replaced with "imprisonment for a term of twenty years." On the surface, Section 377 covers heterosexual conduct as well. However, LGBT activists conclude from their documented incidents over the years that the law is used to target queers who were assigned male at birth.

17. For example, in July 2013, after taking twelve queer persons into custody, Mandalay police officers stripped and photographed the arrestees, hit and grabbed their hair or breasts, interrogated them about how they had sex with men, and then forced them to frog-hop, catwalk, polish officers' shoes, and clean tables (Asian Human Rights Commission 2013; Zarni Mann 2013). If convicted and incarcerated, queers can also be subject to beating and rape in prison (Equality Myanmar 2012), though *apwint* may be placed in separate cells from the gender-normative male population in major Burmese prisons. *Apwint* inmates can also be denied medical treatment. For example, Gun San Naw, an HIV-positive *apwint*, was denied access to antiretroviral medication to suppress the progression of the HIV virus. For more information on Gun San Naw's lawsuit, see the "New Claims" section in this chapter.

18. According to interviews with lawyers and queers who were arrested, bribes usually start from 200,000 kyat (U$200), depending on whether the bribed parties know of the arrestee's financial situation. In fact, the culture of bribery is so entrenched that interviewees do not differentiate between bribes and fines. I had to ask them to clarify what they meant when they said they had made "payment" as the result of an arrest. For a general discussion on police and judicial corruption in Myanmar, see Cheesman (2015) and Prasse-Freeman (2015).

19. See, e.g., Second Police Corporal Nay Zin Tun v. Lin Ko Ko (or) Lin Lin (2012) Major Crime No. 982, Mingalartaungnyunt Township Court, Yangon Division (on file with the author). On the influence of police testimonies in the courtroom and how judges often do not convict based on the law, see Cheesman (2015).

20. Aung Aung's experience in school related in Chapter 2 is one example of ostracism by teachers. For other examples, see Chua and Gilbert (2015, 2016).

21. On the concept of human rights in Myanmar, also see the discussion in "Infused Meanings of Human Rights and LGBT Identities" in Chapter 1.

22. I use "suffering" in the common English meaning of the word, rather than the more complex understandings of "suffering" associated with Buddhism.

23. Burmese subjects in Skidmore's study (2003) used the gesture of the thumb pressed into the palm of the hand when referring to the military to symbolize its brutality. The gesture, Skidmore noticed, was often accompanied by the phrase "pressed down" to indicate the feeling of being trapped and pinned down.

24. See note 2 in "Note on Language" for further explanation of *nat* and *nat* worship.

25. Others follow the less common practices of *weikza* cults. *Weikza* are mystical beings who used to be humans but, through esoteric and occult practices, take themselves out of the karmic cycle of life without dying and remain in this world to await

the coming of the next Buddha (Brac de la Perrière 2009a; also see Brac de la Perrière, Rozenberg, and Turner 2014).

26. I retrieved this set of minutes from a pile of documents discarded by VIVID activists (see the appendix). The minutes were written in English and addressed from Kyaw Kyaw to Seng Naw, so they were probably produced for the purpose of reporting to the international donors of SUNSHINE, whose funds were administered by JUSTICE. The document is not dated, but judging from the contents, it was probably written in 2010.

27. Fletcher (2011) finds that Burmese HIV/AIDS prevention programs extolled "good behavior" and adherence to "cultural" or "traditional" norms.

28. LGBT activists sometimes use *eain dre* and *theit khar* interchangeably as abbreviated forms of *eain dre theit khar*. However, *eain dre* is more concerned with behavior, such as manner of speech, dressing, and walking, whereas *theit khar* indicates a person's moral character. Combined as *eain dre theit khar*, the term connotes both behavior and moral character, but LGBT activists often use the term to refer specifically to *apwint* behavior. The popular *Thalun English-Myanmar Dictionary* (2013) defines "dignity" interchangeably as *eain dre*, *gong*, and *gong theit khar*, which may cause confusion with the reference to "human dignity," *lu gone theit khar*. However, LGBT activists do have in mind different concepts when they speak of *lu gone theit khar*, by which they mean "human dignity" in the context of human rights, and *eain dre theit khar*, by which they mean dignified behavior and moral character.

29. The traditional role and social position of Buddhist kings, including those of Buddhist Burma, also come with obligations (Keown 2012).

30. As this book went to press, Myanmar media reported an alleged same-sex rape by an HIV-positive *gay* man in Yangon. Speaking to a reporter, one LGBT activist described the news as a "huge blow" for the movement's fight for legal reform. He was worried that LGBT people in Myanmar as a whole would now be accused of wanting to repeal Section 377 of the Penal Code in order to engage in nonconsensual intercourse. He pleaded to the public, "Please do not generalize and look down on all LGBTs just because of the action of one LGBT person," and urged LGBT people in Myanmar to "restrain desire with dignity [*theit khar*]" as the actions of one LGBT person could have a negative impact on the entire group (media report, March 17, 2018). On the activist's use of *theit khar*, see note 28 of this chapter.

31. Ferree (2003) points out that some activists pursue culturally resonant tactics to achieve movement success and accept the potential cost of sacrificing more transformative possibilities.

32. Cho Cho, who knew Chan Thar as an HIV/AIDS outreach worker, invited Chan Thar to her one-day discussions in Yangon and put him in touch with VIVID.

33. On the state of Burmese legal education and profession, see Saffin and Willis (2017).

34. For more details on Yamin's gender identity, see Chapters 4 and 5.

35. The phrase can also refer to children generally.

36. In his study on LGBT activism in the Philippines, Thoreson (2011) noticed that affirmations by other people were important to his subjects' sense of dignity. Morreira

(2016) also observed that being able to look after one's family was significant to the Shona understanding of dignity in Zimbabwe.

37. For recent writings about the struggles of everyday "survival," see Maung Thawnghmung (2011) and Prasse-Freeman (2012).

38. The phenomenon of making use of NGO connections at the grassroots to build patronage is not unique to my study or to Myanmar. For example, in Malawi, local residents participate in international NGOs' human rights activities because they want to generate supplementary income from reimbursements and allowances and create opportunities to build up their own patronage networks (Swidler 2009, 2013). See Chapter 5 on tensions between national leaders and grassroots organizers of the movement.

39. LGBT activists from areas in Myanmar with little Internet access make use of better Internet connections in urban areas to catch up on social media during their trips.

40. See Chapter 4 for the second essential component of their distinctive emotion culture, an inclusive manner of queer bonding.

41. See Chapter 5 on LGBT activists' navigation of multiple identities.

42. Informal social networks connected to HIV/AIDS-related community-based organizations and self-help groups include those formed around niche occupations. Some partner with HIV/AIDS programs to provide vocational training for *apwint* and *apone* to achieve economic independence in those occupations. As explained in Chapter 2, during the military regime, HIV/AIDS organizations did not openly speak of human rights or characterize the conditions of queer Burmese as human rights violations. They began to provide human rights training to their beneficiaries and affiliated groups and more openly incorporated human rights discourse into their work after the changeover to semi-civilian governance.

43. Gilbert (2016) observed that the female beauty industry had superseded other niche occupations, including spirit mediumship and sex work. He also noticed, though for reasons that cannot be clearly explained, *apwint* and *apone* have squeezed out cisgender women and dominated these occupations in their stead (also see Ho 2009).

44. However, because *nat kadaw* command respect among *nat* followers, some people may pretend to be *nat kadaw*, causing nonfollowers to dismiss them as "hoaxers," said Zin Yaw, who is a *nat kadaw* (interview, August 3, 2016). Ho (2009) argues that anti-*nat* worship views reflect masculinist disavowal of superstition and femininity (also see Keeler 2017).

45. On other differences between the older queer communities and the LGBT movement's, see Chapters 4 and 5.

46. One group, formed in 2016, advocates for *transgender* Burmese and organizes workshops to educate them about human rights. Upon clarification with the leader, I learned that the group focuses on *trans women* (it does not reach out to *trans men*). It is also a fledging organization, without an expansive network like the LGBT movement's.

47. The lawsuit questioned the trial court's findings of fact and accused the police of misconduct for unduly pressuring the arrestee, Gun San Naw, to plead guilty by withholding his access to antiretroviral medication meant for suppressing the progression of the HIV virus. The morning after pleading guilty and receiving a seven-day sentence,

Gun San Naw asked to contact his family so that they could bring the medication to him. The officer on duty replied that people like him "deserve whatever you've got" and refused to let him contact anybody (Gun San Naw (a) Naw Naw v. Republic of the Union of Myanmar, Mandalay State Court, Appellant Brief). Two months after his release, Gun San Naw's CD4 cell count, which indicates the health of one's immune system, dropped from approximately 350 to 200 (a count below 200 is a qualification for AIDS diagnosis) (Cindy, interview, September 23, 2013). Fortunately for Gun San Naw, his health had improved by the time of our interview on July 4, 2015 (Gun San Naw identifies as *apwint*, even though he refers to himself as *kyun taw*, the male "I," in his affidavit and uses gender-neutral self-referencing in interviews for this study).

48. The quality of the documentation does vary, depending on the activist who wrote the report.

Chapter 4

1. It is possible that some interviewees thought they had to display their approval of "LGBT" to me, an English-speaking foreigner, or to come across as modern (an issue addressed in the appendix). However, the consistency of responses across interviewees and over time in the course of my fieldwork gives validity to the finding. In any case, at the very least, movement leaders espouse and spread this view. Moreover, it is possible that activists increasingly approved of LGBT identity terms as they became more involved with the movement and influenced by other activists, interactions that are part of community building.

2. I asked interviewees who identify as ethnic minorities whether they know of any word in their own languages that refer to queer people. They said they were unsure and that they adopted Burmese words or directly translated the meanings of those Burmese words into their languages; also see note 5 of Chapter 2.

3. During his fieldwork on *trans women* and *apwint* in Yangon, David Gilbert came across such Burmese references as "shit giver," "chick with balls," and "black bean paste" (personal communication, April 2014).

4. Burmese who were involved with international HIV/AIDS NGOs or who could access the Internet would have come across LGBT identities. However, as I emphasize in this chapter, adopting an LGBT identity does not necessarily count as being part of the movement community, which is premised on a shared human rights practice.

5. Sometimes when VIVID leaders jot down notes on attendance lists or write reports, they refer to fellow activists and participants with LGBT identity terms that do not match their self-identifications, but they do not insist that those people adopt their references.

6. Some interviewees regard *meinmashar* ("man acting as woman") and *yaukkashar* ("woman acting as man"), which respectively refer to *apwint* and *tomboys*, as derogatory, while others react to them neutrally or use them for self-ascription.

7. MSM also covers *tha nge, ingahlan*, and *offer*. See the explanations in the List of Terms Related to Queer People, Queer Cultures, or the LGBT Movement in Myanmar.

8. If *trans men* or *tomboys'* feminine-presenting partners identify as heterosexual, like *tha nge*, they would not be regarded as queer.

9. Pyae Soe may have preferred to identify as *gay* to avoid upsetting his mother too much, but this is conjecture and difficult to verify. Pyae Soe refers to himself using the male gender pronoun, uses a male name, and generally keeps a masculine-presenting appearance, occasionally putting on a long-haired wig and women's high-heeled shoes for the camera or special occasions.

10. To be clear, this divide does not concern the debates about trans women and feminism. For an overview of those issues elsewhere, see Connell (2012), Green (2006), and Stryker (2007).

11. Gilbert (2016) documented the queer slang reference to "eating grapes" (having sex with soldiers). Also see Chapter 5's discussion regarding sexual banter among LGBT activists assigned male at birth and its impact on lesbian participation in the movement.

12. But *homo* is sometimes also used as a synonym for *apone*. See the explanation in the List of Terms Related to Queer People, Queer Cultures, or the LGBT Movement in Myanmar.

13. When I asked if they had a Burmese word for themselves, Pyae Soe and Naing Lin chose *apwint*, because the meaning of "open" means they do not hide who they are. It is beyond the scope of this book to examine how people come to understand their sexualities as being independent of their gender identities, such as in the studies conducted by Jackson (2000, 2009), Boellstorff (2005), and Chauncey (1994), respectively on Thailand, Indonesia, and New York.

14. It is also possible that those who claim to be *gay* instead of *transgender* or *apwint* do so to avoid causing distress to their families too much. See the discussion on Pyae Soe in note 9 of this chapter.

15. Cisgender women do serve as *nat kadaw*. Also see the List of Terms Related to Queer People, Queer Cultures, or the LGBT Movement in Myanmar and note 43 of Chapter 3.

16. Although the new *transgender* group formed in 2016 offers human rights training and advocacy work, it targets *trans women*. Also see note 46 of Chapter 3.

17. The quoted statement comes from a video recording provided to the broadcaster by one of two *apwint* beauticians who did not accept the invitation to speak on the panel with LGBT activists.

18. On kinship among beauticians, see Gilbert (2016), and among *nat kadaw*, see Brac de la Perrière (2009b) and Gilbert (2016).

19. Gilbert (2016) argues that the relationships between *nat kadaw* and spirits are affective in nature, whereas the LGBT movement's make demands of one another. In contrast, I find that both the LGBT movement and other queer communities comprise affective relationships, but the relationships are anchored in dissimilar practices.

20. See note 17 of Chapter 3.

21. For an assessment of the Myanmar National Human Rights Commission, see Crouch (2013) and Renshaw (2017).

22. ASEAN governments have resisted the explicit recognition of the human rights of sexual and gender minorities in the declaration. For a discussion, see Langlois (2014).

Chapter 5

1. The wedding was a symbolic one without legal effect because same-sex marriages are not legally recognized in Myanmar.

2. At least one location held a *transgender* beauty pageant during IDAHO 2014 with alternative sponsorship (IDAHO 2014 report, VIVID).

3. Social movements studies observe that activists may have more success at mobilizing rural communities by using traditional forms of communication and expression, such as poetry, music, and dance (Aminzade and McAdam 2001).

4. Also see note 38 of Chapter 3.

5. When SUNSHINE, described in Chapter 2, was based in Ranong, Thailand, it received international funding administered by JUSTICE, VIVID's parent organization, and served as an important base for organizing queer Burmese working in southern Thailand. Following its leaders' repatriation in the mid-2010s, SUNSHINE was relocated to Tanintharyi Region, where it became one of the movement's grassroots organizations.

6. As observed during a phone conversation captured on a film promoted by the LGBT movement about queer Burmese.

7. During the interview on July 8, 2015, Yamin showed me the text messages with her mother. But as pointed out in note 35 of Chapter 3, *tha the me* is also used to refer to children generally.

8. See note 6 of this chapter.

9. Other times Yamin refers to herself in her own name, thus avoiding gendered pronouns. This is not an unusual way in Burmese to refer to oneself.

10. Gilbert (2016) observes that *apwint, apone,* and *trans women* often engage in "penis size banter" and share sexually explicit photographs of their lovers on mobile phones.

11. Whether human rights will be realized by legal reforms or simply be paid lip-service in Burmese politics remains to be seen. On the legacy of abuse of power and arbitrary rule in Myanmar and the challenge for realizing rule of law and human rights, see Cheesman (2015).

12. Lawyers such as Cindy and Ywet War who became activists of the LGBT movement did not learn much about human rights from their formal legal education. They have mainly learned about human rights from the movement and other international NGOs. Also see note 33 of Chapter 3.

13. Women's rights activists who opposed the Laws for the Protection of Race and Religion, regulating interfaith marriage, religious conversion, population control, and polygamy (see note 7 of the Introduction), faced harassment, vilification, and death threats (Walton, McKay, and Daw Khin Mar Mar Kyi 2015).

14. In other societies such as the United States (Wolf 1979; Taylor and Whittier 1992; Esterberg 1994; Gilmore and Kaminski 2007), Indonesia (Blackwood 2007), Singapore (Lyons 2004), India (Dave 2011), and Peru (Jitsuya and Sevilla 2003), women's rights groups have also avoided being publicly associated with lesbian politics for fear that their groups would lose legitimacy.

15. For an older and alternative definition of "homonormativity," see Stryker (2008).

16. For a description of rituals at a *nat* festival, see Brac de la Perrière (2005).

17. However, heteronormative norms are not completely irrelevant to *nat kadaw*. Although being *nat kadaw* helps queers resist heteronormativity and gain visibility, Ho (2009) cautions against reading into the occupation and *nat* rituals unfettered freedom for sexual fluidity and gender transgression. Interpreting the origins of certain female *nat* as tragic mythologies of feminine affect and virtue, she critiques the cult of *nat* worship for disciplining sexuality and gender norms. Gilbert (2016) also notes that *nat kadaw* who are queers assigned male at birth do not marry male spirits, only female ones.

18. See Chapter 3 generally on the lower social status of women.

19. Lesbians generally do not diverge from the two views. Aung Aung, who identifies as a *tomboy* and, later, a *trans man*, is one of the few exceptions (Aung Aung, interview, August 3, 2016). However, I am unsure where Aung Aung stands on the larger issue of heteronormative norms, since he endorses good "behavior" for everyone (interview, August 1, 2016) and wants to behave like "a very good man" and "will never drink [beer] . . . to keep a very good character for a man" (interview, July 2, 2015).

20. A question asking about one's *lu myo* is commonly understood as pertaining to race or ethnicity, and not one's nationality, for which a phrase such as *naing ngan thar* would be used. It is also important to know that government-issued identity cards may be inconsistent with the interview answers. The cards usually specify the person's ethnic descent from both parents, showing a series of hyphenated categories, such as Karen-*Bamar*-Shan-*Bamar* (one parent has Karen and Burman ethnicity, and the other parent has Shan and Burman descent).

21. On discrimination against people of South Asian descent in Burmese society, see Ikeya (2005) and Nyi Nyi Kyaw (2015).

22. My assistants and I did not feel comfortable asking interviewees over the phone, when trying to set up interviews, about their ethnicities or religious affiliations. I left the question to the actual interviews to find out. See the appendix on my fieldwork experience.

23. Cindy happened to be traveling to a few towns in Chin State as part of her work for an international NGO, and she brought Yamin along to introduce her to a few contacts.

Conclusion

1. In reality, the Burmese military's weaponry is probably manufactured in various Western and non-Western countries.

2. I am grateful to the generous comments by both of my publisher's reviewers. They could not have said it better than me in characterizing the strengths of the book, so I have built this section based on their encouraging words.

3. Social movements studies that analyze emotions tend not to focus on close analysis of movements' human rights practices (see, e.g., Gould 2009; Jasper 1997).

4. See note 25 of Chapter 1 about the treatment of the "cultural" in the concept of human rights practice as a way of life.

5. Sociolegal studies find that agents of transformation (Felstiner, Abel, and Sarat 1981), such as family and friends, counselors, activists, social workers, and lawyers, can turn individuals into rights claimants by educating them about their rights and encouraging them to make rights demands (see, e.g., McCann 1994; Merry 2003b; Albiston 2010; Gallagher 2017).

6. In other words, human rights studies on activism or social movements can be differentiated from those concerned with "horizontal consciousness" (Engel 2012), the spread of rights consciousness among people not involved with activism or any movement. However, local activists, including LGBT activists in this book, are usually so-called ordinary folks themselves. Their adoption of rights can also count as the spread of rights' resonance on the ground or at least cannot be easily demarcated from the "horizontal." I am grateful to Michael McCann for our conversation on the issue of local activists and horizontal consciousness.

7. Santos and Rodríguez-Garavito (2005) argue that counterhegemonic actors at the grassroots can only bring about sustained legal change through collective action.

8. Instead, it was the colonial powers, most notably Britain, that denied the universal nature of human rights (Roberts 2015).

9. Comparing the arguments of abortion activists in the United States and Germany, Ferree (2003) argues that what is radical or resonant depends on context and culture. Also see Polletta (2000) and Chua (2014).

Appendix

1. Prior to the September 2012 travels, I received human subjects' approval from my institution to conduct the study for its duration.

2. My detection of little fear does not mean there was no fear in participating in my research at all, as interviewees may have denied or covered it up.

3. Although *anade* does not seem to have an entirely equivalent English term, people in other societies may also feel compelled to behave in a certain manner. In that sense, while *anade* is unique to Burmese society, the researcher's challenges of dealing with human nature to conform or seek approval are not.

4. Moora spent a lot of effort to work out which names on the documents corresponded to which interviewees. We knew some of the interviewees only by their preferred nicknames, which are often nothing close to their formal or given names.

5. When doing research in Thailand, Jackson (2017) noticed that his interviewees might want to figure out what he, the Western researcher, wanted to hear or present to him the impression of possessing "Western rationality."

6. Moora and Khine Khine, both from Yangon, expressed some difficulty with understanding regional accents such as those from Tanintharyi Region.

7. I found out in 2013 that Seng Naw had returned to Kachin State (he later moved to another part of the country, where he died). Because armed conflict between the Kachin Independence Army and the Burmese military was ongoing, visiting him at home would have been difficult and hazardous for a foreigner like me. One possibility would have been to meet him in China across the border from Kachin State. Eventually, with David Gilbert's assistance, I contacted Seng Naw online. He was using a very weak Internet connection, probably along the Myanmar-China border or in a border town on the Chinese side. After several difficult attempts at messaging each other online, he and I finally managed to set up an interview meeting inside Myanmar.

References

Abrams, Kathryn. 2002. "The Progress of Passion." *Michigan Law Review* 100:1602–1620.
———. 2011. "Emotions in the Mobilization of Rights." *Harvard Civil Rights–Civil Liberties Law Review* 46:551–589.
Abrams, Kathryn, and Hila Keren. 2010. "Who's Afraid of Law and the Emotions?" *Minnesota Law Review* 94:1997–2074.
Albiston, Catherine R. 2010. *Institutional Inequality and the Mobilization of the Family and Medical Leave Act: Rights on Leave.* New York: Cambridge University Press.
Alimi, Eitan Y., Bosi Lorenzo, and Chares Demetriou. 2012. "Relational Dynamics and Processes of Radicalization: A Comparative Framework." *Mobilization: An International Journal* 17:7–26.
Allen, Lori. 2013. *The Rise and Fall of Human Rights: Cynicism and Politics in Occupied Palestine.* Palo Alto: Stanford University Press.
Altman, Dennis. 2001. *Global Sex.* Chicago: University of Chicago Press.
———. 2006. "On Global Queering." *Australian Humanities Review.* http://www.australianhumanitiesreview.org/archive/Issue-July-1996/altman.html?ref=Sex%C5%9Ehop.Com (accessed June 11, 2017).
Alvarez, Sonia E., Evelina Dagnino, and Arturo Escobar. 1998. "Introduction: The Cultural and the Political in Latin American Social Movements." In *Cultures of Politics, Politics of Culture: Re-visioning Latin American Social Movements,* edited by Sonia E. Alvarez, Evelina Dagnino, and Arturo Escobar, 1–29. Boulder, CO: Westview Press.
Aminzade, Ron, and Doug McAdam. 2001. "Emotions and Contentious Politics." In *Silence and Voice in the Study of Contentious Politics,* edited by Ronald R. Aminzade, Jack A. Goldstone, Doug McAdam, Elizabeth J. Perry, William H. Sewell Jr., Sidney Tarrow, and Charles Tilly, 14–50. New York: Cambridge University Press.
An-Na'im, Abdullahi A. 2011. *Muslims and Global Justice.* Philadelphia: University of Pennsylvania Press.
Armstrong, Elizabeth A. 2002. *Forging Gay Identities: Organizing Sexuality in San Francisco, 1950–1994.* Chicago: University of Chicago Press.
Asian Human Rights Commission. 2013. "Burma: Police Torture of Gay and Transgendered People." http://www.humanrights.asia/news/ahrc-news/AHRCSTM-137-2013 (accessed July 10, 2014).

Aspinall, Edward, and Nicholas Farrelly. 2014. "Introduction to Special Issue: Myanmar's Democratization: Comparative and South East Asian Perspectives Introduction." *South East Asia Research* 22 (2): 163–169.

Aung San Suu Kyi. 1995. *Freedom from Fear and Other Writings*. London: Penguin Books.

Bandes, Susan A., ed. 1999. "Introduction." In *The Passions of Law*, edited by Susan A. Bandes, 1–16. Chicago: University of Chicago Press.

Bandes, Susan A., and Jeremy A. Blumenthal. 2012. "Emotion and the Law." *Annual Review of Law and Social Sciences* 8:161–181.

Barbalet, Jack. 1998. *Emotion, Social Theory, and Social Structure: A Macrosociological Approach*. Cambridge: Cambridge University Press.

———. 2002. "Introduction: Why Emotions Are Crucial." In *Emotions and Sociology*, edited by Jack Barbalet, 1–9. Oxford: Blackwell.

Barclay, Scott, Mary Bernstein, and Anna-Maria Marshall. 2009. *Queer Mobilizations: LGBT Activists Confront the Law*. New York: New York University Press.

Baxi, Upendra. 2002. *The Future of Human Rights*. Oxford: Oxford University Press.

Benford, Robert. 1997. "An Insider's Critique of the Social Movement Framing Perspective." *Sociological Inquiry* 67 (4): 409–430.

Benford, Robert, and David A. Snow. 2000. "Framing Processes and Social Movements: An Overview and Assessment." *Annual Review of Sociology* 26:611–639.

Bericat, Eduardo. 2016. "The Sociology of Emotions: Four Decades of Progress." *Current Sociology* 64 (3): 491–513.

Berk, Hillary L. 2015. "The Legalization of Emotion: Managing Risk by Managing Feelings in Contracts for Surrogate Labor." *Law and Society Review* 49 (1): 143–77.

Bernstein, Mary. 2005. "Identity Politics." *Annual Review of Sociology* 31:47–74.

Best, Rachel K., Lauren B. Edelman, Linda Hamilton Krieger, and Scott R. Eliason. 2011. "Multiple Disadvantages: An Empirical Test of Intersectionality Theory in EEO Litigation." *Law and Society Review* 45 (4): 991–1025.

Binnie, Jon. 2004. *The Globalization of Sexuality*. London: Sage.

Blackwood, Evelyn. 2007. "Regulation of Sexuality in Indonesian Discourse: Normative Gender, Criminal Law and Shifting Strategies of Control." *Culture, Health and Sexuality* 9 (3): 293–307.

———. 2010. *Falling into the Lesbi World: Desire and Difference in Indonesia*. Honolulu: University of Hawaii Press.

Blackwood, Evelyn, and Saskia E. Wieringa. 2007. "Introduction." In *Women's Sexualities and Masculinities in a Globalizing Asia*, edited by Saskia E. Wieringa, Evelyn Blackwood, and Abha Bhaiya, 1–20. New York: Palgrave Macmillan.

Bob, Clifford. 2005. *The Marketing of Rebellion: Insurgents, Media, and International Activism*. New York: Cambridge University Press.

———. ed. 2009. *The International Struggle for New Human Rights*. Philadelphia: University of Pennsylvania Press.

Boellstorff, Tom. 2005. *The Gay Archipelago: Sexuality and Nation in Indonesia*. Princeton: Princeton University Press.

———. 2009. "The Emergence of Political Homophobia in Indonesia: Masculinity and National Belonging." In *Homophobias: Lust and Loathing Across Time and Space*, edited by David A. B. Murray, 123–145. Durham, NC: Duke University Press.

Boellstorff, Tom, and Johan Lindquist. 2004. "Bodies of Emotion: Rethinking Culture and Emotion Through Southeast Asia." *Ethnos* 69 (4): 437–444.

Bornstein, Brian H., and Richard L. Wiener. 2006. "Introduction to the Special Issue on Emotion in Legal Judgment and Decision Making." *Law and Human Behavior* 30 (2): 115–118.

Bosco, Fernando J. 2007. "Emotions That Build Networks: Geographies of Human Rights Movements in Argentina and Beyond." *Tijdschrift voor Economische en Sociale Geografie* 98 (5): 545–563.

Bosi, Lorenzo, Marco Giugni, and Katrin Uba. 2016. *The Consequences of Social Movements*. Cambridge: Cambridge University Press.

Boutcher, Steven A. 2010. "Mobilizing in the Shadow of the Law: Lesbian and Gay Rights in the Aftermath of Bowers v. Hardwick." In *Research in Social Movements, Conflicts and Change*, edited by Patrick G. Coy, 175–205. Bingley: Emerald Group.

Boyd, Lydia. 2013. "The Problem with Freedom: Homosexuality and Human Rights in Uganda." *Anthropological Quarterly* 86:697–724.

Brac de la Perrière, Bénédicte. 2005. "The Taungbyon Festival: Locality and Nation-Confronting in the Cult of the 37 Lords." In *Burma at the Turn of the Twenty-First Century*, edited by Monique Skidmore, 65–79. Honolulu: University of Hawaii Press.

———. 2009a. "An Overview of the Field of Religion in Burmese Studies." *Asian Ethnology* 68 (2): 185–210.

———. 2009b. " 'Nats' Wives' or 'Children of Nats': From Spirit Possession to Transmission Among the Ritual Specialists of the Cult of the Thirty-Seven Lords." *Asian Ethnology* 68 (2): 283–305.

Brac de la Perrière, Bénédicte, Guillaume Rozenberg, and Alicia Turner, eds. 2014. *Champions of Buddhism: Weikza Cults in Contemporary Burma*. Singapore: National University of Singapore Press.

Brown, Wendy. 2004. " 'The Most We Can Hope For . . . ': Human Rights and the Politics of Fatalism." *South Atlantic Quarterly* 103 (2/3): 451–463.

Bruner, Jerome. 1990. *Acts of Meaning*. Cambridge, MA: Harvard University Press.

Buechler, Steven. 1995. "New Social Movement Theories." *Sociological Quarterly* 36 (3): 441–464.

Butler, Judith. 1993. *Bodies That Matter: On the Discursive Limits of 'Sex.'* New York: Routledge.

Calhoun, Craig. 1991. "The Problem of Identity in Collective Action." In *Macro-Micro Linkages in Sociology*, edited by Joan Huber, 51–75. Thousand Oaks, CA: Sage.

———. 2001. "Putting Emotions in Their Place." In *Passionate Politics: Emotions and Social Movements*, edited by Jeff Goodwin, James M. Jasper, and Francesca Polletta, 45–57. Chicago: University of Chicago Press.

Centre for Peace and Conflict Studies. 2009. *Listening to Voices from Inside: Myanmar Civil Society's Response to Cyclone Nargis*. Phnom Penh: Centre for Peace and Conflict Studies.

Chantavanich, Supang. 2012. "Policy Review on Myanmar Economy: Myanmar Migrants to Thailand and Implications to Myanmar Development." Policy Review Series on Myanmar Economy 7. Bangkok: Bangkok Research Center.

Charney, Michael. 2009. *A History of Modern Burma*. New York: Cambridge University Press.

Chauncey, George. 1994. *Gay New York: Gender, Urban Culture, and the Making of the Gay Male World, 1890–1940*. New York: Basic Books.

Cheesman, Nick. 2015. *Opposing the Rule of Law: How Myanmar's Courts Make Law and Order*. Cambridge: Cambridge University Press.

Cheng, Sealing. 2011. "The Paradox of Vernacularization: Women's Human Rights and the Gendering of Nationhood." *Anthropological Quarterly* 84 (2): 475–505.

Cichowski, Rachel A. 2007. *The European Court and Civil Society: Litigation, Mobilization, and Governance*. Cambridge: Cambridge University Press.

Chua, Lynette J. 2014. *Mobilizing Gay Singapore: Rights and Resistance in an Authoritarian State*. Philadelphia: Temple University Press.

———. 2015. "The Vernacular Mobilization of Human Rights in Myanmar's Sexual Orientation and Gender Identity Movement." *Law and Society Review* 49 (2): 299–332.

———. 2016. "Negotiating Social Norms and Relations in the Micromobilization of Human Rights: The Case of Burmese Lesbian Activism." *Law and Social Inquiry* 41 (3): 643–669.

Chua, Lynette J., and David M. Engel. 2015. "State and Personhood in Southeast Asia: The Promise and Potential for Law and Society Research." *Asian Journal of Law and Society* 2 (2): 211–228.

Chua, Lynette J., and David Gilbert. 2015. "Sexual Orientation and Gender Identity Minorities in Transition: LGBT Rights and Activism in Myanmar." *Human Rights Quarterly* 37 (1): 1–28.

———. 2016. "State Violence, Human Rights Violations, and the Case of *Apwint* in Myanmar." In *Gender, Violence, and the State in Asia*, edited by Amy Barrow and Joy L. Chia, 169–185. New York: Routledge.

Chua, Lynette J., and Timothy Hildebrandt. 2014. "From Health Crisis to Rights Advocacy? HIV/AIDS and Gay Activism in China and Singapore." *International Journal of Voluntary and Nonprofit Organizations* 25 (6): 1583–1605.

Clemens, Elisabeth S. 1996. "Organizational Form as Frame: Collective Identity and Political Strategy in the American Labor Movement, 1880–1920." In *Comparative Perspectives on Social Movements: Political Opportunities, Mobilizing Structures, and Cultural Framings*, edited by Doug McAdam, John D. McCarthy, and Mayer N. Zald, 205–226. New York: Cambridge University Press.

Coe, Anna-Britt, and Annette Schnabel. 2011. "Emotions Matter After All: How Reproductive Rights Advocates Orchestrate Emotions to Influence Policies in Peru." *Sociological Perspectives* 54 (4): 665–688.

Cole, Wade M. 2012. "Human Rights as Myth and Ceremony? Reevaluating the Effectiveness of Human Rights Treaties, 1981–2007." *American Journal of Sociology* 117:1131–1171.

Coleman, Eli, Philip Colgan, and Louis Gooren. 1992. "Male Cross-Gender Behavior in Myanmar (Burma): A Description of the Acault." *Archives of Sexual Behaviour* 21 (3): 313–321.

Collins, Patricia H. 1990. *Black Feminist Thought: Knowledge, Consciousness, and the Politics of Empowerment.* New York: Routledge.

Comaroff, John L., and Jean Comaroff. 2006. "Law and Disorder in the Postcolony: An Introduction." In *Law and Disorder in the Postcolony*, edited by Jean Comaroff and John L. Comaroff, 1–56. Chicago: University of Chicago Press.

Connell, Raewyn. 2012. "Transsexual Women and Feminist Thought: Toward New Understanding and New Politics." *Signs* 37 (4): 857–881.

Corbin-Dwyer, Sonya, and Jennifer L. Buckle. 2009. "The Space Between: On Being an Insider-Outsider in Qualitative Research." *International Journal of Qualitative Methods* 8:54–63.

Cowan, Jane K. 2003. "The Uncertain Political Limits of Cultural Claims: Minority Rights Politics in South-East Europe." In *Human Rights in Global Perspective: Anthropological Studies of Rights, Claims, and Entitlements*, edited by Jon P. Mitchell and Richard A. Wilson, 140–162. London: Routledge.

———. 2006. "Culture and Rights After *Culture and Rights.*" *American Anthropologist* 108 (1): 9–24.

Cowan, Jane K., Marie-Bénédicte Dembour, and Richard A. Wilson. 2001. "Introduction." In *Culture and Rights: Anthropological Perspectives*, edited by Jane K. Cowan, Marie-Bénédicte Dembour, and Richard A. Wilson, 1–26. Cambridge: Cambridge University Press.

Crenshaw, Kimberlé. 1988. "Race, Reform, and Retrenchment: Transformation and Legitimation in Antidiscrimination Law." *Harvard Law Review* 101:1331–1387.

———. 1989. "Demarginalizing the Intersection of Race and Sex: A Black Feminist Critique of Antidiscrimination Doctrine, Feminist Theory and Antiracist Politics." *University of Chicago Legal Forum* 140: 139–167.

Crouch, Melissa. 2013. "Asian Legal Transplants and Rule of Law Reform: National Human Rights Commission in Myanmar and Indonesia." *Hague Journal on the Rule of Law* 5:146–177.

———. 2016. *Islam and the State in Myanmar: Muslim-Buddhist Relations and the Politics of Belonging.* New York: Oxford University Press.

Crouch, Melissa, and Tim Lindsey. 2014. *Law, Society and Transition in Myanmar.* Oxford: Hart Publishing.

Cummings, Scott L. 2017. "The Social Movement Turn in Law." *Law and Social Inquiry.* https://doi.org/10.1111/lsi.12308

Currier, Ashley. 2012. *Out in Africa: LGBT Organizing in Namibia and South Africa.* Minneapolis: University of Minnesota Press.

Dale, John G. 2011. *Free Burma: Transnational Legal Action and Corporate Accountability.* Minneapolis: University of Minnesota Press.

Dave, Naisargi N. 2011. "Indian and Lesbian and What Came Next: Affect, Commensuration, and Queer Emergences." *American Ethnologist* 38 (4): 650–665.

De la Dehesa, Rafael. 2010. *Queering the Public Sphere in Mexico and Brazil: Sexual Rights Movements in Emerging Democracies.* Durham, NC: Duke University Press.

Diani, Mario. 2004. "Networks and Participation." In *The Blackwell Companion to Social Movements,* edited by David A. Snow, Sarah A. Soule, and Hanspeter Kriesi, 339–359. Malden, MA: Blackwell.

Duggan, Lisa. 2003. *The Twilight of Equality? Neoliberalism, Cultural Politics, and the Attack on Democracy.* Boston: Beacon Press.

Durkheim, Emile. 1965. *The Elementary Forms of Religious Life.* New York: Free Press.

Egreteau, Renaud. 2012. "Burma in Diaspora: A Preliminary Research Note on the Politics of Burmese Diasporic Communities in Asia." *Journal of Current Southeast Asian Affairs* 31 (2): 115–147.

Emirbayer, Mustafa. 1997. "Manifesto for a Relational Sociology." *American Journal of Sociology* 103 (2): 281–317.

Emirbayer, Mustafa, and Jeff Goodwin. 1994. "Network Analysis, Culture, and the Problem of Agency." *American Journal of Sociology* 99 (6): 1411–1454.

Emirbayer, Mustafa, and Ann Mische. 1998. "What Is Agency?" *American Journal of Sociology* 103 (4): 962–1023.

Emirbayer, Mustafa, and Chad Alan Goldberg. 2005. "Pragmatism, Bourdieu, and Collective Emotions in Contentious Politics." *Theory and Society* 34:469–518.

Engel, David M. 2012. "Vertical and Horizontal Perspectives on Rights Consciousness." *Indiana Journal of Global Legal Studies* 19 (2): 423–455.

Engel, David M., and Jaruwan S. Engel. 2010. *Tort, Custom, and Karma: Globalization and Legal Consciousness in Thailand.* Palo Alto: Stanford University Press.

Engel, David M., and Frank W. Munger. 2003. *Rights of Inclusion: Law and Identity in the Life Stories of Americans with Disabilities.* Chicago: University of Chicago Press.

Engle, Karen. 2010. *The Elusive Promise of Indigenous Development: Rights, Culture, Strategy.* Durham, NC: Duke University Press.

———. 2011. "On Fragile Architecture: The UN Declaration on the Rights of Indigenous Peoples in the Context of Human Rights." *European Journal of International Law* 22 (1): 141–163.

Englund, Harri. 2006. *Prisoners of Freedom: Human Rights and the African Poor.* Berkeley: University of California Press.

Epp, Charles R. 2009. *Making Rights Real: Activists, Bureaucrats, and the Creation of the Legalistic State.* Chicago: University of Chicago Press.

Equality Myanmar. 2012. "Impact of Section 377 of the Myanmar Penal Code on Discrimination Based on Sexual Orientation and Gender Identity." Yangon, Myanmar: Equality Myanmar.

Esterberg, Kristin G. 1994. "From Accommodation to Liberation: A Social Move-ment Analysis of Lesbians in the Homophile Movement." *Gender and Society* 8 (3): 424–443.

Ewing, Katherine P. 1990. "The Illusion of Wholeness: Culture, Self, and the Experience of Inconsistency." *Ethos* 18 (3): 251–278.

Falk, Monica Lindberg. 2007. *Making Fields of Merit: Buddhist Female Ascetics and Gen-dered Ordered in Thailand*. Copenhagen: Nordic Institute of Asian Studies.

Fantasia, Rick. 1988. *Cultures of Solidarity: Consciousness, Action, and Contemporary American Workers*. Berkeley: University of California Press.

Farrelly, Nicholas. 2014. "Cooperation, Contestation, Conflict: Ethnic Political Interests in Myanmar Today." *South East Asia Research* 22 (2): 251–266.

Farrior, Stephanie. 2009. "Human Rights Advocacy on Gender Issues: Challenges and Opportunities." *Journal of Human Rights Practice* 1:83–100.

Farris, Christopher J. 2014. "Respect for Human Rights Has Improved over Time: Mod-eling the Changing Standard of Accountability." *American Political Science Review* 108:297–318.

Feldman, Eric A. 2000. *The Ritual of Rights in Japan: Law, Society, and Health Policy*. New York: Cambridge University Press.

Felstiner, William L. F., Abel, R., and Austin Sarat. 1981. "The Emergence and Trans-formation of Disputes: Naming, Blaming, Claiming . . ." *Law and Society Review* 15:631–654.

Ferree, Myra Marx. 2003. "Resonance and Radicalism: Feminist Framing in the Abor-tion Debates of the United States and Germany." *American Journal of Sociology* 109 (2): 304-344.

Ferree, Myra Marx, and David A. Merrill. 2000. "Hot Movements, Cold Cognition: Thinking about Social Movements in Gendered Frames." *Contemporary Sociology* 29 (3): 454–462.

Ferree, Myra Marx, and Frederick D. Miller. 1985. "Mobilization and Meaning: Toward an Integration of Social Psychological and Resource Perspectives on Social Move-ments." *Sociological Inquiry* 55: 38–61.

Ferree, Myra Marx, and Aili M. Tripp. 2006. *Global Feminism: Transnational Women's Activism, Organizing, and Human Rights*. New York: New York University Press.

Fineman, Martha A. 2008. "The Vulnerable Subject: Anchoring Equality in the Human Condition." *Yale Journal of Law and Feminism* 20 (1): 1–23.

Fink, Christina. 2009. *Living Silence in Burma: Surviving Under Military Rule*. London: Zed Books.

Flam, Helena. 2005. "Emotions' Map: A Research Agenda." In *Emotions and Social Movements*, edited by Helena Flam and Debra King, 19–40. London: Routledge.

———. 2015. "Micromobilization and Emotions." In *The Oxford Handbook of Social Movements*, edited by Donatella della Porta and Mario Diani, 264–276. Oxford: Ox-ford University Press.

Flam, Helena, and Debra King. 2005. *Emotions and Social Movements*. New York: Routledge.

Fletcher, Gillian. 2011. "The Cultural Queasiness Factor: Intersections of Gender, Sexuality and HIV Prevention in Burma/Myanmar." *Asian Studies Review* 35 (2): 189–207.

Friedman, Debra, and Doug McAdam. 1992. "Collective Identity and Activism: Networks, Choices, and the Life of a Social Movement." In *Frontiers in Social Movement Theory*, edited by A. D. Morris and C. M. Mueller, 156–173. New Haven, CT: Yale University Press.

Fujii, Lee Ann. 2013. "Working with Interpreters." In *Interview Research in Political Science*, edited by Layna Mosley, 144–158. Ithaca, NY: Cornell University Press.

Gallagher, Mary E. 2017. *Authoritarian Legality in China: Law, Workers, and the State.* Cambridge: Cambridge University Press.

Gamson, William A. 1992. *Talking Politics.* Cambridge: Cambridge University Press.

Garcia, J. Neil C. 2009. *Philippine Gay Culture: Binabae to Bakla, Silahis to MSM.* Hong Kong: Hong Kong University Press.

Geertz, Clifford. 1973. *The Interpretation of Cultures.* London: Fontana Press.

———. 1984. "From the Native's Point of View: On the Nature of Anthropological Understanding." In *Culture Theory: Essays on Mind, Self, and Emotion*, edited by Richard Shweder and Robert Levine, 123–136. New York: Cambridge University Press.

Gergen, Kenneth J. 2009. *Relational Being: Beyond Self and Community.* New York: Oxford University Press.

Gilbert, David. 2013. "Categorizing Gender in Queer Yangon." *Sojourn: Journal of Social Issues in Southeast Asia* 28 (2): 241–271.

———. 2016. "Everyday Transgender Belonging in Transitioning Yangon." PhD diss., Australian National University.

Gilmore, Stephanie, and Elizabeth Kaminski. 2007. "A Part and Apart: Lesbian and Straight Feminist Activists Negotiate Identity in a Second-Wave Organization." *Journal of the History of Sexuality* 16 (1): 95–113.

Goodale, Mark. 2006. "Introduction to 'Anthropology and Human Rights in a New Key.'" *American Anthropologist* 108 (1): 1–8.

———. 2007a. "Introduction: Locating Rights, Envisioning Law Between the Global and the Local." In *The Practice of Human Rights: Tracking Law Between the Global and the Local*, edited by Mark Goodale and Sally Engle Merry, 1–38. New York: Cambridge University Press.

———. 2007b. "The Power of Right(s): Tracking Empires of Law and New Modes of Social Resistance in Bolivia (and Elsewhere)." In *The Practice of Human Rights: Tracking Law between the Global and the Local*, edited by Mark Goodale, and Sally Engle Merry, 130–162. New York: Cambridge University Press.

———. 2009. *Surrendering to Utopia: An Anthropology of Human Rights.* Palo Alto: Stanford University Press.

Goodwin, Jeff, and James M. Jasper, eds. 2004. *Rethinking Social Movements: Structure, Meaning, and Emotion.* Lanham, MD: Rowman and Littlefield.

Goodwin, Jeff, James M. Jasper, and Francesca Polletta. 2000. "The Return of the Repressed: The Fall and Rise of Emotions in Social Movement Theory." *Mobilization: An International Journal* 5 (1): 65–83.

———. 2001a. "Introduction: Why Emotions Matter." In *Passionate Politics: Emotions and Social Movements*, edited by Jeff Goodwin, James M. Jasper, and Francesca Polletta, 1–24. Chicago: University of Chicago Press.

———, eds. 2001b. *Passionate Politics: Emotions and Social Movements*. Chicago: University of Chicago Press.

Goodwin, Jeff, and Steven Pfaff. 2001. "Emotion Work in High-Risk Social Movements: Managing Fear in the U.S. and East German Civil Rights Movements." In *Passionate Politics: Emotions and Social Movements*, edited by Jeff Goodwin, James M. Jasper, and Francesca Polletta, 282–302. Chicago: University of Chicago Press.

Gordon, Steven L. 1989 "The Socialization of Children's Emotions: Emotional Culture, Competence and Exposure." In *Children's Understanding of Emotion*, edited by Carolyn Saarni and Paul L. Harris, 319–349. New York: Cambridge University Press.

Gould, Deborah B. 2002. "Life During Wartime: Emotions and the Development of ACT-UP." *Mobilization: An International Journal* 7 (2): 177–200.

———. 2004. "Passionate Political Processes: Bringing Emotions Back in the Study of Social Movements." In *Rethinking Social Movements: Structure, Meaning, and Emotion*, edited by Jeff Goodwin and James M. Jasper, 155–176. New York: Rowman and Littlefield.

———. 2009. *Moving Politics: Emotion and ACT UP's Fight Against AIDS*. Chicago: University of Chicago Press.

Gowans, Christopher W. 2006. "Standing Up to Terrorists: Buddhism, Human Rights, and Self-Respect." In *Comparative Philosophy and Religion in Times of Terror*, edited by Douglas Allen, 101–121. Lanham, MD: Lexington Books.

Gravers, Mikael. 2007. "Introduction: Ethnicity Against the State–State Against Ethnic Diversity." In *Exploring Ethnic Diversity in Burma*, edited by Mikael Gravers, 1–33. Copenhagen: Nordic Institute of Asian Studies.

Green, Eli R. 2006. "Debating Trans Inclusion in the Feminist Movement." *Journal of Lesbian Studies* 10 (1–2): 231–248.

Grewal, Kiran Kaur. 2016. *The Socio-Political Practice of Human Rights: Between the Universal and the Particular*. New York: Routledge.

Gun San Naw. 2013. Naw Naw v. Republic of the Union of Myanmar. Appellant brief, Mandalay State Court.

Harriden, Jessica. 2012. *The Authority of Influence: Women and Power in Burmese History*. Copenhagen: NIAS Press.

Hayfield, Nikki, and Caroline Huxley. 2015. "Insider and Outsider Perspectives: Reflections on Researcher Identities in Research with Lesbian and Bisexual Women." *Qualitative Research in Psychology* 12 (2): 91–106.

Hayward, Susan. 2015. "The Double-Edged Sword of 'Buddhist Democracy' in Myanmar." *Review of Faith and International Affairs* 13 (4): 25–35.

Heyer, Katharina. 2015. *Rights Enabled: The Disability Revolution from the US, to Germany and Japan, to the United Nations*. Ann Arbor: University of Michigan Press.

Hildebrandt, Timothy, and Lynette J. Chua. 2017. "Negotiating In/visibility: The Political Economy of Lesbian Activism and Rights Advocacy." *Development and Change* 48 (4): 639–662.

Ho, Tamara C. 2009. "Transgender, Transgression, and Translation: A Cartography of Nat Kadaws: Notes on Gender and Sexuality Within the Spirit Cult of Burma." *Discourse* 31 (3): 273–317.

Hochschild, Arlie Russell. 1979. "Emotion Work, Feeling Rules, and Social Structure." *American Journal of Sociology* 85 (3): 551–575.

———. 1983. *The Managed Heart: Commercialization of Human Feeling.* Berkeley: University of California Press.

Holzer, Elizabeth. 2013. "What Happens to Law in a Refugee Camp?" *Law and Society Review* 47 (4): 837–872.

———. 2015. *The Concerned Women of Buduburam: Refugee Activists and Humanitarian Dilemmas.* Ithaca, NY: Cornell University Press.

Holzmeyer, Cheryl. 2009. "Human Rights in an Era of Neoliberal Globalization: The Alien Tort Claims Act and Grassroots Mobilization in Doe v. Unocal." *Law and Society Review* 43 (2): 271–304.

Houtman, Gustaaf. 1999. *Mental Culture in Burmese Crisis Politics: Aung San Suu Kyi and the National League for Democracy.* Tokyo: Institute for the Study of Languages and Cultures of Asia and Africa

Human Rights Watch. 2014. "World Report: Burma." http://www.hrw.org/world-report-%5Bscheduler-publish-yyyy%5D/world-report-2014-burma (accessed July 10, 2014).

Hunt, Lynn. 2007. *Inventing Human Rights.* New York: Norton.

Hunt, Scott A., Robert D. Benford, and David A. Snow. 1994. "Identity Fields: Framing Processes and the Social Construction of Movement Identities." In *New Social Movements: From Ideology to Identity*, edited by Enrique Laraña, Hank Johnston, and Joseph R. Gusfield, 185–208. Philadelphia: Temple University Press.

Ignatieff, Michael. 2001. *Human Rights as Politics and Idolatry.* Princeton: Princeton University Press.

Igoe, Jim, and Tim Kelsall, eds. 2005. *Between a Rock and a Hard Place: African NGOs, Donors and the State.* Durham, NC: Carolina Academic Press.

Ikeya, Chie. 2005. "The 'Traditional' High Status of Women in Burma: A Historical Reconsideration." *Journal of Burma Studies* 10 (1): 51–81.

———. 2011. *Refiguring Women, Colonialism, and Modernity in Burma.* Honolulu: University of Hawaii Press.

Jackson, Peter. 1996. "The Persistence of Gender." *Meanjin* 55 (1): 118–119.

———. 1998. "Male Homosexuality and Transgenderism in the Thai Buddhist Tradition." In *Queer Dharma: Voices of Gay Buddhists*, edited by Winston Leyland, 55–89. San Francisco: Gay Sunshine Press.

———. 2000. "An Explosion of Thai Identities: Global Queering and Re-imagining Queer Theory." *Culture, Health and Sexuality* 2:405–424.

———. 2003. "Performative Genders, Perverse Desires: A Bio-History of Thailand's

Same-Sex and Transgender Cultures." *Intersections: Gender, History and Culture in the Asian Context* 9:1–52.

———. 2009. "Global Queering and Global Queer Theory: Thai [Trans]genders and [Homo]sexualities in World History." *Autrepart* 49:15–30.

———. 2017. Seminar. *Capitalist Modernity and the Enchantment of Political Culture: Spirits of Power in Twenty-First Century Thailand.* Singapore: Asia Research Institute.

Jasper, James M. 1997. *The Art of Moral Protest: Culture, Biography, and Creativity in Social Movements.* Chicago: University of Chicago Press.

———. 1998. "The Emotions of Protest: Affective and Reactive Emotions in and Around Social Movements." *Sociological Forum* 13 (3): 397–424.

———. 2011. "Emotions and Social Movements: Twenty Years of Theory and Research." *Annual Review of Sociology* 37:285–303.

———. 2014. *Protest: A Cultural Introduction to Social Movements.* Hoboken, NJ: Wiley.

Jasper, James M., and Jane Poulsen. 1993. "Fighting Back: Vulnerabilities, Blunders, and Countermobilization by the Targets in Three Animal Rights Campaigns." *Sociological Forum* 8 (4): 639–657.

Jenkins, J. Craig, and Charles Perrow. 1977. "Insurgency of the Powerless: Farm Worker Movements (1946–1972)." *American Sociological Review* 42:249–268.

Jitsuya, Nelly, and Rebeca Sevilla. 2003. "All the Bridges That We Build: Lesbophobia and Sexism Within the Women's and Gay Movements in Peru." *Journal of Gay and Lesbian Social Services* 16 (1): 1–28.

Jordan, Glenn, and Chris Weedon. 1995. *Cultural Politics: Class, Gender, Race, and the Postmodern World.* Oxford: B. Blackwell.

Karstedt, Susanne, Ian Loader, and Heather Strang, eds. 2011. *Emotions, Crime and Justice.* Oxford: Hart Publishing.

Kean, Thomas, Toe Wai Aung, and Clare Hammond. 2015. "U.S. Embassy Urges Caution Following Attacks in Taxis." *Myanmar Times,* May 22. http://www.mmtimes.com/national-news/14616-us-embassy-urges-caution-following-attacks-in-taxis.html (accessed June 30, 2018).

Keck, Margaret E., and Kathryn Sikkink. 1998. *Activists Beyond Borders: Advocacy Networks in International Politics.* Ithaca, NY: Cornell University Press.

Keeler, Ward. 2016. "Shifting Transversals: Trans Women's Move from Spirit Mediumship to Beauty Work in Mandalay." *Ethnos* 81 (5): 792–820.

———. 2017. *The Traffic in Hierarchy: Masculinity and its Others in Buddhist Burma.* Hawaii: University of Hawaii Press.

Kemper, Theodore D. 1978. "Toward a Sociology of Emotions: Some Problems and Some Solutions." *American Sociologist* 13 (1): 30–41.

Kennedy, David. 2002. "The International Human Rights Movement: Part of the Problem?" *Harvard Human Rights Journal* 15:101–125.

———. 2012. "The International Human Rights Regime: Still Part of the Problem?" In *Examining Critical Perspectives on Human Rights,* edited by Rob Dickinson, Elena Katselli, Colin Murray, and Ole W. Pedrsen, 19–34. New York: Cambridge University Press.

Keown, Damien. 2012. "Are There 'Human Rights' in Buddhism?" In *Buddhism and Human Rights,* edited by Damien Keown, Charles S. Prebish, and Wayne R. Husted, 15–42. Surrey, UK: Curzon Press.

Keown, Damien, Charles S. Prebish, and Wayne R. Husted, eds. 2012. *Buddhism and Human Rights.* Surrey, UK: Curzon Press.

Keyes, Charles F. 1983a. "Introduction: The Study of Popular Ideas of Karma." In *Karma: An Anthropological Inquiry,* edited by Charles F. Keyes, and E. Valentine Daniel, 1–26. Berkeley: University of California Press.

———. 1983b. "Merit-Transference in the Kammic Theory of Popular Theravada Buddhism." In *Karma: An Anthropological Inquiry,* edited by Charles F. Keyes, and E. Valentine Daniel, 261–286. Berkeley: University of California Press.

———. 2011. "Buddhism, Human Rights, and Non-Buddhist Minorities." In *Religion and the Global Politics of Human Rights,* edited by Thomas Banchoff and Robert Wuthnow, 157–192. New York: Oxford University Press.

Keyes, Charles F., and E. Valentine Daniel, eds. 1983. *Karma: An Anthropological Inquiry.* Berkeley: University of California Press.

Kollman, Kelly, and Matthew Waites. 2009. "The Global Politics of Lesbian, Gay, Bisexual and Transgender Human Rights: An Introduction." *Contemporary Politics* 15 (1): 1–17.

Krinsky, John, and Nick Crossley. 2014. "Social Movements and Social Networks: Introduction." *Social Movement Studies: Journal of Social, Cultural and Political Protest* 13 (1): 1–21.

Kurasawa, Fuyuki. 2007. *The Work of Global Justice: Human Rights as Practices.* Cambridge: Cambridge University Press.

Kyaw Yin Hlaing. 2007. "Associational Life in Myanmar: Past and Present." In *Myanmar: State, Society and Ethnicity,* edited by N. Ganesan and K. Y. Hlaing, 143–171. Singapore: Institute of Southeast Asian Studies.

Lang, Hazel. 2002. *Fear and Sanctuary: Burmese Refugees in Thailand.* Ithaca, NY: Cornell University Press.

Langlois, Anthony J. 2014. "Human Rights, 'Orientation,' and ASEAN." *Journal of Human Rights* 13 (3): 307–321.

Laraña, Enrique, Hank Johnston, and Joseph R. Gusfield. 1994. *New Social Movements: From Ideology to Identity.* Philadelphia: Temple University Press.

Lefebvre, Alexandre. 2013. *Human Rights as a Way of Life: On Bergson's Political Philosophy.* Palo Alto: Stanford University Press.

Lehman, Frank. 1987. "Burmese Religion." In *The Encyclopedia of Religion,* edited by Mircea Elliade, 2:574–580. New York: Macmillan.

Leve, Lauren. 2007. " 'Secularism is a Human Right!': Double-Binds of Buddhism, Democracy, and Identity in Nepal." In *The Practice of Human Rights: Tracking Law between the Global and the Local,* edited by Mark Goodale and Sally Engle Merry, 78–114. New York: Cambridge University Press.

Levitsky, Sandra R. 2008. " 'What Rights?' The Construction of Political Claims to American Health Care Entitlements." *Law and Society Review* 42 (3): 551–589.

———. 2014. *Caring for Our Own: Why There is No Political Demand for New American Social Welfare Rights*. Oxford: Oxford University Press.

Levitt, Peggy, and Sally E. Merry. 2009. "Vernacularization on the Ground: Local Uses of Global Women's Rights in Peru, China, India and the United States." *Global Networks* 9 (4): 441–461.

Liang, Lily, and Sida Liu. 2018. "Beyond the Manifesto: Mustafa Emirbayer and Relational Sociology." In *The Palgrave Handbook of Relational Sociology*, edited by François Dépelteau, 395–411. New York: Palgrave MacMillan.

Lovell, George I. 2012. *This Is Not Civil Rights: Discovering Rights Talk in 1939 America*. Chicago: University of Chicago Press.

Lutz, Catherine. 1988. *Unnatural Emotions*. Chicago: University of Chicago Press.

Lyons, Lenore. 2004. *A State of Ambivalence: The Feminist Movement in Singapore*. Leiden: Brill.

Ma Khin Mar Mar Kyi. 2014. "Engendering Development in Myanmar: Women's Struggle for San, Si, Sa." In *Debating Democratization in Myanmar*, edited by Nick Cheesman, Nicholas Farrelly, and Trevor Wilson, 305–330. Singapore: Institute of Southeast Asian Studies.

MacLean, Ken. 2004. "Reconfiguring the Debate on Engagement: Burmese Exiles and the Politics of Aid." *Critical Asian Studies* 36 (3): 323–354.

Mansbridge, Jane, and Aldon Morris. 2001. *Oppositional Consciousness: The Subjective Roots of Social Protest*. Chicago: University of Chicago Press.

Maroney, Terry A. 2006. "Law and Emotion: A Proposed Taxonomy of an Emerging Field." *Law and Human Behaviour* 30 (2): 119–142.

Massad, Joseph A. 2002. "Re-Orienting Desire: The Gay International and the Arab World." *Public Culture* 14 (2): 361–385.

———. 2007. *Desiring Arabs*. Chicago: University of Chicago Press.

Massoud, Mark F. 2013. *Law's Fragile State: Colonial, Authoritarian, and Humanitarian Legacies in Sudan*. New York: Cambridge University Press.

———. 2015. "Work Rules: How International NGOs Build Law in War-Torn Societies." *Law and Society Review* 49 (2): 333–364.

Matsuda, Mari J. 1989. "When the First Quail Calls: Multiple Consciousness as Jurisprudential Method." *Women's Rights Law Reporter* 11:7–10.

Maung Thawnghmung, Ardeth. 2011. "The Politics of Everyday Life in Twenty-First Century Myanmar." *Journal of Asian Studies* 70 (3): 641–656.

McAdam, Doug. 1986. "Recruitment to High Risk Activism: The Case of Freedom Summer." *American Journal of Sociology* 92 (1): 64–90.

———. 1988. *Freedom Summer*. New York: Oxford University Press.

———. 1992. "Gender as a Mediator of the Activist Experience: The Case of Freedom Summer." *American Journal of Sociology* 97 (5): 1211–1240.

———. 1999a. "Introduction to the Second Edition." In *Political Process and the Development of Black Insurgency, 1930–1950*, 2nd ed. Chicago: University of Chicago Press.

———. 1999b. *Political Process and the Development of Black Insurgency, 1930–1950*, 2nd ed. Chicago: University of Chicago Press.

———. 2003. "Beyond Structural Analysis: Toward a More Dynamic Understanding of Social Movements." In *Social Movements and Networks: Relational Approaches to Collective Action*, edited by Mario Diani and Doug McAdam, 281–298. Oxford: Oxford University Press.

McAdam, Doug, and Ronnelle Paulsen. 1993. "Specifying the Relationship Between Social Ties and Activism." *American Journal of Sociology* 99 (3): 640–667.

McCann, Michael W. 1994. *Rights at Work: Pay Equity Reform and the Politics of Legal Mobilization*. Chicago: University of Chicago Press.

———. 2006. "Law and Social Movements: Contemporary Perspectives." *Annual Review of Law and Social Science* 2:17–38.

———. 2014. "The Unbearable Lightness of Rights: On Sociolegal Inquiry in the Global Era." *Law and Society Review* 48 (2): 245–273.

———. 2017. "Listening for the Songs of Others: Insiders, Outsiders, and the Legal Marginalization of the Working Underclass in America." In *Insiders, Outsiders, Injuries, and Law: Revisiting "The Oven Bird's Song*," edited by Mary Nell Trautner, 139–160. New York: Cambridge University Press.

McCann, Michael W., and Tracey March. 1996. "Law and Everyday Forms of Resistance: A Socio-political Assessment." *Studies in Law, Politics and Society* 15:207–236.

McCarthy, John D., and Mayer N. Zald. 1977. "Resource Mobilization and Social Movements: A Partial Theory." *American Journal of Sociology* 82:1212–1241.

Meinert, Carmen, and Hans-Bernd Zöllner, eds. 2010. *Buddhist Approaches to Human Rights*. Bielefeld: Serie Globaler Humanismus.

Melucci, Alberto. 1980. "The New Social Movements: A Theoretical Approach." *Theory and Methods* 19 (2): 199–226.

Merry, Sally E. 2001. "Rights, Religion, and Community: Approaches to Violence Against Women in the Context of Globalization." *Law and Society Review* 35:38–88.

———. 2003a. "Global Human Rights and Local Social Movements in a Legally Plural World." *Canadian Journal of Law and Society* 12:247–71.

———. 2003b. "Rights Talk and the Experience of Law: Implementing Women's Human Rights to Protection from Violence." *Human Rights Quarterly* 25 (2): 343–381.

———. 2006. *Human Rights and Gender Violence: Translating International Law into Local Justice*. Chicago: University of Chicago Press.

Merry, Sally E., Peggy Levitt, Mihaela Çerban Rosen, and Diana H. Yoon. 2010. "Law from Below: Women's Human Rights and Social Movements in New York City." *Law and Society Review* 44 (1): 101–128.

Mertus, Julie. 2009. "Applying the Gatekeeper Model of Human Rights Activism: The U.S.-Based Movement for LGBT Rights." In *The International Struggle for New Human Rights*, edited by Clifford Bob, 52–67. Philadelphia: University of Pennsylvania Press.

Mische, Ann. 2003. "Cross-Talk in Movements: Reconceiving the Culture-Network Link." In *Social Movements and Networks: Relational Approaches to Collective Action*, edited by Mario Diani and Doug McAdam, 258–280. Oxford: Oxford University Press.

Mogrovejo, Norma. 1999. "Sexual Preference, the Ugly Duckling of Feminist Demands: The Lesbian Movement in Mexico." In *Female Desires: Same-Sex Relations and Transgender Practices Across Cultures*, edited by Evelyn Blackwood and Saskia E. Wieringa, 308–335. New York: Columbia University Press.

Moore, Barrington Jr. 1978. *Injustice: The Social Basis of Obedience and Revolt*. Armonk, NY: M. E. Sharpe.

Morag-Levine, Noga. 2003. "Partners No More: Relational Transformation and the Turn to Litigation in Two Conservationist Organizations." *Law and Society Review* 37 (2) :457–510.

Morreira, Shannon. 2016. *Rights After Wrongs: Local Knowledge and Human Rights in Zimbabwe*. Palo Alto: Stanford University Press.

Moyn, Samuel. 2010. *The Last Utopia*. Cambridge, MA: Harvard University Press.

Mujica, Rosa Alayza, and Mercedes Crisostomo Meza. 2009. "Women's Rights in Peru: Insights from Two Organizations." *Global Networks* 9 (4): 485–506.

Munger, Frank. 2014. "Revolution Imagined: Cause Advocacy, Consumer Rights, and the Evolving Role of NGOs in Thailand." *Asian Journal of Comparative Law* 9:29–64.

———. 2015. "Thailand's Cause Lawyers and Twenty-First-Century Military Coups: Nation, Identity, and Conflicting Visions of the Rule of Law." *Asian Journal of Law and Society* 2 (2): 301–322.

Mutua, Makau. 2002. *Human Rights: A Political and Cultural Critique*. Philadelphia: University of Pennsylvania Press.

———. 2004. "African Human Rights Organizations: Questions of Context and Legitimacy." In *Human Rights, the Rule of Law, and Development in Africa*, edited by Paul T. Zeleza and Philip J. McConnaughay, 191–197. Philadelphia: University of Pennsylvania Press.

———. 2008. "Human Rights in Africa: The Limited Promise of Liberalism." *African Studies Review* 51 (1): 17–39.

Mya Mya Thet, and Piriya Pholphirul. 2015. "The Perception of Myanmar Development on its Return Migrants: Implications for Burmese Migrants in Thailand." *Journal of International Migration and Integration* 17 (4): 995–1014.

Myanmar Ministry of Health. 2011. "Myanmar National Strategic Plan on HIV and AIDS 2011–2015." http://www.jhsph.edu/research/centers-and-institutes/center-for-public-health-and-human-rights/_pdf/NSP%20Full%20Book%20Final.pdf (accessed June 11, 2017).

Nash, Kate. 2012. "Human Rights, Movements and Law: On Not Researching Legitimacy." *Sociology* 46 (5): 797–812.

Nash, Manning, ed. 1966. *Anthropological Studies in Theravada Buddhism*. New Haven: Yale University Press.

Nedelsky, Jennifer. 2011. *Law's Relations: A Relational Theory of Self, Autonomy, and Law*. New York: Oxford University Press.

Nussbaum, Martha C. 2001. *Upheavals of Thought: The Intelligence of Emotions*. New York: Cambridge University Press.

———. 2004. *Hiding from Humanity: Disgust, Shame, and the Law*. Princeton: Princeton University Press.

Nyi Nyi Kyaw. 2015. "Alienation, Discrimination, and Securitization: Legal Personhood and Cultural Personhood of Muslims in Myanmar." *Review of Faith and International Affairs* 13 (4): 50–59.

———. 2017. "A Blow to Buddhist Nationalism in Myanmar." http://www.eastasiafo rum. org/2017/05/27/a-blow-to-buddhist-nationalism-in-myanmar/#more-69979 (accessed June 11, 2017).

Osanloo, Arzoo. 2009. *The Politics of Women's Rights in Iran*. Princeton: Princeton University Press.

Park-Kim, Soo Jin, Soo Youn Lee-Kim, and Eun Jung Kwon-Lee. 2007. "The Lesbian Rights Movement and Feminism in South Korea." *Journal of Lesbian Studies* 10 (3): 161–190.

Pasquetti, Silvia. 2013. "Legal Emotions: An Ethnography of Distrust and Fear in the Arab Districts of an Israeli City." *Law and Society Review* 47 (3): 461–492.

Perera, L. P. N. 1991. *Buddhism and Human Rights: A Buddhist Commentary on the Universal Declaration of Human Rights*. Ann Arbor: University of Michigan Press.

Perry, Elizabeth J. 2002. "Moving the Masses: Emotion Work in the Chinese Revolution." *Mobilization: An International Journal* 7 (2): 111–128.

Petchesky, Rosalind P. 2000. "Sexual Rights: Inventing a Concept: Mapping an International Practice." In *Framing the Sexual Subject: The Politics of Gender, Sexuality, and Power*, edited by Richard Parker and Regina M. Barbosa, 81–103. Berkeley: University of California Press.

Polletta, Francesca. 2000. "The Structural Context of Novel Rights Claims: Southern Civil Rights Organizing, 1961–1966." *Law and Society Review* 34 (2): 367–406.

———. 2004. "Culture Is Not Just in Your Head." In *Rethinking Social Movements: Structure, Meaning, and Emotion*, edited by Jeff Goodwin and James M. Jasper, 97–110. Lanham, MD: Rowman & Littlefield.

Polletta, Francesca, and James M. Jasper. 2001. "Collective Identity and Social Movements." *Annual Review of Sociology* 27:283–305.

Prasse-Freeman, Elliott. 2012. "Power, Civil Society, and an Inchoate Politics of the Daily in Burma/Myanmar." *Journal of Asian Studies* 71 (2): 371–397.

———. 2015. "Conceptions of Justice and the Rule of Law." In *Myanmar: The Dynamics of an Evolving Polity*, edited by David Steinberg, 89–114. Boulder, CO: Lynne Rienner.

Puri, Jyoti. 2008. "Gay Sexualities and Complicities. Rethinking the Global Gay." In *Gender and Globalization in Asia and the Pacific: Method, Practice, Theory*, edited by Kathy E. Ferguson and Monique Mironesco, 59–78. Honolulu: University of Hawaii Press.

Rajagopal, Balakrishnan. 2003. *International Law from Below: Development, Social Movements, and Third World Resistance*. Cambridge: Cambridge University Press.

Rajaram, N., and Vaishali Zararia. 2009. "Translating Women's Human Rights in a Globalizing World: The Spiral Process in Reducing Gender Injustice in Baroda, India." *Global Networks* 9 (4): 462–284.

Renshaw, Catherine. 2017. "Human Rights Under the New Regime." In *Constitutionalism and Legal Change in Myanmar*, edited by Andrew Harding and Khin Khin Oo, 215–234. Oxford: Hart Publishing.

Richards, Patricia. 2005. "The Politics of Gender, Human Rights, and Being Indigenous in Chile." *Gender and Society* 19 (2): 199–220.

Richman, Kimberly D. 2014. *License to Wed: What Legal Marriage Means to Same-Sex Couples*. New York: New York University Press.

Riles, Annelise. 2006. "Anthropology, Human Rights, and Legal Knowledge: Culture in the Iron Cage." *American Anthropologist* 108 (1): 52–65.

Roberts, Christopher N. J. 2015. *The Contentious History of the International Bill of Human Rights*. New York: Cambridge University Press.

Robnett, Belinda. 1996. "African-American Women in the Civil Rights Movement, 1945–1965: Gender, Leadership, and Micromobilization." *American Journal of Sociology* 101 (6): 1661–1693.

———. 1997. *How Long? How Long? African-American Women in the Struggle for Civil Rights*. New York: Oxford University Press.

Rogers, Benedict. 2015. "The Contribution of Christianity to Myanmar's Social and Political Development." *Review of Faith and International Affairs* 13 (4): 60–70.

Rosaldo, Michelle. 1980. *Knowledge and Passion: Ilongot Notions of Self and Social Life*. New York: Cambridge University Press.

———. 1984. "Toward an Anthropology of Self and Feeling." In *Culture Theory: Essays on Mind, Self, and Emotion*, edited by Richard Shweder and Robert Levine, 137–157. New York: Cambridge University Press.

Rosen, Mihaela Serban, and Diana H. Yoon. 2009. " 'Bringing Coals to Newcastle'? Human Rights, Civil Rights and Social Movements in New York City." *Global Networks* 9 (4): 507–528.

Rosenblum, Darren. 2009. "Queer Legal Victories: Intersectionality Revisited." In *Queer Mobilizations: LGBT Activists Confront the Law*, edited by Scott Barclay, Mary Bernstein, and Anna-Maria Marshall, 38–51. New York: New York University Press.

Ross, Becki L., and Catharina Landstrom. 1999. "Normalization Versus Diversity: Lesbian Identity and Organizing in Sweden and Canada." In *Women's Organizing and Public Policy in Canada and Sweden*, edited by Linda Briski and Mona Eliasson, 310–346. Montreal: McGill–Queen's University Press.

Sadan, Mandy. 2013. *Being and Becoming Kachin: Histories Beyond the State in the Borderworlds of Burma*. Oxford: Oxford University Press.

Saffin, Janelle, and Nathan Willis. 2017. "The Legal Profession and the Substantive Rule of Law in Myanmar." In *Constitutionalism and Legal Change in Myanmar*, edited by Andrew Harding and Khin Khin Oo, 235–251. Oxford: Hart Publishing.

Santos, Boaventura de Sousa. 2002. *Towards a New Legal Common Sense*. London: Elsevier.

———. 2015. *If God Were a Human Rights Activist*. Palo Alto: Stanford University Press.

Santos, Boaventura de Sousa, and César Rodríguez-Garavito. 2005. "Law, Politics, and the Subaltern in Counter-Hegemonic Globalization." In *Law and Globalization from*

Below: Towards a Cosmopolitan Legality, edited by Boaventura de Sousa Santos and César Rodríguez-Garavito, 1–26. Cambridge: Cambridge University Press.

Schober, Juliane. 2004. "Burmese Spirit Lords and Their Mediums." In *Shamanism: An Encyclopedia of World Beliefs, Practices, and Culture*, edited by Mariko Namba Walter and Eva Jane Neumann Fridman, 803–806. Santa Barbara, CA: ABC-CLIO.

———. 2005. "Buddhist Visions of Moral Authority and Modernity in Burma." In *Burma at the Turn of the Twenty-First Century*, edited by Monique Skidmore, 113–132. Honolulu: University of Hawaii Press.

———. 2011. *Modern Buddhist Conjunctures in Myanmar: Cultural Narratives, Colonial Legacies, and Civil Society.* Honolulu: University of Hawaii Press.

Schonthal, Benjamin, and Tom Ginsburg. 2016. "Setting an Agenda for the Socio-Legal Study of Contemporary Buddhism." *Asian Journal of Law and Society* 3 (1): 1–15.

Second Police Corporal Nay Zin Tun v. Lin Ko Ko (or) Lin Lin. 2012. Major Crime No. 982, Mingalartaungnyunt Township Court, Yangon Division.

Selby, Don F. 2011. " 'Kat Mai Ploi'—Bite and Don't Let Go: Motherhood and Pursuits of Justice in Thailand." *Citizenship Studies* 15 (6–7): 711–733.

———. 2012. "Patronage, Face, Vulnerability: Articulations of Human Rights in Thailand." *International Journal of Human Rights* 16 (2): 378–400.

Seligman, Adam B. 2000. *Modernity's Wager: Authority, the Self and Transcendence.* Princeton: Princeton University Press.

Selth, Andrew. 2008. "Burma's 'Saffron Revolution' and the Limits of International Influence." *Australian Journal of International Affairs* 62 (3): 281–297.

———. 2012. "Myanmar's Police Forces: Coercion, Continuity and Change." *Contemporary Southeast Asia* 34 (1): 53–79.

Sewell Jr., William H. 1992. "A Theory of Structure: Duality, Agency, and Transformation." *American Journal of Sociology* 98 (1): 1–29.

Silverstein, Helena. 1996. *Unleashing Rights: Law, Meaning, and the Animal Rights Movement.* Ann Arbor: University of Michigan Press.

Sinnott, Megan. 2004. *Toms and Dees: Transgender Identity and Female Same-Sex Relationships in Thailand.* Honolulu: University of Hawaii Press.

Skidmore, Monique. 2003. "Darker Than Midnight: Fear, Vulnerability, and Terror Making in Urban Burma (Myanmar)." *American Ethnologist* 30 (1): 5–21.

———. 2004. *Karaoke Fascism: Burma and the Politics of Fear.* Philadelphia: University of Pennsylvania Press.

———. 2006. "Scholarship, Advocacy and the Politics of Engagement in Burma (Myanmar)." In *Engaged Observer: Anthropology, Advocacy, and Activism*, edited by Asale Angel-Ajani and Victoria Sanford, 42–59. New Brunswick, NJ: Rutgers University Press.

Smith, Alan Smith. 2007. "Ethnicity and Federal Prospect in Myanmar." In *Federalism in Asia*, edited by Baogang He, Brian Galligan, and Takashi Inoguchi, 188–212. Cheltenham, UK: Edward Elgar.

Smith, Miriam. 1998. "Social Movements and Equality Seeking: The Case of Gay Liberation in Canada." *Canadian Journal of Political Science* 31 (2): 285–309.

Snow, David A., and Robert Benford. 1988. "Ideology, Frame Resonance, and Partici-
pant Mobilization." *International Social Movement Research* 1 (1): 197–218.

———. 2009. "Alternative Types of Cross-National Diffusion in the Social Movement
Arena." In *Social Movements in a Globalising World*, edited by Hanspeter Kriesi and
Donatella della Porta, 3–22. New York: Palgrave Macmillan.

Snow, David A., E. Burke Rochford Jr., Steven K. Worden, and Robert D. Benford. 1986.
"Frame Alignment Processes, Micromobilization, and Movement Participation."
American Sociological Review 51 (4): 464–481.

Snow, David A., Louis A. Zurcher Jr., and Sheldon Ekland-Olson. 1980. "Social
Networks and Social Movements: A Microstructural Approach to Differential Recruitment." *American Sociological Review* 45 (5): 787–801.

Solomon, Robert C., ed. 2003. *What Is an Emotion? Classic and Contemporary Readings*,
2nd ed. Oxford: Oxford University Press.

Somers, Margaret R., and Christopher N. J. Roberts. 2008. "Toward a New Sociology of
Rights: A Genealogy of 'Buried Bodies' of Citizenship and Human Rights." *Annual
Review of Law and Social Science* 4:385–425.

South, Ashley. 2004. "Political Transition in Myanmar: A New Model for Democratization." *Contemporary Southeast Asia* 26 (2): 233–255.

———. 2008. *Ethnic Politics in Myanmar: States of Conflict*. Abingdon-on-Thames:
Routledge.

Speed, Shannon. 2008. *Rights in Rebellion: Indigenous Struggle and Human Rights in
Chiapas*. Palo Alto: Stanford University Press.

Spiro, Melford E. 1967. *Burmese Supernaturalism: A Study in the Explanation and Re-
duction of Suffering*. Englewood Cliffs, NJ: Prentice Hall.

Steinberg, David I. 1992. "The Role of International Aid in Myanmar's Development."
Contemporary Southeast Asia 13 (4): 415–432.

———. 2001. *Burma: The State of Myanmar*. Washington, DC: Georgetown University
Press.

———. 2008. "Globalization, Dissent, and Orthodoxy: Burma/Myanmar and the Saffron
Revolution." *Georgetown Journal of International Affairs* 9 (2): 51–58.

———. 2010. *Burma/Myanmar: What Everyone Needs to Know*. New York: Oxford University Press.

Stern, Rachel. 2005. "Unpacking Adaptation: The Female Inheritance Movement in
Hong Kong." *Mobilization: An International Journal* 10 (3): 421–439.

Stockdill, Brett C. 2003. *Activism Against AIDS: At the Intersections of Sexuality, Race,
Gender, and Class*. Boulder, CO: Lynne Rienner.

Stryker, Sheldon. 2004. "Integrating Emotion into Identity Theory." *Advances in Group
Processes* 21:1–23.

Stryker, Susan. 2007. "Transgender Feminism: Queering the Woman Question." In
Third Wave Feminism, edited by Stacy Gillis, Gillian Howie, and Rebecca Munford,
59–70. New York: Palgrave Macmillan.

———. 2008. "Transgender History, Homonormativity, and Disciplinarity." *Radical History Review* 100:145–157.

Stychin, Carl F. 2004. "Same-Sex Sexualities and the Globalization of Human Rights Discourse." *McGill Law Journal* 49: 951–968.

Subramaniam, Ajantha. 2009. *Shorelines: Space and Rights in South India.* Palo Alto: Stanford University Press.

Swidler, Ann. 2009. "Dialectics of Patronage: Logics of Accountability at the African AIDS-NGO Interface." In *Globalization, Philanthropy, and Civil Society: Projecting Institutional Logics Abroad,* edited by David C. Hammack and Steven Heydemann, 192–222. Bloomington: Indiana University Press.

———. 2013. "African Affirmations: The Religion of Modernity and the Modernity of Religion." *International Sociology* 28 (6): 680–686.

Swiebel, Joke. 2009. "Lesbian, Gay, Bisexual and Transgender Human Rights: The Search for an International Strategy." *Contemporary Politics* 15:19–35.

Tambiah, S. J. 1970. *Buddhism and the Spirit Cults in North-East Thailand.* Cambridge: Cambridge University Press.

Taylor, Alan. 2014. "Ten Years Since the 2004 Indian Ocean Tsunami." [Photos.] https://www.theatlantic.com/photo/2014/12/ten-years-since-the-2004-indian-ocean-tsunami/100878/ (accessed June 11, 2017).

Taylor, Robert. 1995. "Disaster or Release? J. S. Furnivall and the Bankruptcy of Burma." *Modern Asian Studies* 29 (1): 45–63.

———. 2009. *The State in Myanmar.* Singapore: National University of Singapore Press.

Taylor, Verta A. 1989. "Social Movement Continuity: The Women's Movement in Abeyance." *American Sociological Review* 54 (5): 761–775.

———. 1996. *Rock-a-By Baby: Feminism, Self-Help, and Postpartum Depression.* New York: Routledge.

Taylor, Verta A., and Leila J. Rupp. 2002. "Loving Internationalism: The Emotion Culture of Transnational Women's Organizations, 1888–1945." *Mobilization: An International Journal* 7 (2): 141–158.

Taylor, Verta A., and Nancy Whittier. 1992. "Collective Identity in Social Movement Communities: Lesbian Feminist Mobilization." In *Frontiers in Social Movement Theory,* edited by Aldon D. Morris and Carol McClurg Mueller, 104–130. New Haven: Yale University Press.

Thalun. 2013. *Thalun English-Myanmar Dictionary.* Yangon, Myanmar: Thalun Publishing.

Than, Tharaphi. 2014. *Women in Modern Burma.* New York: Routledge.

———. 2015. "Nationalism, Religion, and Violence: Old and New Wunthanu Movements in Myanmar." *Review of Faith and International Affairs* 13 (4): 12–24.

Thoits, Peggy A. 1989. "The Sociology of Emotions." *Annual Review of Sociology* 15:317–342.

Thoreson, Ryan. 2011. "Capably Queer: Exploring the Intersections of Queerness and Poverty in the Urban Philippines." *Journal of Human Development and Capabilities* 12 (4): 493–510.

———. 2012. "Realizing Rights in Manila: Brokers and the Mediation of Sexual Politics in the Philippines." *GLQ: A Journal of Lesbian and Gay Studies* 18 (4): 529–563.

———. 2014. *Transnational LGBT Activism: Working for Sexual Rights Worldwide*. Minneapolis: University of Minnesota Press.

Tilly, Charles. 1984. "Social Movements and National Politics." In *Statemaking and Social Movements*, edited by Charles Bright and Susan Harding, 297–317. Ann Arbor: University of Michigan Press.

Tin Htet Paing, 2016. "Burma Removes Hundreds of Names from Blacklist." http://www.irrawaddy.com/burma/burma-removes-hundredsof-names-from-blacklist.html (accessed July 28, 2016).

Tripp, Aili M. 2004. "Women's Movements, Customary Law and Land Rights in Africa: The Case of Uganda." *African Studies Quarterly* 7 (4): 1–19.

Tripp, Aili M., Isabel Casimiro, Joy Kwesiga, and Alice Mungwa. 2009. *African Women's Movements: Transforming Political Landscapes*. New York: Cambridge University Press.

Tsutsui, Kiyoteru. 2017. "Human Rights and Minority Activism in Japan: Transformation of Movement Actorhood and Local-Global Feedback Loop." *American Journal of Sociology* 122 (4): 1050–1103.

Tsutsui, Kiyoteru, Claire Whitlinger, and Alwyn Lim. 2012. "International Human Rights Law and Social Movements: States' Resistance and Civil Society's Insistence." *Annual Review of Law and Social Science* 8:367–396.

Turner, Jonathan, and Jan Stets. 2005. *The Sociology of Emotions*. New York: Cambridge University Press.

UNAIDS. 2012. *National AIDS Programme, Global AIDS Response Progress Report: Myanmar*. March 31. http://www.unaids.org/en/dataanalysis/knowyourresponse/countryprogressreports/2012countries/ce_MM_Narrative_Report.pdf (accessed June 11, 2017).

United Nations Human Rights Council. 2011. "Human Rights, Sexual Orientation and Gender Identity." UN Doc. A/HRC/RES/17/19 (July 14, 2011).

———. 2014. "Human Rights, Sexual Orientation and Gender Identity." UN Doc. A/HRC/RES/27/32 (October 2, 2014).

———. 2016. "Protection Against Violence and Discrimination Based on Sexual Orientation and Gender Identity." UN Doc. A/HRC/32/L.2/Rev.1 (28 June 28, 2016).

Vanhala, Lisa. 2011. *Making Rights a Reality? Disability Rights Activists and Legal Mobilization*. New York: Cambridge University Press.

Waites, Matthew. 2009. "Critique of 'Sexual Orientation' and 'Gender Identity' in Human Rights Discourse: Global Queer Politics Beyond the Yogyakarta Principles." *Contemporary Politics* 15 (1): 137–156.

Walton, Matthew J. 2013. "The 'Wages of Burman-Ness': Ethnicity and Burman Privilege in Contemporary Myanmar." *Journal of Contemporary Asia* 43 (1): 1–27.

———. 2017a. *Buddhism, Politics and Political Thought in Myanmar*. Cambridge: Cambridge University Press.

———. 2017b. "Misunderstanding Myanmar's Ma Ba Tha." *Asia Times*, June 9.

Walton, Matthew J., Ma Khin Mar Mar Kyi, and Aye Thein. 2017. "Ma Ba Tha." *Mekong Review* 2 (3): 14–15.

Walton, Matthew J., Melyn McKay, and Daw Khin Mar Mar Kyi. 2015. "Women and Myanmar's 'Religious Protection Laws.'" *Review of Faith and International Affairs* 13(4): 36–49.

Watkins, Susan C., and Ann Swidler. 2012. "Working Misunderstandings: Donors, Brokers, and Villagers in Africa's AIDS Industry." *Population and Development Review* 38 (Suppl.): 197–218.

Whittier, Nancy. 2001. "Emotional Strategies: The Collective Reconstruction and Display of Oppositional Emotions in the Movement Against Child Sexual Abuse." In *Passionate Politics: Emotions and Social Movements*, edited by Jeff Goodwin, James M. Jasper, and Francesca Polletta, 233–250. Chicago: University of Chicago Press.

Wieringa, Saskia E., and Evelyn Blackwood. 1999. *Introduction in Female Desires: Same-Sex Relations and Transgender Practices Across Cultures*, edited by Evelyn Blackwood and Saskia E. Wieringa. New York: Columbia University Press.

Williams, David C. 2009. "Constitutionalism Before Constitutions: Burma's Struggle to Build a New Order." *Texas Law Review* 87:1657–1693.

Williams, Patricia J. 1991. *The Alchemy of Race and Rights*. Cambridge, MA: Harvard University Press.

Wilson, Richard A. 1997. "Human Rights, Culture and Context: An Introduction." In *Human Rights, Culture and Context: Anthropological Perspectives*, edited by Richard A. Wilson, 1–27. London: Pluto Press.

Wilson, Richard A., and Richard D. Brown, eds. 2009. *Humanitarianism and Suffering: The Mobilization of Empathy*. New York: Cambridge University Press.

Wilson, Richard A., and Jon P. Mitchell. 2003. "Introduction: The Social Life of Rights." In *Human Rights in Global Perspective: Anthropological Studies of Rights, Claims, and Entitlements*, edited by Jon P. Mitchell and Richard A. Wilson, 1–15. London: Routledge.

Wolf, Deborah G. 1979. *The Lesbian Community*. Berkeley: University of California Press.

Women's League of Burma. 2014. *Same Impunity, Same Patterns*. Chiang Mai: Women's League of Burma.

Wong, Yuenmei. 2012. "Islam, Sexuality, and the Marginal Positioning of Pengkids and Their Girlfriends in Malaysia." *Journal of Lesbian Studies* 16 (4): 435–448.

Wood, Elizabeth Jean. 2001. "The Emotional Benefits of Insurgency in El Salvador." In *Passionate Politics: Emotions and Social Movements*, edited by Jeff Goodwin, James M. Jasper, and Francesca Polletta, 267–281. Chicago: University of Chicago Press.

Zarni Mann, 2013. "Gay Rights Activist to Sue Mandalay Police for Alleged Abuse." http://www.irrawaddy.org/women-gender/gay-rights-activists-to-sue-mandalay-police-for-alleged-abuse.html (accessed July 16, 2013).

Zurcher, Louis A., and David A. Snow. 1981. "Collective Behavior: Social Movements." In *Social Psychology: Sociological Perspectives*, edited by David E. Rohall, Melissa A. Milkie, and Jeffrey W. Lucas, 447–482. New York: Basic Books.

Index

Note: The italicized letter *m* following page numbers refers to maps. The letter "n" following page numbers refers to endnotes.

abortion, 168n13, 176n9

achauk: as derogatory term, 56, 79, 91, 93, 104; karma and, 73, 167n8; meaning of, xv, 45, 91; in *nat* worship, 158n5; in ethnic minorities, 163n5; as term of endearment, 115, 154

activists, LGBT: agency and, 19–20, 38–40, 131–132, 138–139, 175–176nn5–7; backgrounds of, 2, 112–113, 128–130, 150; behavior change and, 74–78, 126–127, 170nn27–30; fear of getting caught, 22, 42, 58–60, 96–97; gender norms and, 37, 66, 118–120, 126–128, 162–163n33; heterosexual, cisgender, 54–55, 79–80, 84, 116, 125, 129; lawyers for, 84, 87, 123–125, 129, 150; multiple identities of, 10, 114–117, 141, 153; paid versus volunteer, 112–113; police and corruption and, 122–123, 169n18; recruitment of, 21–22, 51–53, 55, 56–60, 118, 130; repression of, 5–6, 58–60, 164–165n17, 166nn30–32; in study interviews, 148–149. *See also* grassroots activists

agency and human rights: collective action and, 176n7; complications of, 10, 38–40; education and encouragement, 138, 175n5; horizontal consciousness and, 176n6; in human rights practice as a way of life, 10, 131–132, 138–140; in the three processes, 19–20

anade, 149, 167–168n9, 176n3

apone, xv; AIDS in, 53–54; beauty pageants,

85–86, 105; employment of, 85; grassroots activism by, 52; informal social networks of, 52; *nat* worship, 85–86, 105–106, 127; new terminology for, 93; in recruiting lesbians, 56–57, 118; in social hierarchy, 37, 95

apwint, xv; AIDS in, 53–54; assaults on, 49, 54, 66; beauty pageants, 85–86, 110–114; behavior change in, 75, 77, 116, 126, 170n28, 170n30; body modification by, 157n1 (List of Terms); Buddhism and, 127–128; derogatory terms for, 91, 93, 172n3, 172n6; distress in families of, 66; employment of, 67, 85, 171n42; gender divide and, 119, 121; grassroots activism among, 47, 52, 55, 111–112; informal social networks of, 52, 55; in recruiting lesbians, 56–58, 105, 118, 121; in movement social events, 100, 110–112, 113, 121; *nat* worship by, 34–35, 85–86, 127, 171n44; new terminology for, 93, 167n2; in older queer communities, 35, 85–86, 111–113; persecution and arrest of, 66–67, 70, 87, 122–123, 169n17; sex and relationships of, 94; in social hierarchy, 65–66, 95; *tha nge* and, 158n3 (List of Terms)

ASEAN Human Rights Declaration (2014), 107–108

Aung Aung: as activist, 57–58, 83, 84, 87, 120, 175n19; karma and, 65; as *trans man*, 104, 166n28, 167n7

Aung San Suu Kyi, 5–6, 43, 68, 159n6

baw pyar, xv, 91, 104
beauty industry: emotion culture and,
    34–35, 85–86; employment in, 67,
    105–106, 112, 141, 171n43; as sanctuary,
    34–35, 85–86, 106. *See also* niche occu-
    pations; older queer communities
beauty pageants, 85–86, 102–103, 110–114,
    174n2
bisexual, as new terminology, 92
bribes, 123, 169n18
BRIGHT, 58, 118, 120
Buddhism, in Myanmar: Buddhist
    privilege, 37–38, 128–130, 149–150,
    175nn20–22; on change behavior, 76–77;
    on collective responsibility, 25, 80; *nat*
    worship and, 127, 157n2; women and,
    65, 127–128, 167nn5–6. *See also* karma
Burman *(Bamar)*, identification as, 129, 150

change behavior, 74–78, 126–127,
    170nn27–30
Chan Thar: as LGBT activist, 79, 98–99,
    170n32; self-transformation of, 71, 81,
    170n32
Chiang Mai. *See* Thailand
Cho Cho: activist work of, 165n24, 166–
    167n37, 170n32; empathy in, 79–80; on
    lesbians dropping out, 56, 102, 118, 121;
    in movement founding, 54–55; REGAL
    founding by, 60, 79, 96; smuggling
    human rights materials, 61, 165n24; on
    women's rights activists, 125
Christians: 6, 45, 66, 130, 147, 159n10,
    163–164n6, 168n10; in LGBT move-
    ment, 45, 129, 130, 150
Cindy: empathy in, 79–80; legal work of,
    87, 124, 171–172n47, 174n12, 175n23
cognition, emotion versus, 18–19,
    161nn13–15
collective action: community building and,
    90, 98; emotions and, 22–23, 25, 31,
    98, 106, 131; framing, 160n5, 161n15,
    162n21; human rights practice and, 10,
    16–17, 20, 32, 137–139, 176n7; human
    rights scholarship and, 134, 136; self-
    transformation and, 73–74, 139; reso-
    nance and, 137–139; Westernized ideas
    and, 14

collective identity: as LGBT, 26, 90–96;
    as Burmese, 30; in community build-
    ing, 26–28, 90–96; countering deroga-
    tory terms, 90–93, 172nn1–8; internal
    prejudices and gender divide, 37–38,
    94–96, 117–121; LGBT as inclusive,
    90–91, 93–94, 172n1; political unity in,
    93–96; self-transformation and, 33–34,
    103–104, 162nn27–28
community building: 89–108; collective
    identity in, 26–28, 90–96; dropping out,
    101–103, 106, 117–121, 151; emotional
    bonds in, 26–27, 31–32, 89–90, 96–103;
    in human rights practice, 8, 12, 26–28,
    103–108; new collective identity in,
    26–28, 90–96; in other rights move-
    ments, 32; political unity in, 93–96; soc-
    cer matches in, 96; study methods, 136;
    totems in, 28, 60–61, 92, 166nn34–35,
    166–167n37
corruption, 122–123, 169n18
crying, 27, 46, 71, 79, 97–98
cultural schemas: in grievance transforma-
    tion, 23, 64, 68–70; human agency and,
    19–20, 38, 131–132; in human rights
    practice, 19–20, 38, 135, 137, 138, 140,
    162n25
Cyclone Nargis crisis (2008), 54–55

Dar Dar, 51, 57, 166n27
demonstrations of 1988, 1, 42–43, 52–53,
    63, 158n2 (Introduction), 163n1
dignity: in activism, 141–142; in changed
    behavior, 75–76, 126; collective action
    and, 73–74, 78–80; compassion and,
    140; as human right, 9–10, 28–31, 64,
    68–71, 111, 136; local understandings of,
    9, 30, 151–152, 170n28; loss of, in queer
    Burmese, 23–24, 25, 68–69, 70, 87; new
    collective identity and, 30–31, 90–96,
    103–104; in personal relationships, 82;
    self-transformation and, 33–34, 68–71,
    73–74, 103; social prestige and, 83–84,
    171–2n36
dubbing, 30, 93

eain dre theit khar, 75, 116, 126, 170n28;
    See also theit khar
"eating oranges", 102, 147
emotional bonds: collective emotion labor,

139; in community building, 26–27, 31–32, 89–90, 96–103; dropping out and, 101–103, 106, 151; from fear of getting caught, 96–97; making friends, 99–100; in movement founding, 20–22, 47, 51–53, 56–58, 64; older queer communities and, 35, 106, 114, 141, 153, 173n19; from queer suffering, 97–99; in self-transformation, 33–34, 81–84; study methods, 146; from trust, affection, and respect, 99–101. *See also* emotion culture

emotional fealty to human rights, 8–9, 40, 63–88, 114, 118, 131, 135–136, 138, 154

emotion culture: creation of, 7–9, 12, 62; feeling rules in, 34–35, 64, 81, 84–86, 162n30; in grievance transformation, 62, 64, 84–86, 90, 110–114, 132, 136–139, 162nn29–32; internal contestations, 110–114; multiple identities and, 114–117; new claims from, 31–32, 35–36, 86–87, 103, 137; observations of, 153–154; older queer communities and, 85–86, 104–106, 111–112, 153; other elements of, 162n30; queer bonding in, 34–35, 90, 104–106

empathy: in collective responsibility, 25, 78–79; in heterosexual, cisgender activists, 79–80; in human rights, 161n19; in queer suffering, 97–99

employment: in beauty industry, 85, 106, 112, 141, 171n43; discrimination in, 6, 66–67, 76, 107; as LGBT activist, 82–84, 170–171nn36–38; self-employment, 85; in Thailand, 47–48

families: disapproval by, 43, 45, 69–70, 164n7; fear of distress to, 66, 68, 164–165n17, 166n30, 173n9, 173n14; in multiple identities, 117; obligations of lesbians to, 66, 118–120; in self-transformation, 33–34, 76, 82–83, 170–171n36; violence in, 66

fashion shows, 47, 110–113, 174n2

fear and anxiety: of being queer, 19, 42, 44, 49, 57, 67; bonding over, 96–97, 154; community building and, 27, 96–97; of distress to families, 66, 68, 164–165n17, 166n30, 173n9, 173n14; feeling rules changes and, 70–71, 81, 91, 111; of getting caught, 22, 42, 56, 96–97; in griev-

ance transformation, 23–24, 33; karma and, 64; overcoming, 58–60

feeling rules changes: emotion culture and, 34–35, 64, 81, 84–86, 162n30; fear and anxiety and, 70–71, 81, 91, 111; in grievance transformation, 23–25, 33–34, 68–73, 85, 115–116, 151; internal contestations and, 111, 113–114; by national and grassroots activists, 36–37, 38–39; self-hatred and, 24, 70–73, 91, 111; in self-transformation, 33–34, 81–82

fieldwork and methods, 145–156; assistants in, 125, 130, 147–148, 153–154, 176n4, 176n6; documents, photographs, and videos, 154–156; focus and analysis in, 146–147; gaining access, 147–149; initial contact, 145, 147; interviews and interviewees, 149–153; observations, 153–154; outsider view in, 146–147; scope of, 145; time in field, 148; translation issues in, 147; willingness of informants, 148–149

formation processes: movement founding and, 8, 20–22, 41–62; emotional bonds in, 20–22, 47, 51–58, 64; multiplier effect in, 60–62, 166n33; political disaffection in, 42–44; recruiting lesbians, 56–59; study methods, 135–136; ties of altruism and escape from pain, 21–22, 51–56; ties of disaffection and self-hatred, 44–46; ties of survival and escape from despair, 46–51

gandu, xv, 49, 91, 158n2 (List of Terms)

GARUDA, 58

gay, xv; family distress and, 173n9, 173n14; identity as, 45, 89, 93, 104, 109, 166n27, 167n2; oppression and abuse, 43–44; in social hierarchy, 95, 173n9, 173n14; older queer communities and, 105–106

gender divide in the LGBT movement, 37, 38–39, 117–121, 146, 162–163n33

gender norms: change behavior and, 75, 126–128; lesbian activists and, 37, 66, 118–119, 120, 162–163n33

Gilbert, David, xii, 158nn2–3, 158n5, 164n7, 165n21, 167–168nn9–10, 171n43, 172n3, 173n11, 173n19, 176n7 (Appendix)

grassroots activists, 13–14; *apwint* as, 47,

52, 55, 111–112; backgrounds of, 2, 112–
113; locations of, 3, 4*m*; in Myanmar's
IDAHO celebrations (2012), 2; national
activists versus, 10, 36–37, 111–114
grievance transformation, 8, 22–25, 63–88;
changing behavior, 74–78, 126–127;
claiming LGBT rights, 78–80, 86–87;
cultural schemas in, 23, 64, 68–70; dignity
in, 68–71, 73–74; emotion culture in, 62,
64, 84–86, 90, 110–114, 132, 136–139,
162nn29–32; expansion of individual to
collective, 73–80; feeling rules changes in,
23–25, 33–34, 68–73, 85, 115–116, 151;
responsibility in, 73–80; self-transformation in, 33–34, 81–84; study methods,
136; suffering in, 22–25, 63–70, 169n23;
VIVID workshops in, 69–70, 72–73, 78
Gun San Naw, 169n17, 171–172n47
Gyo Kyar: in beauty industry, 84, 100; on
gay pride parades, 75; on human rights,
71; as LGBT activist, 53–54, 59

heterosexual, cisgender activists: empathy
in, 79–80; as lawyers, 84, 129, 174n12;
motivation of, 54–55, 79–80
HIV/AIDS programs: HIV/AIDS in
Myanmar, 51, 165n18; in LGBT movement founding, 51–52, 53, 54–56, 147,
164n16; LGBT activists designated male
at birth in, 120; men who have sex with
men (MSM) in, 51, 93, 165n21; niche
occupations and, 171n42
homonormativity, 77, 126
homophobia, in rebel army, 44
horizontal consciousness, 176n6
Htut Htut, 86, 93, 101–102, 123
human rights: agency and, 175n5, 176n7;
ASEAN Human Rights Declaration, 108,
173n22; contemporary versus modern,
160n1; empirical study of, ix, 7, 13,
14–16, 134–137, 139–144; government
suppression of, 6, 58–60, 164–165n17,
166nn30–32; horizontal consciousness
of, 176n6; ignorance about, 6, 13–14, 68;
promises and pitfalls of, 3–5, 12–14, 131;
vernacularization of, 15, 16, 136–137,
160nn4–6; Westernness of, 5, 13–14,
29–30, 133–134, 160n3, 172n1. *See also*
human rights practice as a way of life;
UDHR; Yogyakarta Principles

human rights groups: Burmese, in Thailand,
44, 163n3, 166n30; LGBT activism and,
44–46, 164n16
human rights practice as a way of life:
agency and, 10, 19–20, 38–40, 131–132,
138–140; Burman and Buddhist privilege in, 10, 37–38, 128–130, 143, 146,
149–150, 175n20, 175n22; Burmese culture and, 9–10, 28–30, 38–40, 121–126,
131–132; community building in, 8, 12,
26–28, 103–108; cultural schemas in,
19–20, 38, 135, 137, 138, 140, 162n25;
documentation programs, 78–79,
83–84, 87, 108; formation processes in,
8, 12, 20–22, 41–62; dignity in, 9–10,
28–31, 64, 68–71, 73–74, 90, 108, 111,
136, 146; grievance transformation in,
8, 12, 22–25, 63–88; infused meanings
of human rights, 9–10, 28–31, 39, 64,
73–74, 88, 90, 108, 136, 146; outcomes
from, 9, 12, 31–36, 80–87, 103–108, 131,
137; limitations of, 10, 36–38, 131–132;
responsibility in, 9–10, 28, 73–80, 136;
See also queer suffering

IDAHO (International Day Against
Homophobia), xvi; activities at, 96,
106–107, 110–111; LGBT identity in,
90; in Myanmar (2012), 61; paraphernalia distributed at, 92; solidarity at,
70, 98
ingahlan, xvi, 158n3 (List of Terms), 172n7
interpersonal ties: of altruism and escape
from pain, 51–56; in community-
building, 26–27, 31–32, 89–90, 96–103;
in escape from self-hatred, 27, 44–46,
48–49; in formation processes, 20–22,
47, 51–58, 64; importance of, 8, 16–19,
32–33, 135–139, 160n9, 162n22; among
lesbians, 56–58; observation of, 154;
queer bonding, 34–35, 37, 39, 90, 103,
104–106, 141; study methods and, 146;
in survival and escape from despair,
46–51. *See also* social belonging
intersex people, 157n4
interviews, 149–153; analysis of, 151,
152–153; data verification, 152–153;
informants in, 149–150; "long", 151–152;
questions in, 150–151, 153
"in-the-shadow" laws, 67, 80, 123

JUSTICE: activist recruitment by, 44–47, 49–51, 54–55; assistance in author's research, 149–150; employment by, 50–51, 164n13; no-vote campaign of, 54–55; training manual, 92

karma of queers: beliefs on, 6, 24, 65–66, 70, 72, 142, 167n8; stigmatization and, 6–7, 64–68
Kaung Sat, 53, 57, 59, 167n1
Khant Nyar: assistance in author's research, 155–156; on change behavior, 77–78; grassroots organizers and, 110–113, 155; leadership role of, 101, 102, 107, 164n15; on older queer communities, 86, 112–113; on outreach to Muslims, 129–130; supportive family of, 124
Khine Khine (study assistant), xi, 147, 148, 153–154, 156, 176n6 (Appendix)
Khin Kyine, 75, 84, 96, 130
Kyaw Kyaw: activist employment of, 50–51, 83, 164n13; on changing behavior, 74; as grassroots organizer, 83, 164n11; in movement founding, 47–49, 50–51, 91–92, 164n11; SUNSHINE leader, 61, 74, 164nn12–13, 170n26

Laws for the Protection of Race and Religion (2015), 5, 159n7, 174n13
lawyers: lack of training in human rights, 80, 174n12; for LGBT activists, 84, 87, 123–125, 129, 150; in recruiting activists, 175n5; workshops for, 78, 124–125
lein tu chit thu ("those who love the same sex"), xvi, 26, 92, 94, 114–115
lesbians, xvi; adhering to gender roles, 66, 175n19; dropping out of movement, 102, 117–120, 151; employment by movement, 83, 84; family obligations of, 66, 118–120; family violence against, 57–58, 66, 70, 168n12; financial dependence of, 119–120; gender divide in LGBT movement and, 37, 102, 117–121, 131, 162–163n33; grassroots activism by, 57–58, 83; 84, 87, 96, 118, 120, 130; in IDAHO soccer games, 96; informal social networks of, 27, 106, 116; interviewing, 148; lesbians versus, xvi, 93, 94, 158n4 (List of Terms); niche occupation exclusion of, 105, 141; recruiting, 35, 56–58,

83–84, 117–118; sexual violence against, 66, 118, 168n12; in gendered hierarchy, 66, 95, 105, 127–128, 175n19; terminology of, xvi, 92–93, 115, 158n4 (List of Terms); trans women, apwint, apone, and, 95–96, 100, 102, 105, 116; women's rights activism and, 125–126, 174n14. See also tomboys
LGBT: new claims and claimant, 9, 12, 35–36, 86–87, 107–108; as new identity, 33–34, 90–93; used outside the movement, 93, 96, 161n20
LGBT activists. See activists, LGBT
LGBT movement: on change behavior, 74–78, 126–127, 170nn27–30; Burman and Buddhist privilege in, 37–38, 128–130, 149–150; class and urban-rural divisions in, 112–114; documentation of, 155–156, 170n26, 176n7 (Appendix); dropping out of, 101–103, 106, 108, 117–120, 151; employment in, 60, 83–84, 109, 113; fashion shows and beauty pageants in, 110–114, 174n2; gender divide in, 37, 38–39, 117–121, 146, 162–163n33; HIV/AIDS programs and, 51–52, 53, 54–56, 120, 147, 164n16, 165n20; human rights workshops or trainings by, xvii, 2–3, 11, 21–22, 25, 27–28, 37–38, 41, 49, 51–59, 62, 69–72, 74–76, 78–79, 81–82, 84–85, 89, 92, 95–102, 104, 108, 114–118, 119, 124–125, 127, 130, 145, 147–150, 152–155; international connections of, 107–108, 137; legal cases, 87, 171–172n47; locations of, 3, 4m, 158–159n4; materials distributed by, 59–61, 79, 99, 107, 166n34, 166–167n37; national versus grassroots activists, 10, 36–37, 111–114; totems in, 28, 60–61, 92, 166nn34–35, 166–167n37. See also human rights practice as a way of life; terminology
list of terms, xv–xvii. See also terminology

Ma Ngwe Taung, 86, 158n5
Maung Maung, 103–104
Maung Nyan, 53, 57, 58, 167n1
meinmashar, xvi, 82, 93, 104, 115, 167n2, 172n6. See also apwint
men who have sex with men (MSM), xvi, 51, 93, 165n21, 172n7
merchandise. See totems

Min Min, 71, 104, 115

Moe Moe, 47, 51

Moe Saing, 102–103, 106

Moora (study assistant), xi, 125, 130, 147–148, 153–154, 176n4, 176n6 (Appendix)

movement founding. *See* formation processes

MSM (men who have sex with men), xvi, 51, 93, 165n21, 172n7

Muslims: 6, 66, 159n10; in LGBT movement, 129, 130, 149, 150, 168n11

Myanmar: 1988 demonstrations, 1, 42–43, 52–53, 63, 158n2 (Introduction), 163n1; elections, 2, 3, 5–6, 43, 54, 125, 158n3, 159n8; constitution in, 5, 54–55, 159n8, 162n23, 163n4, 165n22; economic despair in, 41, 46–48, 164n9; ethnic minorities in, 5–6, 36–37, 43, 44, 45, 46, 106, 128, 129, 130, 149, 150, 157n1, 163nn4–5, 172n2, 175n20; gendered hierarchy in, ix, 6–7, 37–38, 65–66, 94–96, 127–128; history of, 5–6; Laws for the Protection of Race and Religion (2015), 5, 159n7, 174n13; police persecution in, 6, 24, 66–67, 69, 70, 87, 107, 122–123, 168–169nn14–18, 171–172n47; suppression of human rights in, 6, 58–60, 164–165n17, 166nn30–32; use of term, 157n3. *See also* Buddhism, in Myanmar

Naing Lin, 75, 104, 173n13

nat festivals, 85–86, 116, 127, 154, 174n16

National League for Democracy (NLD): election victory of, 3, 5–6, 43; actions as government, 122, 159nn6–7, 163n2; LGBT rights position, 107, 122, 124, 126; on no-vote on constitution, 54; leaders, 162n28. *See also* Aung San Suu Kyi

nat kadaw, xvi, 6, 157n2, 158n5; affective ties around, 52, 158n5, 173nn18–19; cisgender women as, 85, 171n43, 173n15; employment as, 52, 67, 84–85, 105, 116; heteronormative norms and, 106, 158n5, 175n17; LGBT activists as, 2, 84–85, 116–117, 150; social status of, 6, 67, 85, 105, 106, 117, 127, 171n44

nat worship, 34–35, 39, 72, 85–86, 117, 127, 157n2, 171n44, 175n17

Nay Win, 53–54, 55, 60, 73, 76, 123

niche occupations: affective ties in, 102–103, 105, 106; stereotypes and, 85–86, 105–106, 111–112, 171n43; social networks of HIV/AIDS NGOs, 52, 171n42; multiple identities of activists in, 114–117, 153. *See also* older queer communities

NLD. *See* National League for Democracy

non-Buddhists: 147, 159n10; in author's study, 149, 150; forward-looking perspective and, 72; LGBT movement and, 38–39, 45, 128–130, 163–164n6, 168n11; on queers, 6, 10, 45, 66

Nyan Lin, 104, 119, 168n12

older queer communities: emotion culture and, 35, 85–86, 104–106, 111–112, 153; lesbians and, 105, 141; as sanctuaries and support, 85–86, 106, 112, 141. *See also* niche occupations

Pa Dauk, 58, 59, 118–120

police actions toward queers, 6, 24, 66–67, 69, 70, 87, 107, 122–123, 168n14, 168–169nn16–19, 171–172n47

Pyae Soe: on Buddhist rules for women, 128; on Burmese queer terms, 91; childhood of, 48–49, 91, 164n10; early ignorance of human rights, 68; on empathy, 78–79; interpersonal ties in the LGBT movement, 49, 97, 112; on karma, 72; on living well, 74; in movement founding, 47–51; on reaching non-Buddhists, 130; self-identification of, 95, 104, 173n9, 173nn13–14; VIVID television show, 60–61, 166n35; VIVID human rights workshops, 69–70, 78, 130

queer bonding, 34–35, 37, 39, 90, 103, 104–106, 141

queers: bullying and harassment of, 57, 59, 67, 69, 169n20; bringing family distress, 66, 68, 166n30, 167–168n9, 173n9, 173n14; older communities of, 35, 85–86, 104–106, 111–112, 141, 153; police actions toward, 6, 24, 66–67, 69, 70, 87, 107, 122–123, 168n14, 168–169nn16–19, 171–172n47; self-hatred by, 7, 24, 42, 45, 49, 67–68, 79, 140–141; sexual violence against, 66, 118, 168n12;

in gendered hierarchy, 6, 37–38, 65–66, 94–96, 127–128, 140–143, 173n9, 173n14, 175n19; terminology (*See* terminology). *See also* queer bonding; queer suffering; terminology; *specific terms*
queer slang, 102, 116, 147, 173n11
queer suffering: absence of dignity in, 23–24, 25, 68–69, 70, 87; in community building, 27, 91, 97–99, 106; in grievance transformation, 22–25, 68–70, 169n23; karma and, 6, 24, 64–68, 70, 72, 140–141; in movement founding, 19, 41, 52, 57–58; LGBT identities and, 91

rainbow flag, 28, 92, 99, 106
REGAL: birthday party of, 89, 99; founding of, 60, 96; grassroots activism of, 113, 116; lesbians and, 118, 121, 125; LGBT claims by, 108; voter education and registration, 125
responsibility: collective, 25, 28, 78–80, 136; in human rights practice as a way of life, 9–10, 28, 64, 73–74, 90, 136; to the self, 28, 74–78

Saffron Revolution (2007), 49–50
self-hatred: change behavior and, 77; ties in escape from, 18, 44–45, 48–49; karma and, 6–7, 64–65, 67, 70, 141; feeling rules and, 24, 27, 33, 70–72, 81, 91, 111 by queer persons, 7, 24, 42, 45, 49, 67–68, 79, 140–141
self-transformation: in community-building, 33–34, 103–104; dignity and, 33–34, 82–84, 103–104; families and, 33–34, 76, 82–83,; in grievance transformation, 33–34, 81–84; LGBT identities and, 33, 90, 103–104, 136; multiple identities in, 114–117; social prestige and, 83–84. *See also* community-building; grievance transformation
Seng Naw: collective identity and, 92, 93; as Christian in LGBT movement, 128–130, 163–164n6; on expansion to the collective, 73; family of, 45–46, 66, 112, 164n7; on fear of being caught, 97; illness and death of, 164n7, 164n14, 176n7 (Appendix); human rights workshops by, 47, 48, 55, 73, 97; movement documentation by, 156, 170n26, 176n7

(Appendix); in movement founding, 44–48, 50–51, 92, 156; recruitment by, 49, 51, 55, 56; self-identity, 91–92, 163n5; VIVID television show, 166n35
sexism. *See* gender divide
sexual attraction, terminology and, 94
Shwe Wah, 57–58, 119–120
Sint Sint, 115
social belonging: in activism, 82, 114, 136; change behavior and, 76, 126; dignity and, 7, 10, 28, 33, 73, 82, 126, 133, 136, 152; grievance transformation and, 73, as human rights meaning, 9–10, 28–29, 33, 64, 73, 88, 90; as movement goal, 2, 7, 9, 25, 32, 73, 74, 87, 132, 143, self-transformation and, 33–34, 82, 152; social prestige and, 83–84.
social prestige, 83–84, 111, 170–171n36, 172n38
Song for Unity dance, 106–107
State Law and Order Restoration Council, 43
suffering. *See* queer suffering
SUNSHINE: activists of, 50–51, 61, 74, 84, 164nn12–13; founding of, 50–51, 164nn12–13, 174n5; move to Myanmar, 61, 174n5; report (2010), 74, 170n26
Swe Lin Aung, 115, 123

TDoR (Transgender Day of Remembrance), xvi, 73, 84–85, 89, 92, 96, 98–99, 100, 105, 122–123
terminology, xv–xvii; as alternatives to self-hate and shame, 26, 90–93, 141; in community building, 26–27, 90–93; derogatory Burmese, 90–91, 93–94; in ethnic minorities' languages, 163n5, 172n2; list of terms, xv–xvii; local versus international, 30, 39–40, 92–93, 94; sexual attraction in identity, 94; when not in activist mode, 114–116. *See also* specific terms
Thailand: border crossings, 53, 59–60, 97, 164n11, 165n24; Buddhism and women in, 167n6; economic migrants in, 21, 46–48, 164n9; Burmese human rights activism in, 44, 166n30; JUSTICE in, 44–51, 54–55, 59, 79, 147, 149, 164n13, 166n33; SUNSHINE in, 50–51, 61, 74, 96, 164nn12–13, 170n26, 174n5; tsu-

nami in 2004, 46, 164n8; Tun Tun in exile in, 2, 42–44, 47; VIVID in, 2–3, 11, 60–61, 69, 102, 145, 147; women's rights in, 125

tha nge, xvi, xvii, 158n3, 172nn7–8; *apwint* and, xvi, 54, 75, 85–86, 94, 95, 116, 121, 158n3 (List of Terms), 158n6; relationships of, 54, 85–86, 95, 158n6

Thein Gi, 75, 105

theit khar, 170n28, 170n30. *See also eain dre theit khar*

Thiha Aung, 91, 96, 105

Tin Hla: on 1988 demonstrations, ix, 1, 63, 68–69; at airport checkpoint, 59–60; as a Burman Buddhist, 129; as grassroots organizer, 10, 11, 21, 37, 60; on human rights, 63, 133–134, 141; identity adoption, 89, 109; in lesbian outreach, 35, 118; life of, ix, 1–2, 56, 69, 109, 133–134, 151; in movement founding, 2, 8–9, 11, 55–56, 59–60, 133; pathway to the movement, 55–56, 59–60, 109; at REGAL, 60, 89, 96, 98; 118

tomboys: in author's study, 148; *apwint* and, 102, 105, 121; change behavior and, 75, 77; employment of, 67, 83, 105; harassment of, 57, 59, 66, 169n20; karma and, 65; rape by relatives, 168n12; in gendered hierarchy, 65–66, 67, 105, 121, 167n3, 175n19; terminology of, xvi, xvii, 91, 93–94, 104, 115, 158n4 (List of Terms), 166n28, 172n6. *See also trans men; yaukkashar*

totems, 28, 60–61, 92, 166nn34–35, 166–167n37

transgender (T.G.), xvi, xvii; in Buddhist temples, 127–128; fashion shows and beauty pageants, 47, 110–113, 174n2; as new terminology, 93, 117, 173n14. *See also apwint.*

trans men, xvii; gender divide and, 102, 121; employment of, 105; rape by relatives, 168n12; recruitment of, 57–58, 119; in study, 148; terminology of, xvii, 93, 104, 158n4 (List of Terms), 166n28, 167n7. *See also tomboys*

trans women, xvii, 82, 93, 95; beauty pageants, 85–86, 127; change behavior and, 75, 82; derogatory terms for, 172n3; gender divide and, 56, 96, 102, 116, 118–

119, 121; multiple identities of, 116–117; as *nat kadaw,* 105, 116–117, 127; *nat* worship and, 85–86, 127; in other *transgender* groups, 171n46, 173n16. *See also apwint*

Tun Tun: on change behavior, 74, 76; in community building, 8–9, 37, 92, 97–98, 100–102, 105; in demonstrations of 1988, ix, 1–2, 41–43, 69, 133, 143–144; death of boyfriend in rebel army, 43–44; death of friend in 1988, 41–43; family of, 43, 143; in grievance transformation, 8–9, 63–64, 68–69, 71, 74, 76; on human rights, 68, 69, 141, 143; influence of, 8, 45–46, 49, 92, 100–101, 109, 143–144; interaction with author, 147–148; among dissidents, 2, 44, 47–49, 52–53, 112; JUSTICE and, 44, 45, 46, 47, 49, 54, 92, 147; in movement founding, 2–3, 8–9, 20–21, 25, 45–49, 52–53; new terminology and, 92; on prejudices of allies, 123; return to Myanmar (2012), 43, 143; VIVID and, 2, 11, 61–62, 92, 101, 102

UDHR (Universal Declaration of Human Rights), 12, 141–142, 160n3; use by LGBT movement, xvii, 11, 23–24, 29–30, 70–71, 87, 154

VIVID: on changes to the laws, 124; on collective responsibility, 78–79; employment at, 50–51, 101–102, 113; contestation with grassroots organizers, 110–114; friendships at, 97, 100; human rights documentation program, 79, 87; under JUSTICE, 51; lesbian participation in, 57, 118–121; materials distributed by, 60–61, 79, 99, 107, 166n34, 166–167n37; move to Yangon, 2, 61–62, 101, 156; legal reform recommendations of, 86–87; television show, 60–61, 166n35. *See also human rights practice as a way of life; LGBT movement*

weikza cults, 169–170n25
Win Sein, 83, 84, 87, 120
women's rights activists, LGBT rights and, 120, 125–126, 174n14

Yamin: gender identity of, 93, 167n2,

174n9; on community building, 128,
130; on extreme Buddhist nationalists,
159n7; multiple identities of, 116–117,
167n2, 174n9; in pageants, 112; on queer
suffering, 64, 67, 70; relationship with
mother, 82, 117, 174n7; self-transformation of, 81–82

yaukkashar, xvii, 93–94, 104, 172n6. *See
also tomboys*

Yogyakarta Principles, xvii, 13, 23–24,
160n2; use by LGBT movement, xvii,
23–24, 29–30, 70–71, 91

Ywet War, 84, 116, 124, 174n12

Zarni Mann, 115

Zin Yaw: on Buddhism and women, 127–
128; childhood of, 76; on gender divide,
105–106, 118–119, 127–128; as LGBT
activist, 99, 107; multiple identities of,
116–117; as *nat kadaw*, 84, 117, 171n44

Zwe Naung: in community building, 97;
empathy in, 79; as monk, 49–50; in
movement founding, 47, 49–51, 61; on
LGBT identities, 91

Branding Humanity: Competing Narratives of Rights, Violence, and Global Citizenship
Amal Hassan Fadlalla
2019

Remote Freedoms: Politics, Personhood and Human Rights in Aboriginal Central Australia
Sarah E. Holcombe
2018

Letters to the Contrary: A Curated History of the UNESCO Human Rights Survey
Mark Goodale
2018

Just Violence: Torture and Human Rights in the Eyes of the Police
Rachel Wahl
2017

Bodies of Truth: Law, Memory, and Emancipation in Post-Apartheid South Africa
Rita Kesselring
2016

Rights After Wrongs: Local Knowledge and Human Rights in Zimbabwe
Shannon Morreira
2016

If God Were a Human Rights Activist
Boaventura de Sousa Santos
2015

Digging for the Disappeared: Forensic Science after Atrocity
Adam Rosenblatt
2015

The Rise and Fall of Human Rights: Cynicism and Politics in Occupied Palestine
Lori Allen
2013

Campaigning for Justice: Human Rights Advocacy in Practice
Jo Becker
2012

In the Wake of Neoliberalism: Citizenship and Human Rights in Argentina
Karen Ann Faulk
2012

Values in Translation: Human Rights and the Culture of the World Bank
Galit A. Sarfaty
2012

Disquieting Gifts: Humanitarianism in New Delhi
Erica Bornstein
2012

Stones of Hope: How African Activists Reclaim Human Rights to Challenge Global Poverty
Edited by Lucie E. White and Jeremy Perelman
2011

Judging War, Judging History: Behind Truth and Reconciliation
Pierre Hazan
2010

Localizing Transitional Justice: Interventions and Priorities after Mass Violence
Edited by Rosalind Shaw and Lars Waldorf, with Pierre Hazan
2010

Surrendering to Utopia: An Anthropology of Human Rights
Mark Goodale
2009

Human Rights for the 21st Century: Sovereignty, Civil Society, Culture
Helen M. Stacy
2009

Human Rights Matters: Local Politics and National Human Rights Institutions
Julie A. Mertus
2009